# A
# SCREAM
# AWAY FROM
# HAPPINESS

# A SCREAM AWAY FROM HAPPINESS

## Daniel Casriel, M.D.

GROSSET & DUNLAP, INC.
A National General Company
Publishers          New York

*To the bonded:*
To Olivia, my wife; Seth, my son; Carl, my brother; to my co-workers, friends, professional associates and patients; and to all the other societies, professional and social, to which I belong.

# Acknowledgments

First and foremost are my thanks to my collaborators, Margaret and Derry (Seumas) Daly, without whose knowledge and dedication this book would not have been written.

Thanks, too, to Felix Morrow for his advice and consultation. And thanks to Tom Fraser, professor in the Department of Anthropology, University of Massachusetts, who read and provided advice on the anthropological material in the book. My special appreciation extends to the many perceptive and emotionally open group leaders and group members who contributed new insights and techniques to the development of the process. New Identity groups constitute an emotional peer process—and emotional peers have made (and will continue to make) invaluable contributions to the therapy that goes on. I am grateful to Christopher Cross, who brought us together with the publisher, and to Victor D. Solow, who got us together with Christopher Cross. Special thanks to all the people who gave me autobiographical sketches. Although not all of them appear in the book, they were of great value in the preparation of the manuscript.

# Contents

1. A Scream Away from Happiness      **1**
2. A Group in Action      **11**
3. An Analyst's Journey: From Couch to Encounter      **45**
4. Emotional Health      **66**
5. Beyond the Symptom      **82**
6. The Human Need for Bondedness      **97**
7. A Character-Disordered Society      **120**
8. Neurosis and Character Disorder      **132**
9. The Limitations of Psychoanalysis
   and Individual Psychotherapy      **162**
10. Triangular Man: Behavior, Feelings, Attitudes      **181**
11. Acceptors and Rejectors      **202**
12. The Process: Taboos, Structure, Leaders, Marathons      **219**
13. Signals: The Foundation
    of the Group Therapy Process      **242**
14. The Process: Exercises      **253**
15. From Now On      **276**
    Bibliography      **297**
    Index      **301**

We are here because there is no refuge, finally, from ourselves.
Until a man confronts himself in the eyes and hearts
    Of his fellows,
    He is running.
Until he suffers them to share his secret,
    He has no safety from it.
Afraid to be known, he can know neither himself nor any other.
    He will be alone.

Where else but in our common ground can we find such a mirror?
Here, together, a man can at last appear clearly to himself.
    Not as the giant of his dreams
    Or the dwarf of his fears,
        But as a man, part of a whole, with his share in its purposes.
In this ground we can each take root—and grow
    Not alone anymore, as in death,
        But alive, a man among men.

—RICHARD BEAUVAIS
Group Member, 1963-1964

# A SCREAM AWAY FROM HAPPINESS

# CHAPTER 1

# *A Scream Away from Happiness*

A BOOK ABOUT SCREAMING? Yes, in part. To put the matter precisely, this book is about a kind of group therapy that uses screaming as a tool to help patients express long-buried emotions.

But it is also a book about people—not just a few hardy souls who opt for the group psychotherapy process because privacy isn't important to them, but all of us who live today in a complex society. It is about the problems of staying emotionally and psychically healthy in a culture that has tried to turn off man's deepest-level survival-based feelings.

In the psychotherapy process described here, there is not just one kind of scream. There are several screams, each embodying different sounds and different emotions. There are basic screams of fear, of pain, of need and entitlement, and four different screams of anger—the deepest one accompanied by strong feelings of pleasure. There are also the joyous sounds of pleasure—pleasure in the awareness of oneself freed of the distortions of a misprogrammed childhood, in the awareness of the choices open to the emotionally adult and of the feelings of true bondedness to other human beings.

Screaming is not the only tool employed in our group therapy. As in other forms of psychotherapy, talking—especially about misprogrammed attitudes—is part of the process. At the beginning, however, the emphasis is on screams, for screams can express or uncover emotions that cannot easily be put into words. The stress is on *showing* feelings, not talking about them.

The idea of expressing feelings with nonverbal screams is pivotal to the process. A newcomer will be startled to hear loud cries of "I'm angry," "I'm scared," "I'm a woman," and so forth. Often the words end up in sounds that are shrieks or wails, sounds beyond words, arising from depths of pain, anger, fear, or from the need for love. These sounds may frighten an unsuspecting visitor or cause him to dismiss the process as pointless or dangerous. But the screams are part of a structured process. There are reasons for the screams, reasons for the words, reasons for particular emotional exercises. Any person open to his own emotions will resonate to some of these sounds.

At the Casriel Institute, where this form of therapy was developed, we concentrate on "full-measure" expression of feelings. Screams can release emotions repressed since childhood, and the freedom of release can effect significant positive changes in personality. It can do so if the experience takes place within a responsible environment where the individual is involved in a continuing process of psychotherapy.

My approach to treating emotionally discomforted people did not spring full-blown from my personal experience or insight. It began with my experience as a psychoanalyst, when I saw patients who had lost contact with their deepest-level emotions and were playing "word games" with me. My dissatisfaction with one-to-one therapy was nourished by discussions with colleagues who were experiencing the same frustrating patterns with patients. It was aggravated further by my work with drug addicts who, as "character-disordered personalities," seemed impervious to treatment.

Why were "character disorders" so difficult to treat successfully? Psychiatric literature has never been very precise about the matter. The label has served as a way of saying "untreatable," and has therefore been somewhat self-serving. The term itself has unfortunate connotations, suggesting flaws in an individual's personality. In common-sense terms, these "flaws" are in the area of what I call the two "Rs": "Responsibility" and "Relationship." Character-disordered personalities have been emotionally damaged in infancy and childhood, through deprivation. Their emotional needs (and sometimes their physical needs, as well) were not filled by the significant persons in their lives. Thus character-disordered personalities become disconnected from their deepest-level emotions. Psychoanalysis invariably is unsuccessful with them, chiefly because transference (the process upon which an effective analysis depends) cannot take place. Transference is effected when the individual being analyzed begins to relate emotionally to the analyst the way he did with significant persons in his early life.

The character-disordered individual has encapsulated his fear, pain, and anger *inside* his personality. His symptoms are "ego-syntonic," or part of his personality. They cause him no terrible pain, but rather relieve the emotional stress which builds up inside him. A person with a severe character disorder may shoot dope, drink heavily, or be sexually promiscuous. But many a successful businessman working fifteen hours a day is also character-disordered. So are a lot of compulsive housecleaners, mild-mannered bookworms, reckless drivers, long-term underachievers, overeaters, and unhappily married people. The common denominator is anaesthetization of basic emotions and encapsulation of the feelings behind a defensive shell that is extremely hard to penetrate in traditional psychotherapy situations.

On the other hand, the neurotic suffers from symptoms which are "ego-alien." The symptoms are foreign to his personality and cause considerable pain. Because the neurotic does not want the symptoms, he is more likely to seek help. "Why am I so afraid?" a neurotic may ask. "Why do I feel so lonely all the time?" Neurotics *feel* their fear, their pain, their anger. They may have trouble expressing it (especially in a healthy way), but they *experience* it, nevertheless.

While most persons have a combination of neurotic and character-disordered problems, I find that character-disordered personalities comprise the majority of my practice. As my group process developed, I became aware that our techniques were able to break rapidly through the defenses of character-disordered persons and bring them into contact with the repressed feelings from which they had withdrawn. By this I do not mean to imply "instant health." A vast number of problems remained to be worked through. I mean only that the encapsulation which prevented effective psychotherapeutic treatment had been broken through—and, as a result, emotional contact with an individual could be made on a completely new basis.

The genesis of my approach to therapy was a visit I made in 1962 to Synanon, a therapeutic community for rehabilitating drug addicts. By its nature, Synanon consisted of nothing but character-disordered personalities—hard-core dope fiends whom psychiatrists and psychologists considered to be untreatable. I was therefore amazed at the success of the community in rehabilitating its inmates.

Encounter groups were a basic ingredient in the Synanon way of life. While there, I first experienced the emotional "high" which a group can create. Later, when the therapeutic community of Daytop Lodge was started in New York City, I served as psychiatric consultant and had the opportunity to see encounter groups in operation for a longer time. It was not until 1963, a year after my visit to Synanon, that I experimentally introduced group therapy to my private practice in Manhattan.

From the fall of 1962 until now, my approach to group therapy has evolved, one step at a time, from an experimental design that combined verbalizing with some encounter techniques to a "scream-oriented" method which minimizes words and stresses the expression of basic emotions. While we still use some encounter techniques, they are integrated today into a process which takes place in a central atmosphere of acceptance and love. The evolution of this process has involved trial-and-error learning, significant contributions from group leaders, and to a minor extent, experimentation with techniques developed in other group therapy or sensitivity training centers.

My group process is based on the knowledge that emotions are common to all mankind. Emotions know no age differences, no social distinctions, no differentiations in intelligence. A sixty-year-old man may "feel" nineteen one day, full of energy and joy, then revert to feeling his true age the next day. No matter how much we have been trained to repress conscious awareness of them, emotions will be generated by stimuli. And consciously or unconsciously, our deepest-level feelings will affect our lives.

We may strive to repress certain feelings, only to have them manifest themselves in ways we don't know about. We may distort the expression of emotions in behavioral modes that seem strange to many people. But our basic feelings of fear, anger, pain, love, and pleasure are remarkably similar to those of other human beings. It is what each individual has learned to do with these feelings that causes the problems of alienation and anxiety so widely prevalent in our culture.

Emotionality is the one domain in which all human beings are capable of being peers. When you compare adults in any complex society, there are obvious differences in intelligence, physical capabilities, formal education, social skills, physical attractiveness, and socio-economic positions. All are variables which, under some circumstances, can create inequalities. Emotionality also correlates importantly with conditioning. Chances are, the children of a highly emotional mother will be able to express their emotions intensively. They are programmed to do so, from infancy on. And, in this sense, there appear to be significant differences in the emotionality of individuals. However, there is an important difference between being capable of emotion and actually feeling and expressing it. Yet it takes a surprisingly short time for even stolid, "non-emotional" people to be reprogrammed so that they are in contact with their own emotions, *and* with the emotions of others.

In a group situation, a Ph.D. and a ninth-grade dropout can be bonded through empathy for each other's pain and need for love. An individual's honest joy can exhilarate a roomful of people, however varied their tastes and intellects and life styles may be. A fifty-year-old mother and a fifteen-year-old girl can share the same anger at *their* mothers. A man programmed to believe that showing fear is unmanly, and another man whose fear has been a lifelong burden of hysteria, can understand each other through the common expression of their fear, once the barrier of their conditioning has been broken through.

In my groups, the focus is on the interaction of human beings as emotional peers. Through emotionally-charged exercises, I have seen shy, introverted, bland persons become—for a while—genuine *tigers!* When they have truly expressed themselves once, they are better able to do so again. With practice, they can significantly expand their emotional range. And through re-education of their emotions, they can gain access to important new options. In my groups, I have seen henpecked men learn to show anger to their emasculating wives—with astonishing results. (In one instance, I saw a woman cry with pleasure. Assertion of honest anger was what she had always wanted—not only from her husband, but also from *her father*. The incident, which was repeated many times in subsequent groups, was a beginning of a tremendously more rewarding marriage for the couple.)

The peer process has another therapeutic aspect. It tends to cause participants (even those who are adolescents) to become emotionally adult. It is significant that here people are not relating to a single authority figure, as in psychoanalysis. Inevitably there are some people in the group (including the leader) who are more significant than others, in the viewpoint of most participants. But since the common ground is emotion rather than professional judgment or experience, peerdom is demanded. Group leaders work on their own fear, anger, pain, love, and pleasure, just the way others work. Group leaders, too, are confronted angrily and accused of distorted feelings and perceptions. (I have been confronted in groups several times, and I have found myself discomforted by these confrontations. My failure has usually involved the holding back of anger and assertions toward a group member.)

The essential position of adults who have remained emotional children or emotional adolescents is to revere or blame parents and authority figures, rather than to assume personal responsibility for what goes on. We are all the products of our heredity and environment; therefore, in a sense, we are not responsible for what we do. But in a much larger sense, each of us *is* responsible—at a given point in time—for his actions. We must take responsibility for ourselves, or we will not grow up and become adults. This is the human condition all of us share.

Emotionally-oriented group therapy highlights this human condition, I believe, in a therapeutic way. It causes people to be responsible for what they feel, say, and *do*. Despite the dangers of the process, it causes participants to be confronted with their manipulations, emotional withdrawals, distorted emotions, faulty perceptions, and self-defeating attitudes faster than any other method I know about. There are many personalities who should not be in the kind of group therapy going on at the Casriel Institute. But for the majority of emotionally discomforted persons in our society, the peer process offers many advantages—at least, as a starting point on the road toward improved emotional health.

Despite the widely-publicized successes of organizations like Esalen and National Training Laboratories, the acceptance of groups as a way to reprogram pathological feelings and attitudes and to develop new emotional resonance and range is still quite new. To some of my professional colleagues, I realize that the use of group (as opposed to one-to-one) therapy borders on the heretical. That is, they recognize group psychotherapy as a sometimes valuable *adjunct* to individual psychotherapy; but they do not believe group therapy can be effective as an exclusive mode of treatment. It is my conviction that group therapy can be enormously effective when used by itself, without individual treatment. It can be effective because it is able to bring people into contact with long-repressed and vitally important emotions which affect how they think and how they behave. (Later, individual treatment may be valuable for many people.)

The operative word is "can." No matter how it is practiced, group therapy is no panacea, no easy cure for the problems of our society. Especially when it employs encounter techniques, group therapy is potentially dangerous. Some people do not have the ego strength to withstand it without a great deal of accompanying emotional support. For example, participants are under twenty-four-hour-a-day surveillance in communities like Synanon,* Daytop,† and AREBA (a therapeutic community established by Ron Brancato and myself specifically for drug addicts and other infantile, nonfunctioning personalities from the middle class). In contrast, most members of regular groups, once a session is over, return to a regimen in their personal lives

---

*D. H. Casriel, *So Fair a House: The Story of Synanon,* (New York: Prentice-Hall, 1963).

†D. H. Casriel and Grover Amen, *Daytop: Three Addicts and Their Cure,* (New York: Hill & Wang, 1971).

that may be isolated, closed, and depressing. Supervision and care are called for. Without them, the results of the group process can be (at best) nontherapeutic and (at worst) tragic.

Today group psychotherapy is vastly more important and more prevalent than it was three or four years ago. It is my conviction that organized group interaction will soon explode into a force of massive significance in the United States. (An article in *The New York Times* recently reported that six million Americans are today involved in what it calls encounter groups.) There are a number of reasons why this explosion will take place. First, almost everyone is emotionally discomforted—isolated, insecure, unfulfilled, out of contact with his basic feelings. Second, individual psychotherapy is generally ineffective for the majority of patients, who, in diagnostic terms, are "character-disordered personalities." Third, even if individual treatment were effective, there are simply not enough psychiatrists and psychologists available to provide the help demanded by a culture in which destructive attitudes and behavior are the rule, rather than the exception. And, fourth, if by some miracle enough professionals could be trained, individual therapy would continue to be too expensive for most emotionally troubled people. This becomes dramatically clear in the case of families. When one member of a family is emotionally ill, it is almost a certainty that others need help, too. How can the average family afford to pay for extensive individual therapy for four or five of its members at the same time? (I once knew a man who was trying to do so on $45,000 a year, and he could not afford to buy lunch in a restaurant. When he wasn't going to eat a company-financed business lunch, he carried a sandwich inside his attaché case!)

There is still another reason, one that I find the most important: The group process is humanizing. It is designed to establish trust and promote "bondedness" among participants. It is aimed at achieving emotional openness, the ability to express one's own feelings, and to resonate to the emotions of someone else. The process also can rid one of phantom figures in the belly and head—parents, siblings, authorities, previous mates and lovers—which prevent effective crystalization of reality. The focus of successful group therapy must be on the here-and-now. The expiation of historic feelings of fear, anger, and pain produces a clear head and, at least for a while, a clear belly. *The result is pleasure, not pain.* And the pleasure is coupled with the capacity to think about a problem more clearly and meaningfully. The ability yields obvious in-the-world benefits.

To me, widespread use of group therapy does not mean a diminution of the importance of psychiatrists and psychologists. On the contrary, it means better use of their time and skills. My group process involves the re-education of what I call "Triangular Man." The ABC's are man's Affect, Behavior and Cognition. In groups, *affect,* or emotionality, is the name of the game. The dynamic primarily involves the expression of feelings, both to expiate distorted, misprogrammed feelings and to exercise new, healthy feelings. We deal with *behavior* by demanding that newcomers give up their "symptoms," their destructive patterns of conduct. We also ask group members to behave like responsible adults. If they don't know how, then they should "act as if" they do. Emotionally open group leaders who have been trained in this process and are professionally supervised can deal effectively with both feelings and behavior. But *cognition,* which involves the superstructure of attitudes each of us carries with us, is more difficult to treat. Each destructive attitude must be identified, then overcome. Such a process takes a long time—at least twelve months, in my judgment, after a patient has given up damaging symptoms and gained access to his gut-level emotions. An emotionally healthy or well-analyzed psychiatrist or psychologist is best qualified to help a patient get through this struggle with maladaptive attitudes.

One-to-one treatment of an insightful, emotionally open patient is a stimulating and beautiful experience. Before I started my group process, I would experience such a moment only fleetingly with a patient. Now, with "advanced" patients from my groups, it is a normal experience in an individual session. Not all group patients want or need individual therapy at the end. For those who do, there are insights galore; new perceptions about jobs, children, relatives, mates; creative ideas about living patterns; and a gratifying sense of movement and change in the person's life.

Beyond all the professional verbiage, the success of any form of psychotherapy must be gauged by its ability to generate positive changes in a patient's life pattern. This is what it is all about. We must exorcise maladaptive emotions, behavior, and attitudes— ferret them out—then replace them with healthy emotions, behavior, and attitudes. If the result fails to show up in a person's conduct—and in the "signals" he or she transmits through physical gestures, eye contact, and tone of voice—then something is wrong. The psychotherapy has not worked.

This book is about a process of psychotherapy that is proving itself to be unusually effective. It is about why the system works, how it works, and what the process really entails. The book also deals with some failures of the system, and indicates when it may not work. Basically, I believe most people, if dedicated to changing and willing to work hard, will benefit from the process if they stick with it. Even many who have not been highly motivated at the beginning become irrevocably involved within only a few group sessions. People cannot help but react to group. One person may be frightened, another claim that "it's silly," another say that "this is what I've been looking for all my life." But the reaction is there, and even someone who just sits in will be learning a great deal.

When all is said and done, this process is experiential. It takes place primarily in the feelings of people, and it is hard to translate it into words. In our groups we go beyond the social façade, beyond the quick-and-ready responses we have been programmed to use as camouflage, beyond the symptom, beyond the pattern of individual behavior, to the essential feelings underlying the personality. And when the façade is stripped away, the feelings we all share are astonishingly similar.

What is left is the vital, vulnerable core of man: his survival-based need to trust and be bonded to others, his need to love and to be loved without the claptrap camouflage of a sick culture.

CHAPTER 2 | *A Group in Action*

MOST NEWCOMERS to the Casriel Institute are in for a shock.

The screaming they hear can be very loud. And it can continue for a long time. (When the Institute was in another building without soundproofing, the police used to arrive once or twice a month to investigate reports that someone was being beaten up or murdered.) There are likely to be angry encounters, painful sobbing, outbursts of street invective. There may be hugging, touching, and other expressions of affection and love.

The process is not a social get-together. Nor does it involve a meeting in which participants talk about their feelings for two or three hours. Honest feeling is the motif (as it can never be at the vast majority of social gatherings). Therefore the new participant must expect people to say things which are blunt, to the point, sometimes rude, often irritating and abrasive. Emotionality is the name of the game, so he won't be allowed to talk for very long about his attitudes and theories.

During a participant's first or second session in group, others will usually be rather gentle with him. (An exception is when a newcomer has unusually irritating defenses, and the defenses remind a couple of group members of a significant person with whom they are angry—a mother, a former wife, an older brother, and so on.) Usually, a new group member is permitted to ramble a bit, verbalize his feelings without showing emotions, and avoid the dynamics of interaction with others. After he has been in group for a while, however, he is expected to be an active and responsible participant.

Let me escort you through a typical group, so that you will have a chance to see what it is like. Before you enter a group, you will have had a private meeting with me or one of my staff. Therefore you will understand the nature of the process you are entering. You will also have had a chance to read a brochure that explains something of the process and sets forth the rules you will be obliged to follow. No drugs—including pills—or alcohol before coming to a group. No smoking during a session. (It is more therapeutic to let the tensions that cigarettes release build up.) You're supposed to be honest—about your own emotions, *and* about your reactions to others in the group. You are committed to relating to *feelings,* as opposed to attitudes and facts. And you must avoid physical violence regardless of how angry you get.

As you enter the brownstone which is the Casriel Institute, you will usually see people waiting for a group to begin. If it is a typical evening group, you'll hear conversations going on in clusters which have formed in the reception area. A few people may be sitting in lonely isolation, psychologically separated from the chatter. But most will be talking, laughing, telling stories— interacting. Most of the time there is an emotional warmth in the room that is contagious. You can sense it. People reach for each other—with their eyes, with their smiles, with embraces. As newcomers enter the reception room, they frequently make eye contact with someone who is in a conversation. There is a visual signal, and the two people walk toward each other and embrace.

A slight majority of those in the room are female. (More women than men come to my groups.) Most of the people are in their twenties or early thirties. But there are people of other ages here, too: teenagers (many of whom are siblings of members participating in the AREBA program), people in their forties and fifties, and occasionally someone in his sixties. The oldest patient to be in my practice was seventy-seven—the youngest, in our childrens' group, was five.

The range of clothing styles is considerable. Women may be in dresses or slacks. Some look as though they have come from work. Others have obviously come from home. In general the women are attractively groomed. Businessmen wear suits and ties. Younger men and teenagers tend toward loose-fitting shirts and bell-bottom pants. A few who walk up from the Village have beards and wear sandals. Occasionally, a group member will have a chauffeured limousine waiting outside.

The ending of a preceding group is signaled by the sounds of people coming down the steps. Some people in the group just ending have friends among those who are waiting, so there will be more greetings, more embraces, additional banter and laughter. Then those who have been waiting will mount the stairs and enter the room in which their group is to be held.

In this room ten or fifteen chairs have been placed in a circle. Eight to twelve people make up a two-hour group; thirteen to eighteen people group for three hours. There are coffee tables and ash trays. (Sometimes, a group room will be empty prior to a session, and people may smoke in it while they are waiting.) There are many boxes of facial tissue in the room (for participants often cry) and at least one waste paper basket. (Sometimes a group member will gag—although one rarely throws up.) Usually, the coffee tables will contain empty paper cups. It is not unusual to see three or four group members drinking coffee at any given point during a session.

When everyone is settled inside the room, the group leader says: "Let's have a group" or "Let's start the go-around." The group leader gestures toward someone, and that person tells how he feels and what has happened to him since the last group session. Then, one by one, the people in the circle follow suit. One individual may say, "I'm feeling great tonight." Another may tell about a fight with a spouse and end up saying: "I want to work on my anger tonight." Another person may talk about feelings of fear and pain generated by a work situation. A go-around of fifteen minutes provides an opportunity for each individual to focus briefly on the special problems and special emotions facing him at this moment in his life.

In order to convey a sense of what one of my groups is like, I've transcribed portions of several tapes of actual groups which took place several months ago. These group scenes are more verbal than some, but they reflect what takes place in the process. And because a series of screams without sufficient verbalization to indicate what the screams were about would not make illuminating reading, I have interpolated descriptions of what was occurring in the room.

In what follows (and throughout the book) the names of group members have been changed to protect their identities. The dialogue here begins with the last person in a "go-around" talking about herself. The individual is a newcomer named Gretchen.

GRETCHEN: I'm Gretchen. And I'm here because of my husband. He's having an affair with a twenty-two-year-old college girl in Boston every week when he goes there on business. I found out by reading a letter in his attaché case. It was from *her.*

(*Gretchen is an attractive, intelligent thirty-five-year-old college graduate, mother of two, married eleven years, upper middle class.*)

NANCY: That must be a terrible feeling, Gretchen. How do you feel right this minute?

(*Nancy, thirty-nine, has been married close to twenty years and has one child. She works part time in advertising, is college educated, although not graduated, and is from the middle economic class. She is not as attractive as Gretchen but is equally as intelligent. Nancy has been in groups several months, depressed by an unemotional, nonfeeling marriage. Basically, she is a woman who has felt alien since childhood, unentitled to ask to have her needs filled. She now gives to her daughter what she wants for herself.*)

GRETCHEN: Well, it means I can't trust him anymore. About *anything*, I mean. He's a liar . . . . He spent a day and two nights with that bitch and told me it was business.

NANCY: You sound angry, Gretchen.

GRETCHEN: (*After a prolonged silence*) Well, I feel pretty lousy, if that's what you mean.

NANCY: You're scared to death, aren't you? That's the way I felt my first night in group.

(*There is no verbal response. Gretchen has nodded yes.*)

BARRY: You mean this is your *first* group? Your *very* first?

GRETCHEN: Yes, my first.

BARRY: I'm Barry, and I've been in groups about six weeks. I can remember how it was in my first group. I started to speak and some kids kept yelling I was a phony. I didn't know what was going on.

(*Barry is in his early thirties and has just gotten a divorce after eight years of marriage. He has two children, is a white collar executive, and has had several jobs and business adventures in the past ten years. Although none was really successful, he has managed to make a living for himself and pay child support. His wife wanted the divorce. She claimed he was a phoney, and she was right. But his exaggeration has subsided and he is beginning to change, thanks to his intensive group experience.*)

CASRIEL: Okay, who has a feeling? Who wants to work?

VILMA: I do. I don't feel good. I don't feel sexual at all. When I don't want to screw, my boy friend gets mad and stomps out. It's happened *twice* this week.

(*Vilma is an attractive, twenty-four-year-old secretary who does not feel truly adequate. She uses sexuality as a lure for men, rather than as a pleasure for herself. Once she has hooked her man, she turns off her sex "desire."*)

NANCY: Happened last month, too, didn't it?

(*There is no response. Vilma nods yes.*)

NANCY: What did the group tell you, Vilma?

VILMA: That I was angry, because Mitchell wouldn't marry me. And that I didn't want to screw because I was angry.

CASRIEL: Is it true? What do *you* think?

VILMA: But I've told him several times I'm angry. It doesn't do any good. He doesn't pay any attention to me.

CASRIEL: You don't seem angry. Are you angry right now?

VILMA: Yes, I *think* I am.

CATHY: (*Screaming*) Vilma, I can't stand your turned-off tone —you never get to a feeling. Scream, you bitch! If you're angry, *GET ANGRY!*

(*Cathy is an eighteen-year-old hellcat—bright, irritable, intolerant of authority. She can become angry quickly at anyone who annoys her. She never received love or concern from her parents—both of whom are successful and busy professionals. Cathy learned early to assert herself and take what she wanted. Although only an adolescent, she has had more experiences with people than any woman in the group. She is quick to identify other people's problems, and all keep their eyes on her. Cathy and Peter, another member of the group, are teenagers who each spent approximately two months in residence in the AREBA program. Both got into contact with intensive amounts of historic anger. They experimented with drugs, but were not heavily involved.*)

VILMA: (*Standing up to scream*) I'm angry. I'm ANGRY. I'm ANGRY.

(*Vilma continues to scream for thirty-five seconds. She is performing an exercise she has seen others do in group.*)

PETER: The hell you're angry! You're about as angry as a pussy cat! (*Leaping to his feet*) If you're angry, *sound* angry! Like this. . . !

(*Peter lets out an intense scream that lasts ten seconds, then a second ten-second scream, and finally a third that lasts about twelve seconds.*)

CATHY: That's not all, Peter. Go on.

*(Peter continues to scream, looking at each group member as he does so. His screams get increasingly higher-pitched and filled with pain. Before he is finished, he has screamed for over three minutes.)*

CASRIEL: Go on, scream it *all* out Peter.

*(Peter screams again, this time with some tears in his eyes. Cathy rises and takes him in her arms, and he begins to scream with pain. Finally, there is only the sound of his sobs.)*

CASRIEL: That's *your* pain, Peter. It's okay. It brings people close to you when you show it. Look around the room and see for yourself. All your life you felt alone because you couldn't show your real feelings. Now you're not alone.

*(There is a pause of thirty seconds while Peter checks the eyes of everyone in the group. He is a twenty-year-old who had been to college. An angry young man, he could never show his anger or assert himself on his own behalf. Instead, he was a champion for other people's causes for social justice. Although he worked on his college newspaper and was a debater, he rarely had the courage to ask a girl he liked for a date. Cathy and Peter are beginning to look at each other in a perspective that goes beyond the limits of the group meeting.)*

CASRIEL: What do you see, Peter?

PETER: I don't know. People feel close to me, I guess.

NANCY: Try again!

PETER: They feel what *I* feel, I mean.

CASRIEL: How about that they love you? Can you say *that?*

PETER: *(After a pause)* Well, I guess *some* of the people do. Nancy does, I think. But not everybody.

CASRIEL: Who *doesn't* feel close to you?

PETER: Vilma.

CASRIEL: Vilma, how *do* you feel about Peter?

VILMA: (*Looking at Casriel.*) I feel close to him. I felt his anger. *And* his pain.

CASRIEL: Tell Peter.

VILMA: I feel close to you, Peter.

PETER: (*Looking her in the eyes*) Okay. I have a little trouble believing it, but I trust what you say.

CASRIEL: You *can* trust it, Peter. People want to share your feelings with you. Your openness is a pleasurable thing for people to experience.

(*As the group continues, Peter goes to a few people—who embrace him.*)

CASRIEL: You seemed angry, Cathy. What's been going on with you?

CATHY: I am angry, Dan. (*She gets up to exercise her anger.*)

CASRIEL: What are you angry about?

CATHY: I don't want to talk about it. I just want to scream. I'm *angry*. I'm ANGRY! I'm ANGRY! I'm AANNGRYYYEE!

(*Cathy screams for more than a minute, with each scream lasting six or seven seconds. No words now, just sounds. She stops, out of breath.*)

CASRIEL: What are you angry *at*, Cathy? Try to talk about it. I think it's important.

CATHY: I don't know. I'm just angry. At my parents. At my brother. At the principal of my school. At the turned-off people I had as friends. At the whole damned world!

CASRIEL: I feel your anger. It's very real. But who is hurting you?

PETER: (*Interrupting*) My goddam parents pushed me and nagged me and lectured me. About a lot of shit. Like cleaning up my room. Or getting better marks in English. Do you know what we were reading? *Dickens,* for Christ's sake! A guy who's as relevant to today's world as the buggy whip! But they don't understand what's going on out there. What the world's about, I mean.

NANCY: What's the world about, Peter?

PETER: Nobody cares! They want to get everything they can from you. They manipulate you, kid you, fake you out, play everything for laughs and a good time. But nobody's *real*. Nobody *cares*.

CASRIEL: *This* group cares, Peter. And you know it, because you've been getting feelings from people here—taking in a lot of warmth. You know we care.

(*There is no verbal response. Peter grins, agreeing that his attitude doesn't conform to the realities in the room.*)

NANCY: How about you Cathy? Do you agree with Peter? Is that why you're angry?

CATHY: Well, not exactly. My parents care, but that doesn't make things right. At least, my father leaves me alone. My mother always controls me and makes me do what she wants. Everything *I* want to do, *she* won't let me do. Every boy I like, *she* won't let me date. She always wants to know who I go out with, when I get in, what I do, why I do it. It stinks!

CASRIEL: But, the other night in group, she admitted it. She said it's because she cares about you a lot and doesn't know how to show it except with control. She even admitted she's a bit jealous of the fun you have which she didn't when she was a girl. Remember?

CATHY: Yes, I remember. But she's an awful bitch with me.

CASRIEL: How did you feel about her admitting she was jealous of you?

CATHY: Surprised, I guess.

CASRIEL: And how do you feel about her loving you?

CATHY: (*Enraged again*) I don't *want* her to love me!

NANCY: But she *does* love you. So why do you reject her that way?

PETER: What's your stake, Nancy?

NANCY: That's what *my* daughter is doing to me. She rejects me, every time I reach out to her. My own behavior toward her has turned her against me.

CASRIEL: Let out the pain.

NANCY: (*Crying*) It hurts like hell. I need Patricia to love me.

BARRY: (*Reaching out to her, holding her hand in his*) It's okay, Nancy, it really is. Things will get better.

(*Comforted by Barry's concern, feeling the years of lack of concern for her, Nancy cries harder.*)

CASRIEL: Push it out Nancy.

NANCY: (*Sobbing*) What'll I yell?

CASRIEL: Just make a louder sound. Push it out. Hold her Barry.

(*Nancy's scream is a loud screech of pain.*)

CASRIEL: More. Louder.

(*Nancy begins to sound like a wounded animal. She continues to scream five, six, seven times, and then is quiet.*)

NANCY: Wow—where did that come from! I thought I've gotten all my pain out before. I feel better . . . a lot better. But I still hurt.

CASRIEL: Why don't you get down on the mat, Nancy—get those historical feelings out?

(*Mats are placed on the floor during some nonverbal emotional exercises. The mats permit individuals to thrash about, pound, and kick, while they are screaming—without doing injury to themselves or others in the room. The stress is on expressing intense preverbal emotions—for example, the kind of temper tantrum an infant can have in its crib.*)

NANCY: I don't feel like it. My dress will get wrinkled. And I'm embarrassed—I don't have slacks on.

CASRIEL: Well, keep your skirt down and you can have the dress pressed. You're ready emotionally. You'll feel a lot better after you've worked through that feeling.

NANCY: I don't know, Dan. I'm really embarrassed.

BARRY: Come on, Nancy. It'll help you.

VILMA: Do it, Nancy. I'll help you. I'll hold your skirt down.

ROGER: *Work,* Nancy. You've been choked up about Patricia and your mother for weeks.

(*Roger is a successful businessman in his forties—quiet, efficient. When he came in he was turned off to his children from a previous marriage. He has since opened up and has a good relationship going with them.*)

CASRIEL: Nancy, it's your decision. And I think you should take a few moments to think about it. The feelings won't begin to go away until you work through it. You can't control what Patricia is going to do, you know. You've got to begin to confront the feeling here, in this room—the feeling interfering with your relationship with your daughter.

ROGER: My experience has been different. When I got divorced, my kids turned off to me. But I kept calling them, trying to see them, offering to take them to ball games, and so on. Now, things are pretty good between me and my kids.

NANCY: What made the difference?

ROGER: Well, my present wife did, really. She's great with the kids. Therapy helped, too. Ever since I got into groups a year ago things began to be better, really.

CASRIEL: But when the trouble with your children started, were you able to do anything that made things better?

ROGER: No, I wasn't. My wife—my *former* wife, that is—painted a ratty picture of me. She told them I had been running around with other women, and that I had been unfaithful. It was true. But I *did* care about the kids. The kids didn't have a chance to make up their own minds. . . .

CASRIEL: How long did the situation go on?

BARRY: Four years. A long time. Once, I didn't see the kids for three months.

NANCY: It must have been an awful thing to go through, Roger.

ROGER: It wasn't so good for my kids. But it wasn't all that terrible for me, Nancy. I went to ball games with friends. I had two or three girl friends to share my bed with me. I was enjoying my job. So I didn't have to pressure my kids to love me—as if they were all I had in the world. That's what *you* do.

VILMA: Roger's right. You *do* put pressure on Patricia, Nancy.

CATHY: Yes, you sure do! If *I* were Patricia, I wouldn't know what to do. That pressure would just push me away. I couldn't *stand* it!

NANCY: Is what they're saying true, Dan?

CASRIEL: I understand your feeling, Nancy. You never had a close relationship with your mother. Patricia's your only child, and you *need* her to love you. You never loved your mother and you know the waste and the pain you felt. When Patricia doesn't love you, you think she's alone on a desert island, as *you* once were. You think she feels as though there's no one else in the world. That's the way *you* felt. You're trying to treat your historical pain as if it resided in Patricia. You have to treat *yourself*, not Patricia. It's as if when you get a cold, she has to drink hot tea and go to bed.

NANCY: I never looked at it in that way.

CASRIEL: No wonder there's pressure on Patricia. No matter how much tea and sympathy she gets from you, *your* cold gets worse.

NANCY: I wasn't aware of it. What do I do about it?

CASRIEL: Get to the mat . . . and *work!*

NANCY: All right, I'll try.

(*The mats are brought out. When an individual is working on the mat, group members gather around the person to provide emotional, and sometimes physical, help.*)

NANCY: What do I do?

CASRIEL: What do you *feel* like doing?

NANCY: I feel a bit silly.

CATHY: You damn bitch!

(*She gets up and leaves the group of people kneeling around Nancy on the mats.*)

CASRIEL: Begin by expressing a sound, Nancy. Just yell! The sound will get to the feelings.

(*Nancy screams three times.*)

CASRIEL: I can feel your anger in that sound.

PETER: I do, too.

BARRY: I agree. There's anger in your yells.

CASRIEL: What do *you* feel, Gretchen?

GRETCHEN: I'm not sure I qualify as a judge. But I sense your anger, too, Nancy.

CASRIEL: Why don't you try to really let go of the anger, Nancy? You'll enjoy feeling free.

(*Nancy is now given instructions about how to relax and let out a sound; how to move her head; how to move her arms; how to kick her feet. During the time, Nancy makes some false starts, and her movements are corrected. Now the temper tantrum begins. Nancy is screaming wildly and thrashing all over the mat.*)

A VOICE: Push that other pillow closer!

NANCY: It's no good. I'm too afraid to let all the anger out.

(*She stops her movements.*)

CATHY: (*From the far corner of the room*) You're a no-good, controlling cunt! I *knew* you couldn't get to that feeling!

NANCY: (*Sitting up*) And you're a bratty adolescent girl with a nasty tongue.

(*Some of the group members are looking angrily at Cathy. Peter goes to her and is quietly talking to her.*)

CASRIEL: (*Shifting back to Nancy*) Nancy, you *were* getting somewhere. Lie down on the mat again.

(*Nancy takes a moment to gain her composure and lies down. Then, charged with new anger toward Cathy, the tantrum starts again, louder than before. Soon, she is out of conscious control, pounding her fists against the mat while her stockinged feet smash into the bottom of the mat. Her head is turning loosely from side to side. Then, suddenly, her screams stop and she is in tears.*)

NANCY: (*One arm over her eyes, one over her abdomen—legs drawn up, lying slightly to one side*) My mother! It's my *mother!* I loved her *so* much. I needed her *so much* . . . and she was terrible to me. She hurt me all the time. She shut me up in the closet. She told Daddy lies about me. But what could I do about it? I *needed* her!

(*Screams of anger and pain turn to scream of painful need.*)

CASRIEL: Yell out that need. Allow that little girl to express her need full measure.

NANCY: I *need* you! I *need* you!

CASRIEL: How old do you feel when you say that?

NANCY: Six, seven, maybe eight.

CASRIEL: What did you call your mother then?

NANCY: Mommy.

CASRIEL: Say: Mommy, I need you.

NANCY: I need you, Mommy. I *need* you. Mommy, I *need* you. *See* me. Mommy, I *need* you. *SEE* me. I *need* you. Mommmmmyyyyyyy. (*The room is frozen into silence. Cathy is crying. Nancy is oblivious to her surroundings.*) See me. See *ME,* Mommy! *See* me. *See* me. See *me.* Mommmmmyyyyyyyyyeee—see meeeeeeeee! (*She cries again. Now the emotional barriers between many members of the group dissolve.*)

ROGER: (*Putting his arms around Nancy*) It wasn't fair, Nancy. It wasn't fair.

(*He sobs, too. Their faces touch, their emotions bond together for the moment.*)

CASRIEL: You're *entitled* to make that demand, Nancy. You really are. It wasn't *your* fault she didn't love you or *see* you. You never felt love from your mother. Your daughter represented a last chance for you to feel love from your mother. Your daughter became you—and you became your own mother. You were desperate for her to love you. What you really wanted from your daughter was the reassurance that you are lovable. No wonder your daughter felt uncomfortable and rebelled. You were feeding *her*—when it was *you* who was hungry. With all your love for your daughter, you haven't seen her—*her* needs. And you didn't feel entitled to ask for or accept love from your husband. It brought up too much need, too much historical pain if you accepted some of the love he gave you early in the marriage. He felt your pain, but misunderstood it. Then he stopped expressing his love for you. You're *entitled* to love, Nancy. And you're very lovable right now. That anger, tension, and control are gone. You're *very* soft and *very* lovable.

(*One by one, the members of the group hug Nancy as she lies on the mat. Everyone hugs her except Gretchen and Cathy.*)

CASRIEL: Would you like to hug Nancy, Gretchen?

GRETCHEN: I feel a little self-conscious about it, Dr. Casriel.

CASRIEL: Okay, you don't have to do it. But it would make you feel better if you could experience the feeling of closeness, of bondedness. Touching is different from hearing, seeing or smelling. It would make you feel differently about Nancy if you could hold her.

NANCY: I feel so good, I'll get up and hug *you*. I don't need my daughter's love to prove I'm lovable.

(*Nancy gets up off the mats and walks over and hugs Gretchen. The group now reconvenes around the circle of chairs.*)

CASRIEL: Who has a feeling they'd like to work on?

CATHY: I do. I'm angry and I don't know why. I want to work out on the mats too.

CASRIEL: O.K., let's work on that anger.

(*Cathy gets down onto the mat.*)

CATHY: I don't really think I'm angry, I think I'm *scared!*

PETER: Stop thinking—and *work!*

CASRIEL: Just scream, Cathy. Your feeling will come out in the scream. Come on—*yell!* The sound will find the feeling . . . and the feeling will uncover your thoughts.

(*Cathy begins to scream. Each sound lasts about four seconds, with a few seconds of silence between. After nine screams Cathy is breathing deeply, but is still very much aware of herself and her environment.*)

PETER: What's wrong, Cathy?

CATHY: I don't know. It doesn't sound right.

PETER: Stop controlling. Let go.

(*Cathy screams, this time louder than before. Others encourage her. Now the screams become sounds of fear, then loud screams of anger, then finally, the anger becomes pain. Cathy is now sobbing.*)

PETER: (*Hugging Cathy*) It's O.K. Cath, it's O.K. It's *your* pain that you feel.

CASRIEL: It really *is*, Cathy. With all your angry bravado you have a great deal of pain.

CATHY: (*Laughing as she cries.*) It's good to feel my pain, and not be frightened by it. I'm sorry I was so angry at anyone who got near it. That must have brought out my mother in me.

(*Cathy now goes over to Nancy, hugs her, and kisses her on the cheek.*)

There is now a lot of interaction as the group members break into small groups of threes and fours. The more experienced members enjoy teaching what they have learned to the newer members. I go and join the ones who seem most isolated, perplexed, or emotionally uncomfortable. Much therapy gets done at this point. The more advanced, emotionally mature, and knowledgeable the group, the longer this kind of grouping. In marathons it may be two to three hours before the group is reconvened as a total group and an emotional reading of each person is called for in a go-around. In groups that meet for two or three hours, this period of breaking into small units may not occur at all. If it does, I may allow it to continue for as little as a minute or as long as an hour or two, depending on the therapeutic benefits that evolve.

In this group, the intense emotional honesty expressed by Nancy and Cathy has affected other group members. They can no longer remain passive participants. Six of them feel a need to talk and express their feelings. From the various little clusters of three and four people, screams arise spontaneously. Each group is oblivious to the others. Each is intent on the emotionality and the intellectual insights that their feelings uncover.

From time to time, I was asked to answer a question, explain an attitude, or help someone gain deeper feeling. Group members were also asked to do this and some volunteered. Sometimes I'm amazed at the feelings group members elicit. It has become obvious to me that peer concern and peer interaction bring to the surface feelings and attitudes that I, as the leader, would not be able to catalyze. On the other hand, I strive as expeditiously as possible to clear any emotional or attitudinal blocks present in the group. And I try constantly to be aware of anyone who— because of painful feelings—starts to isolate himself from his peers. Also, I keep an ear out for bad, irresponsible, or destructively directive "therapy."

The group of four that includes Nancy is now yelling in unison, "I'm entitled . . . I'm entitled!" and there is a feeling of joyousness in the room. Nancy has shed her self-image of a stoic, middle-class, drab matron, and is euphoric. She has become the vibrant, attractive, mature, and dynamic woman she has always hoped to be.

Cathy is quietly radiating warmth, peace, love and good will. She has positioned herself among the forty- and fifty-year-olds in the group and is hugging the men and women alike. It is rewarding to watch her accept and show her pleasure and need of the love shared between the older group members and herself. She is no longer at war with the "older generation" (her parents), and no longer compelled to self-destruction as a way to prove she doesn't care what "they" think. Cathy will no longer let her mother control her.

Cathy's story is a good illustration of the changes which our group process can bring to a maladjusted personality. Before she entered group, Cathy was on a disaster course. Hostile, uncontrollable, acting out in defiance, she had already gone through two abortions. She managed to obtain fairly good grades in college without too much effort, but the men she got involved with contributed to a symbolic situation—a constant battle to prove she couldn't be subdued. Nor would she show fear. Always in search of the invincible man, she would emotionally castrate any boy or man who would not get angry at her. If a man became furious, she would withdraw from the battle she provoked, thus validating to herself that men were bastards. She could not sustain more than four or five dates with any man, though she had been dating since the age of twelve, having coitus since fourteen.

A great deal of Cathy's mother's anxious control resulted from her daughter's behavior. The mother, feeling unconsciously responsible for Cathy's actions tried (even by brutal means) to keep her from self-destructive actions. But it was too late.

Cathy came from a home considered liberal, cultured, educated. Both parents were professional—her mother, an M.A., teacher, economist; her father, a successful lawyer. Although Cathy was their only child, she was raised by uncaring maids. Cathy didn't feel love. She rejected her need for it and defended herself with anger rather than fear or withdrawal. She would be angry at anyone who became or tried to become emotionally important to her.

Cathy, age eighteen, chose to live at home and go to a city college. She chose to provoke her mother, with whom she had been in emotional warfare for six years. Neither of her parents had been emotionally responsive to her during her formative years, and by the time she was twelve her hostile, delinquent behavior with boys became very evident to her mother. (Her father has remained detached.) This delinquent behavior initiated psychotherapy which Cathy continued sporadically with various therapists for five and a half years. All gave up in defeat.

It was Cathy's mother who, suffering from an agitated and depressed state, first entered the Institute. After two months of groups, the mother's feelings changed sufficiently for even Cathy to notice. Because the warfare with her mother no longer always ended up with the mother's unconditional surrender, Cathy became curious about what was happening at "that Casriel place."

Cathy was counterphobic. That is, to prove she wasn't afraid, she would jump off roofs, take walks in the East Village and East Harlem, and by the age of sixteen she had tried all drugs, including skin-popping heroin. Fortunately, she was not an addictive personality. (Except for some occasional pot she doesn't touch any drugs or chemicals today.) And she acted out sexually. It was not only the sex, but the kind of men she dated, that upset her mother. Cathy was lucky. She might have been severely beaten up, knifed, even killed. Instead, she had three cases of V.D. and two abortions.

Cathy dated the most dangerous men she could find: men from the Mafia, Harlem pimps, Village misfits, drug addicts and pushers, married men old enough to be her grandfather. She really didn't care who they were as long as they represented a danger and a challenge and were not her peers. She stated that she couldn't feel anything for the men she went to college with. The truth is, she was too frightened of her male peers to feel any warmth or love for them. Peter, in the group, was the first eligible, socially acceptable male she ever admitted feeling anything for. It was easy for her to have sexual feelings; that was the only part of her body she felt couldn't get hurt. But she never loved any of the dangerous misfits she went out with. Though socially dangerous, they were emotionally safe. Paradoxically, the socially safe and acceptable men were, to her, unconsciously dangerous.

Each patient has a psychodynamic history which is as unique as Cathy's. And only one small area of her psychotherapy has been given here. When therapy is over for Cathy she will understand most of it, as will I. The group members will get to understand her feelings and some of her behavior and attitudes, but they will never know her total history. Even I will not know all the dangerous episodes of her life. Nor do I need to know, in order to help her. Once I understand the pattern and the emotional dynamics, the details are unimportant. An initial interview will usually give me all the background I need to get a new patient started toward a re-education of his affect, behavior, and cognition.

*(After the subgroupings had continued for forty minutes, I reconvened the group. Cathy was the first to speak.)*

CATHY: I want you all to know I love you, and that I need to be loved by you and people like you. *(She begins to choke up, overwhelmed by the strength of her insight.)* And . . . *(Now she is crying hysterically like a little girl)* and my. . . mother . . . . My mother. . . .

*(Four of the women in the group—all of them mothers— go to Cathy and smother her with hugs and kisses. All are crying and Cathy goes limp as a rag doll. Years of deprivation melt away in the warmth of the love these women give her. And Cathy gives them back not only hope, but also proof that it is not too late for themselves and their children. There is a feeling of love and joy in the air; it is contagious. Vilma is hugging Nancy. Nancy then goes to Barry. Cathy, too, now goes to hug Barry.)*

BARRY: It's what I always wanted—to be loved like this. I've needed it so badly all my life. All my goddam life. I'm a fucking desert. A fucking desert!

NANCY: *(Walking over to hug Barry)* I'm going to hug you too.

*(Barry cries louder. These are tears of historic pain. They are a sure sign that Barry is taking in the love being given him.)*

CASRIEL: Take in the love, Barry. Take it all in.

BARRY: I am, Dan. I need it. Come here, Nancy. Come on, Dan. Pile on!

CASRIEL: Okay, let's have a group again . . . let's have a group.

NANCY: Who wants to? I've taken in all the love I can in one night!

BARRY: So have I! I'm so open you could run a tank through me.

CASRIEL: I know, but some people need to get out their feelings. I noticed three people who haven't done any work for themselves. Are *you* feeling anything, Tim?

TIM: I feel a lot for *Barry,* Dan. I really do.

(*Tim is twenty-three and single. He is a high school graduate and works as a technician. He came to groups through the urging of a male friend. Tim is a quiet person. He feels alienated, relates to women poorly, and detaches himself from people.*)

CASRIEL: Do you want to work it through?

TIM: I don't want to.

CASRIEL: You're full of pain, Tim. Try to get it out. . . .

GRETCHEN: What's the pain about, Tim?

TIM: My life, I guess. . . . My mother and father. I never got what I wanted from them.

NANCY: What *do* you want from them?

TIM: Understanding. I was a screwed-up kid, I guess. They were divorced, and each of them tried to turn me against the other one.

VILMA: Boy, do I know that scene!

CASRIEL: You mean, Tim, that you got left out. No one was concerned with your needs.

TIM: That's it. My mother used to tell me how irresponsible my father was; how he didn't give her enough money, and how he was chasing after other women. That's why she asked for a divorce. I turned against him. I gave him a hard time. Now it's too late. . . .

BARRY: Why the hell is it too late?

TIM: He's remarried and living in California. I haven't had a letter from him in over two years. He doesn't even know my address. He doesn't care a damn about me.

CATHY: Maybe he thinks you feel the same way. Have you thought of that?

(*There is no answer from Tim.*)

GRETCHEN: What happened the last time you heard from him?

TIM: It was Christmas time. He sent me a present. It was a book I didn't want to read. A book that was too young for me. He should have known better.

CASRIEL: I can understand your feeling, Tim. How long had it been since he'd seen you?

TIM: Five years, maybe six. Something like that. He was passing through town.

BARRY: The present was an easy mistake to make. I've made the same one with my kids.

TIM: Yeah, I know. But he should have thought about it more.

GRETCHEN: What did you get *him* for Christmas?

(*Tim fails to answer.*)

BARRY: You didn't get your old man a present, did you?

TIM: No.

BARRY: Did you send him a thank-you note for the present he sent you?

(*Tim does not answer.*)

BARRY: How about birthdays? Did he send you cards and presents on your birthdays?

(*No answer. Tim nods yes.*)

BARRY: Have you written him, phoned him, or made any kind of contact with your father in the past two years?

TIM: No, I guess I haven't.

BARRY: You expect him to psyche you out. You want *him* to do all the reaching, don't you? That way, you can be in the catbird's seat.

(*There is no answer.*)

GRETCHEN: What do you *want* from your father, Tim?

TIM: I don't know. I want him to care about me, I guess.

CASRIEL: It sounds as though he once cared, Tim. What about love? Do you want him to love you?

TIM: (*After a long pause*) I guess I do.

NANCY: (*Remembering her own group work*) Say, "please love me, Daddy."

TIM: That's hard to say.

CATHY: Say it anyway.

PETER: Try it, Tim. Try it.

TIM: Please love me, Dad. . . . Please love me. . . . Love me, Dad. Love me. Love me. . . . Love me. . . . Love *me!*

(*With each refrain, his voice has gotten louder.*)

CASRIEL: Say it softer, Tim. You want to ask him—not shout at him.

(*Tim says the words slower and softer, looking at each group member as he says them. When he gets to Barry, his voice chokes. He begins to sob.*)

BARRY: Scream out your pain, Tim. Scream it out!

TIM: (*Screaming*) Please love me, Dad.

BARRY: Just yell. No words.

(*Tim screams six times. There is excruciating pain in the voice. Barry rises and walks to Tim's chair. He pulls Tim up into his arms. The emotional resonance in the group has succeeded in giving Tim the reassurance he needed to ex-*

*pose his own need for love and give up his angry, impotent
defense against it. Tim continues to scream—there are twelve
more screams, with each scream lasting about six seconds.
The screams become higher and higher, until they are
mingled with sobs and finally with laughter.*)

BARRY: How do you feel now, Tim?

TIM: A hundred pounds lighter. Wow!

NANCY: (*Coming up beside Barry and Tim*) I'd like to hug
Tim, too.

CASRIEL: That's *your* pain, Tim, and *your* need. They're beautiful. They make other people feel needed and important,
Tim. Do you know that? When you couldn't show your
pain, you couldn't expose your need so you remained alone,
isolated even at a party. You don't have to be that way.

    You were withdrawn in group this evening. It's true you
reached out to give love to some of the others, but you didn't
allow anyone to reach you until now. But the people here
were concerned enough to help you dissolve your defenses
and get out of the shell you wore as a child. That shell will
form again from habit, and you will have to practice over
and over again, just like tonight, to remove it. Unless, at a
particular time, you want it to be there. You will have to
learn to control your defensive shell rather than let your
defensive shell control you. Do you understand what I'm
trying to tell you?

TIM: I guess I do. I feel pretty good.

CASRIEL: Barry, tell Tim how you feel about him.

BARRY: I feel good that I was able to help you. I feel better
about myself. Important because you needed me.

NANCY: You're so beautiful when you're open, Tim.

    (*Tim laughs and he and Nancy hug each other.*)

TIM: I feel absolutely great . . . but a little weak.

CASRIEL: Here's something important to know, Tim. People will
respond to your needs when you're open and straight about
them. *Your father* will probably respond, if you're open and

straight with him. People will *enjoy* filling your needs, because it will make them feel important. Remember that. It's like a cook who likes herself better when people enjoy the food she has cooked for them.

BARRY: Find out where your father lives and give him a call, Tim. I'll bet he wants to hear from you. Give it a try!

TIM: (*Slowly, and a little fearfully*) All right, I will.

CASRIEL: Tim, you're very open right now. Go around the group and take in some more love. Practice.

(*Tim starts going around the room, hugging each group member.*)

CASRIEL: Gretchen, how are *you* feeling?

GRETCHEN: (*After a prolonged silence*) Pretty good, Dr. Casriel. Self-conscious right now. But I'm moved by Tim. And, earlier, I was very moved by Peter. Peter reminds me of my son, Mickey. He. . . .

CASRIEL: Tell Peter, Gretchen.

GRETCHEN: Yes. . . . Well, my son Mickey is a lot like you, Peter. He hates school—especially subjects like English, history, and algebra. I seem to be lecturing him all the time about cleaning up his room. His hair is long, too. And I guess he feels I don't understand him, either. . . .

CATHY: *Do* you understand him?

GRETCHEN: Well, I try to. I know the world is different from when I was a kid. I understand about the hair—it's a way of asserting independence. A style that says young people are separate from the Establishment. But I don't understand about the lack of articulateness—the failure to try for a dialogue.

PETER: Oh Christ! That's what my mother says when she's trying to manipulate me. She talks faster than I do. She knows more big words, but the words are full of shit. There's shit in what you're saying, too. You know damned well your son's hair makes you uptight. *My* hair makes *my mother* uptight.

GRETCHEN: All I'm saying is, I'm involved with you. I never met you until tonight, yet I feel I know you. I care about you.

PETER: Okay. But there's a lot of shit in what you're saying. I know it's your first group and all that. But cut out all that condescending crap about "understanding" me. No wonder your old man sneaks out. You probably give him a dose of "understanding" every night.

CATHY: (*Quickly*) Tell her, Peter.

PETER: Well, what have you got to say, Mrs. *Manipulator?*

GRETCHEN: You're being very rude.

PETER: Yeah, I'm rude, all right. But what about what I say? I've got your number. You don't know how to get mad. You can't get mad at your son. You can't get mad at your husband. So you manipulate the way my mother does. You're a bullshit manipulator!

CASRIEL: Gretchen isn't your mother, Peter.

PETER: (*Calmer*) I know . . . but she brought back my feelings about my mother.

CASRIEL: If you're angry at your mother, why not get angry at her? Imagine that your mother is sitting out in the middle of the room. Now tell her that you're angry!

PETER: (*Shouting*) I'm angry. I'm angry! You hurt me and I'm angry, Mother! (*He continues to shout until he breaks down crying. His anger has been tremendously strong, tremendously powerful. Sobbing*) Why does it hurt so much?

CASRIEL: Your anger is now in touch with your pain, that's all.

BARRY: I get angry when I feel hurt.

CASRIEL: Do you hear that, Peter? All of us get hurt. Often, we defend the hurt with anger or fear or withdrawal. It's just plain human. Take that in and understand it. Then try to share it with the group directly. Say "My mother hurt me." Can you tell the group those words?

PETER: It's hard, but I think I can do it. . . . My mother hurt me. . . .

*(He turns to say the words to each group member, looking the person in the eyes as he does so.)*

BARRY: Go ahead, tell Gretchen.

*(Peter has stopped at Gretchen and is struggling to say the words.)*

PETER: *(Crying)* My mother hurt me.

GRETCHEN: *(Getting up from her seat to embrace Peter)* I know she did. I know ... I know.

PETER: *(Crying)* She hurt me. . . .

GRETCHEN: I know, but she did the best she could.

CASRIEL: Just hold him, Gretchen. Just hold him. Don't talk. He doesn't need words. Just touch—develop a feeling of bondedness. Comfort him and give him your love.

*(Peter cries for a while in Gretchen's arms. Then he goes around the room to ask for love. Tim is also circling the room, requesting love. There are jokes in the background. Many group members are talking to relieve their tension.)*

CASRIEL: How do you feel, Gretchen?

GRETCHEN: Loving. . . . It made me feel good to hold Peter that way. I felt a lot of love for him.

CASRIEL: Yes, you look very open. You're rosy-cheeked. It makes you look beautiful.

BARRY: Sure does, Gretchen.

CASRIEL: We haven't helped you with your problem about your husband being unfaithful. That's a terrible problem and a terrible feeling, I know. What do you expect us to do about it?

GRETCHEN: I don't know . . . let me talk about it, I guess. Help me understand it better.

NANCY: Go ahead and talk.

BARRY: You talk, Gretchen. We'll listen.

*(Gretchen proceeds to relate details of a twelve-year mar-
riage that was punctured by her discovery of infidelity. The
group is sympathetic and asks questions. Gretchen rambles a
bit, trying to focus on details in order to avoid the pain.)*

CASRIEL:  Gretchen, do you feel you want to leave your husband?

GRETCHEN:  I feel it's all over. But I'm not sure I want to leave. I
love him. Or, I think I love him. I don't know.

CASRIEL:  I know it's a confusing situation. But it would be pretty
normal to be angry at your husband. Do you think you're
angry?

GRETCHEN:  No, I don't think so. Angry? It depends on what you
mean. I'm disturbed that he's been a liar and a cheat. It
hurts me that he's been a bad father. And that he's being
made a fool out of by a twenty-two-year-old kid. I don't see
what she *sees* in him. He's not so much, really. He's getting
bald—and he's pudgy around the waist.

CASRIEL:  You won't need to put him down, Gretchen, when you
let your anger out. What's his name?

GRETCHEN:  Chuck.

CASRIEL:  Say the words, "I'm angry at you" and think of Chuck.
No need to shout. Just say the words to each member of the
group.

*(Gretchen does what is requested. But there is pain in her
words—not anger. She is controlled about the way she says
the words—and very scared.)*

CASRIEL:  Try these words, Gretchen, "I'm afraid to get angry at
Chuck."

*(Gretchen does a go-around, using the new words. The fear
in her voice becomes stronger. People tell her: "Louder."
She speaks louder, and is almost shouting at the end.)*

CASRIEL:  Now try just the words, "I'm afraid." And say them loud
to each person.

(*Gretchen complies. Group members keep yelling, "louder," and she gets louder. Finally, she is screaming, "I'm afraid!"*)

CASRIEL: That's the truth, Gretchen. You're afraid to get really angry, because you were programmed to believe that anger is wrong—or that anger means abandonment.

(*Gretchen nods in agreement.*)

CASRIEL: Also, I bet you and your parents had a contract going not to get angry at each other.

GRETCHEN: Well, I never got angry at them—especially not at Daddy. I never got angry at Daddy. Not ever.

CASRIEL: You were afraid if you got angry, you would lose your Daddy's love.

GRETCHEN: Yes . . . well, I don't know. My Daddy *did* love me. I know he did.

CASRIEL: Why couldn't you get angry at him?

GRETCHEN: If I even complained to him, he got sullen and withdrawn. He'd look stern. Then, I wouldn't see him. I'd have to eat dinner without him for days, and it seemed like ages.

CASRIEL: How old were you?

GRETCHEN: Five or six.

CASRIEL: No wonder you have trouble with demands—and with anger! When you love somebody, it's normal to make demands or to get angry at him sometimes. If you hold back your anger, you become hostile, or manipulative, or turned off, or withdrawn, or frightened. How does that idea feel?

GRETCHEN: I never thought about it that way.

CASRIEL: Think about it. In the meantime, I'd like to give you a homework assignment. Tell your husband you're angry at him, but that you're afraid to express it. See what happens.

Then, come into your next group prepared to express your anger. All right?

GRETCHEN:  O.K., I'll try.

VILMA:  Don't just *try*. Come in and do it.

CASRIEL:  Vilma, you're the only one who hasn't worked tonight. Do you want to work?

VILMA:  Yes, I *do*, Dan. I want to work on my anger.

BARRY:  That's what you said, Vilma. But you've sat there all night without working.

PETER:  Yeah, Vilma, you play a "catch-me, fuck-me" game, and I don't like it.

TIM:  I don't like it either, Vilma. You're an attractive chick, but I wouldn't want to have anything to do with you.

VILMA:  Nobody asked you to.

PETER:  Yeah, well then how come you twitch your ass at Tim every week? Just to get some exercise for your muscles?

VILMA:  I don't! I enjoy talking to Tim. You're just jealous because I don't talk to you, you little prick.

CASRIEL:  How did you feel when Gretchen said she was afraid to get angry at her husband?

VILMA:  It sounded right. I think she *is* afraid to get angry at him.

BARRY:  How did *you* feel?

VILMA:  Sorry for her. It's normal to get angry.

BARRY:  Why don't you get angry, then? Why don't you get angry at Mitchell?

VILMA:  It's hard for me to get really angry. I mean, I can yell in here and get sarcastic, but I have trouble with anger in the outside world—where it counts.

CASRIEL:  Vilma, if you're angry, get up and get it out. You'll feel better after you do, and you'll learn something that will help you in the "outside world."

BARRY: Yeah, Vilma, if you can yell in here, get up and yell! You're making me anxious, just sitting here.

VILMA: I don't want to. I don't feel like it, right now. I did earlier, but the group wouldn't let me do it.

PETER: That's a lie!

CATHY: Liar, manipulative bitch!

NANCY: You had a choice. You could have worked if you wanted to, but you chose to sit there. Why don't you get up and work now!

VILMA: I don't want to.

GRETCHEN: I'd feel better if you worked on your anger, Vilma. It would help me.

VILMA: I'm not here to help you. Help yourself. I'm here to help *me*.

BARRY: Then, do it! Get up and yell, for God's sake!

VILMA: No, it's the end of the group. I'm anxious about that. I feel pressured. I don't want to.

CATHY: But you *always* wait until the end of the group! You act like a damned baby! Why don't you grow up and act as though you're at least *thirteen?*

CASRIEL: Nancy's right, Vilma. You do have a choice. It's up to you. You can work or not work. But don't manipulate the group by getting them to coax you. Do you want to work!

VILMA: Yes, I do, but I'm afraid.

(*Vilma's "yes-no" feelings bring up strong tension in the group.*)

PETER: Then get up and work on your fear, you cock-teaser!

CATHY: Get up on your feet, you damned bitch! Work!

BARRY: (*On his feet, shouting hoarsely*) Get up and work! I'm sick of the way you manipulate. It's *your* life—you should be the one who wants to get it straight. You're living with a sadistic shit who dumps all over you. You want to know what Mitchell is—he's an uneducated, sadistic, third-rate slob who doesn't have a job. And you support him! If he ever asked you to marry him, you'd go up the wall. The truth is, he fits your bag. You're *afraid* to get married.

VILMA: That isn't true. Mitchell is hunting for a job. If he asked me to marry him, I'd say yes—as soon as he gets a job and some money in the bank.

CASRIEL: That's pretty safe, Vilma. What if Barry were right?

VILMA: He's not right.

CASRIEL: Well, think about it. What if he were right?

VILMA: Then I should drop Mitchell and hunt for someone else. Someone who would marry me. But Mitchell will marry me. I know it.

*(At this point, several group members became extremely angry at Vilma, accusing her of controlling Mitchell and the group through her manipulations.)*

CASRIEL: Look, Vilma, it's time for the group to end. You have a way of setting up a group against you because you are frightened of showing your real need. I know you feel pretty bad, and I don't want you to go home feeling that way. Why don't you stay for the next group. We'll make room for you. It'll be a different group of people. This time, don't set them up and you'll have an easier time showing your feelings. You would rather be defensively hostile than feel the anger you are entitled to feel.

Let's have a group scream, remove this tension, and call it a night.

*(The group screams. The tension is dissipated in a few seconds and the feeling of love permeates the room. People feel it as the group ends. They get up from chairs to put on their coats. There is hugging, laughter, banter. Cigarettes are lighted. Vilma sits alone, in isolated pain. She has used her defenses to "win out" over the group—but in doing so, she has lost. Her hope is the next group. There she may overcome long-time defenses against the anger which was too frightening for her to express when she was a child.)*

These scenes are typical of what happens in my groups all the time. The amount of screaming may have been surprising, but it was actually less than the amount that goes on in most groups. Emotional—not verbal—expression is the foundation of my group process.

How did such a process come into existence? What are its theoretical underpinnings? Why is so much screaming therapeutic?

It is the purpose of this book to answer these questions. There is a history to the development of my process. There are specific reasons, both experiential and theoretical, that explain why I believe the process has been so effective with personalities with such a wide variety of symptoms.

Perhaps the greatest breakthrough came when I realized that it was not enough just to talk about feelings, or even to express them through encounters among group members. I remember one early group, for instance, when a young man was rambling on about how angry he was at his wife. (She was not in the group.) The other people in the room were getting restless, and I knew the young man was just going in circles.

"Wait a minute, Ned," I said. "You say you're angry, but I don't feel it. Don't just talk about the anger. Try to express the feeling itself. *Scream* it out!"

Within seconds, he was bellowing at the top of his lungs, his body coiled in a rage I had rarely seen. When all the screaming was done, he collapsed in tears, full of the pain which years of emotional deprivation and stifled anger had caused.

This was the kind of experience that led me to see that the expression of feelings *full measure* is essential to bring about therapeutic change. Deeply-felt feelings of pain, anger, fear, and the need for love must be ferreted out from the unconscious. Otherwise, they will continue to rule the individual's behavior, feelings, and attitudes in ways over which he has little conscious control.

Once someone experiences his deep feelings by screaming them out, he is relieved of a great part of the burden. His defensive shell begins to disintegrate. Gradually he gains insight into his behavior and attitudes. He sees options in his life which he had felt were impossible before. He can learn to exercise healthy feelings, to express anger when he feels it, to show a vulnerable need to be loved, to be in bonded contact with other human beings.

Most important, within this process he learns to feel genuine pleasure—the pleasure of being himself, full of choices about his life, including the possibility of having meaningful relationships with other people. It is this pleasureable sense of self and others which can lead to a freer, happier life. Although it takes hard work to change lifelong patterns, in the most basic sense, any human being can be just *a scream away from happiness.*

# CHAPTER 3

# An Analyst's Journey: From Couch to Encounter

IT SOMETIMES SEEMS STRANGE to me that I should be writing a book about group therapy. My professional involvement with psychiatry began over twenty-three years ago, yet I started using group therapy as a therapeutic technique only nine years ago.

I graduated from the University of Cincinnati College of Medicine in 1949. For the next four years, I was in training at the Columbia Psychoanalytic Institute for Training and Research and the Kingsbridge Veterans' Administration Hospital, and I served in the U. S. Army as a psychiatrist for a year and a half. I was in Okinawa during that military service, and this experience with another culture led me to seek out Dr. Abram Kardiner, well known for his anthropological work. I was in psychoanalysis with him for seven and one-half years. In the winter of 1953, I set up my private practice as a psychiatrist in New York City. But I did not run my first group for private patients until ten years later.

During those ten years, I relied on psychoanalysis, sometimes mixing it with the less exacting techniques of individual psychotherapy. In some instances, I supplemented these methods with the relief offered by psychopharmacology. I did not conduct any group sessions. At Columbia and Kingsbridge I had been taught to be wary of groups. More people in the therapeutic process meant more variables, and that meant extra problems injected into what was already enormously complicated.

Even today, suspicion of group therapy is not unusual among the most conservative of psychoanalytic professionals. Prior to World War II, S. R. Slavson and Alexander Wolf had experimented with groups, but group therapy found wider support as a makeshift outgrowth of World War II, acceptable as a way to help the flood of neuropsychiatric patients produced by a war. But groups were viewed then only as a temporary therapeutic technique. In recent years, despite the expanding number of classical, encounter, sensitivity and T-groups going on throughout the United States, a significant number of psychiatrists and psychologists judge group therapy as, at best, an expedient technique and, at worst, a dangerous method of treatment.

Probably I would have gone on holding such a view, had I not become professionally involved with problems related to drug addiction. Soon after setting up my private practice, I had taken on an assignment as consulting psychiatrist to a pilot program in New York. The program was set up in three city schools to test the effectiveness of concentrated psychiatric services as a means of reducing delinquency among young people. I was attached to a mental health staff of a high school in a delinquent area. Later, I took a job as psychiatrist to the Court of Special Sessions in Manhattan, where an estimated 70 percent of the cases involved addicts. The ways in which addiction contributed to teenage delinquency were shocking. I saw firsthand how kids would become part-time prostitutes or pimps, pickpockets, burglars, muggers, even armed robbers, in order to pay for the drugs they craved. The price in suffering and in lost human potential was horrendous. It became obvious to me, as it had to many others, that laws and police courts could never be the answer to the problem of addiction. Once hooked, youngsters turned to crime to sustain their habits. Then, to avoid or delay being found out, they would use lies, tears, angry bravado, emotional blackmail, charm, ingratiation, sullen silence—an almost endless series of manipulations. The attempt to break through such defenses required countless hours of professional time—and seemed foredoomed to failure.

Seeking a different approach to the problem, I took a part-time job on the staff of Metropolitan Hospital, at the time New York City's most modern and competent center for medical treatment and research on drug addiction. It was a new hospital under the supervision of Flower Fifth Avenue Hospital, New York Medical College. My experience at this center made me increasingly pessimistic about the possibility of successfully treating addicts. Almost all addicts were "character disordered personalities," and classic psychiatric techniques for treating that character type had proved depressingly ineffective. I began to understand the view held by a majority of psychiatrists: drug addiction was impossible to cure.

While delivering a series of lectures to probation officers, I met a remarkable man who shared my conviction that new techniques of treatment must be found. The man was Dr. Alex Bassin, at that time research psychologist for the Probation Department of the Second Judicial District of the New York State Supreme Court. (He is currently a professor of criminology at the University of Florida.) Dr. Bassin asked if I would be willing to act as psychiatric consultant to a kind of "halfway house" for addicts, if one were to be set up in New York City. It was an iffy question, but I told him yes.

This was the beginning of what was to become Daytop Lodge. (The word "Daytop" stood for "Drug Addicts Treated on Probation.") When presented with a request for funds, the National Institute of Mental Health liked the proposal, but suggested that we first survey existing organizations which were set up to control and treat addiction in major areas throughout the United States. The Institute provided the money for such a survey, and we embarked on the exploration.

The highlight was a July 1962 visit to Synanon, a West Coast community for rehabilitating drug addicts and alcoholics. For by the time I arrived at Synanon, I was more discouraged than ever about the chances of converting addicts into healthy people.

# Synanon and Encounter Groups

To my surprise, at Synanon I saw former addicts changing into functioning human beings. Synanon appeared to be succeeding with more than rehabilitation. Some addicts had actually remained symptom-free since their entry into Synanon, which was then four years old. (The medical criterion for "cure" is five years.)

My first impression was of bustling, hectic activity. I saw males and females, blacks and whites, people of varied ages. They were painting, sawing, hammering. As they worked, they chatted enthusiastically with each other. Their facial expressions were healthy and animated. They greeted visitors with open friendliness. It was all a startling contrast to the sullen, guarded, often lethargic personalities we had encountered elsewhere during the survey.

Most significant, I was overjoyed to see addicts whom I had known in New York City now functioning as productive human beings. What made Synanon successful? I was so intrigued that I asked Chuck Dederich, the founder and guiding light of Synanon, if I could move into the community for "a closer look." I was especially curious about the "Synanon Games" which took place three times a week. These were actually "encounter groups" —a new concept which I had never before witnessed. Several members would get together for at least a couple of hours and confront each other, often with loud emotionality, about anything that was bothering them.

Chuck approved my request, and so began the adventure which was to change my approach to psychiatry. I moved into the Synanon beachfront complex, then a community of less than a hundred souls in Santa Monica. No encounter group was scheduled for that particular day, but I found the discussions pleasurable and informative.

The following day, I was terrified when I joined my first "Synanon Game." The verbal attacks were so intense and so frequent that I began to fear for my safety. A number of times, I considered running out the door or jumping down to the beach below. But I was too fearful of ridicule to risk such action.

During the group, I had remained quiet until a director of Synanon whom I will call Roger looked at a black member of the group and suddenly asked: "Hey, nigger, how do you like being called a black motherfucker?" Shocked, I broke my silence, telling

Roger there were already enough problems in the group without introducing the element of racial prejudice.

Slowly—and surprisingly without anger—the entire group turned its eyes toward me. A man asked: "Do you feel *you* are prejudiced against blacks?"

"No," I answered without hesitation.

"Do you feel Wilbur is less equal than Roger?" asked another group member.

"No, I don't," I mumbled, feeling uncomfortable about the attention I was receiving.

"Do you think he is less adequate than Roger?"

"No," I said once again, a bit annoyed, but still remaining polite.

"Do you think he is less intelligent than Roger?" a voice shot at me.

"Basically, no," I rapidly responded.

The group exploded at me. "Then why do you have to go to Wilbur's defense?" "Can't Wilbur speak for himself, without *you* to defend him?" "Who gave you the right to be Uncle Tom?"

Loud voices pelted angry questions at me. My attitude was bad, they said; I was prejudiced if I felt the need to defend a black man against a white man's name-calling.

The attack was frightening, but it also was strengthening. I had been tested with anger and had not run away or disappeared. I really felt very good—actually exhilarated. Afterwards, when the group members were enjoying coffee and cake together, I found it easy to feel a part of their camaraderie and well-being.

Enjoying the sense of closeness, I wondered how the patients in my private practice would react to such an encounter. It seemed to me that so many of my patients were seeking the warm, close feeling I was now experiencing. The difference was they wanted to share the feeling with the loved ones to whom they were bonded by social ties.

Several other provocative encounter groups at Synanon left me with the same warm glow. I also felt the same kind of fear I had experienced in the first session. Verbal attacks were savage. There was shouting, screaming, swearing, name-calling. Often, as a professional, I felt encounters were too strong, too personal, and too self-serving. I questioned the therapeutic value of a number of attacks. Yet encounters were an important part of the total Synanon treatment. Unquestionably, they served a vital purpose in the community.

# An Emphasis on Behavior

As important as the encounter groups were, the most important thing I saw at Synanon was the focus on behavior. The addicts were told to stop taking dope, to stop telling lies, to stop stealing, to stop drinking alcohol—or to get out! Simply stated, Synanon's basic idea seemed to be: Change an addict's behavior and you can *start* to make him a healthy human being. Without behavioral change, there was no hope of cure. An addict was emotionally a child who would steal, lie, cheat, beg, swindle, and betray in order to sustain his habit.

To any traditionally-trained psychiatrist like myself, the commonsense approach to conduct at Synanon was fresh and fascinating. I lacked such a focus in my approach to analysis and therapy, and so did most of my colleagues.

My private patients weren't addicts, but many had defenses which involved highly objectionable behavior. Suppose they were simply told to stop the behavior cold turkey, the way newcomers to Synanon were told to change their destructive behavior? How would my patients react to the criticism? How hurt would they be? How angry? How would they express the anger? How much damage might be done? How many would react positively to the challenge? The questions were fascinating to ask, but difficult to answer. Because of the nature of the analyst-to-patient relationship, it seemed impossible that I should challenge my patients emphatically about their behavior, right on the spot.

Significantly, most of the confrontations at Synanon focused on conduct. What aroused intense anger was what group members were doing—or *not* doing—in the community. For example, one group member thought another member was being irresponsible about his job at Synanon. Somebody else felt threatened by a defeatist attitude another group member was displaying.

For the most part, the confrontations seemed successful in effecting immediate behavioral change. When confronted with his irresponsibility on the job, a man concentrated on working harder. One individual began to change actions which had been causing others to feel slighted. Another ex-addict sincerely tried to struggle with the self-defeating attitudes others had pointed out to him. In these encounters, I observed more supercharged emotions than I had ever experienced in private practice. I was startled to see how often angry confrontations produced later feelings of affection—both in the attacker and in the person being attacked. I saw intense rage promote healthier attitudes and new insights. High-velocity feelings actually generated therapeutic relationships and results.

But there was another side of the coin. Many of those in the encounters used rage defensively, skillfully, as a weapon. Their angry outbursts were invariably unfair. Often they were not therapeutic for anyone. In many instances anger produced terrifying fear in those attacked. This concerned me. The fear might be so strong that it would cause someone to leave the Synanon community. Worse, the victim might try suicide, or perhaps do physical damage to the person who had attacked him.

In the atmosphere of the Synanon community, I began to sense the strength of the human psyche. I saw people withstand pulverizing verbal attacks on lifetime defenses, yet return to the next encounter with greater—not less—ego strength. Watching the vicious anger within some of the members turn into tender affection after the group also gave fresh insights into the human need to be bonded with others.

I returned to New York full of impressions and notes about Synanon. These became the basis of my book, *So Fair a House,* which was published in late 1963. The National Institute of Mental Health survey report was written and submitted earlier as part of Dr. Bassin's revised proposal, and the Institute had provided funds to support a five-year research study on ways to rehabilitate addicts. I became psychiatric consultant on the project, which was to test four different approaches to treating convicted felons who were addicts. One of these approaches involved a special halfway house, called Daytop Lodge, later to become Daytop Village.

Daytop Lodge was founded in the summer of 1963. It combined a vocational-training program with some of the dynamic
and structure of Synanon—all set up with considerable security
controls. Unfortunately, during the next year the six directors—
only one of whom had been partially trained at Synanon—could
not make the experiment at Daytop Lodge therapeutically viable.

During that same year I was in continuing contact with Chuck
Dederich. I asked Chuck what it would take to start a Synanon
facility on the East Coast. His answer was typically abrupt:
$2,000—enough money for two months' rent, a second-hand sta-
tion wagon, gas, and food for seven members of Synanon who
would drive to the East Coast. I gave them the money, and they
opened a community in Westport, Connecticut, in February of
1963. The continued contact with Synanon groups in Westport
caused me to think further about setting up groups for my
middle-class patients, but the dangers and limitations of the
attack-encounter method concerned me a great deal. At Synanon
there was a twenty-four-hour-a-day, highly regulated, work-orien-
ted therapeutic environment. I could not recreate such a community
for my patients. There was no system for repairing possible
damage to self-esteem caused by group attacks, no way to watch
over patients after they had left a group session. Some of my
patients, I knew, were strong enough to withstand encounter
attacks. But others might not have sufficient ego strength. I
needed a way to offer my patients support and love as well as
challenge.

The problems my patients had with giving and receiving love
were many. One housewife said she craved affection from her
husband and complained that he engaged in sex without
showing her his loving feelings. Yet when I talked to him in one
session, he said *he* felt his wife rejected affection when he offered
it. Another patient had been separated from his wife for over two
years without getting a divorce. He was locked with his wife in a
hurtful power struggle. He seemed unable to understand the
nature of his wife's needs or her loving feelings.

Group therapy might help patients like these, but I felt groups
should incorporate softer and more tender feelings than those I

had seen in Synanon encounters. At the same time, the value of a hard-nosed, no-nonsense focus on behavior was evident. And anger seemed to be a basic human emotion requiring expression. At Synanon I had often seen people become frightened and burst into tears when they became angry. Intensive fear emerged in some members when they were challenged with anger. Others not directly involved in an angry exchange would suddenly start crying or trembling with intense feelings. Clearly anger was the prelude to many other emotions.

# An Encounter Group for Private Patients

In the fall of 1963, I incorporated an experimental group-therapy session into my practice. I chose eight basically character-disordered obsessive personalities who had been in analysis with me for from two to five years. Unsure about the damage that might result if I encountered one of my analytic patients directly, I asked two Synanon catalysts to be part of the group. One was a graduate of Synanon. The other was a criminologist who had joined the Westport Synanon encounter groups with me.

The group was an electrifying success. All eight patients related in a way that was startlingly different from their reactions in analytic sessions. On the couch they had been able to control their emotions and verbalize more methodically. In the group, reactions were quicker, more intense, more emotional.

One obsessive man named Jack had the habit of exercising a self-control by using a sing-song monotone. When the catalyst confronted him and Jack objected, the entire group confirmed that the catalyst's judgment was correct. For the first time since I had seen him, Jack's intellectualized verbal control broke down and the angry control lying behind it was exposed. His voice became so loud, so piercing, that it shocked everyone in the group. Then Jack showed signs of the exhilaration I had seen, and personally experienced, at Synanon. He made warm and vulnerable eye contact with others in the room and was fully

attuned to the accepting feelings being shown toward him. Subsequent private sessions revealed the group incident to be a
pivotal factor in changing Jack's attitudes about anger and love.
The pattern of his life then began to undergo important
changes.

June, a grade school teacher, also surprised me. In private
sessions she had maintained firm control of everything she said,
displaying only a modest amount of emotion. She always attempted to focus on immediate problems in her life which
needed to be solved. In the group she broke down in hysterical,
fearful tears, and from then on her private sessions were different. She showed feelings of fear and inadequacy, a sense of being
unlovable. Her therapy began to be much more productive. We
could deal with her genuine sense of insecurity, rather than her
rationalization about problem solving.

I decided to keep the same people together in a once-a-week
session. In private sessions there continued to be a remarkably
greater access to emotions with no damage to the patients'
psyches. Without exception, the insights my patients achieved as
a result of group encounters proved therapeutic. All eight patients were making greater progress toward emotional health in
private analysis because they had greater access to their feelings.

In retrospect it is evident that Synanon and Daytop, as well as
the groups I was running, were part of something going
on—not just with addicts—but with *people*. The "Human
Potential Movement" had begun. The National Training Laboratory was growing fast. Followers of Maslow and Rogers had
founded the Association for Humanistic Psychology.
Esalen, started in Big Sur in 1959 by Michael Murphy and
Richard Price, was becoming known under the direction of
William Schulz. Dr. Frederick S. Perls practiced his Gestalt
therapy in group workshops. Especially on the West Coast, a few
pioneering psychiatrists and psychologists were developing
group-therapy innovations. Classical groups, encounter groups,
and "T-groups" (training groups) were no longer the only kinds
of groups. In many instances, "sensitivity" was the direction
groups were taking. These last groups, more exploratory than
provocative, were not primarily therapeutic in design. Instead,
they concentrated on developing awareness of one's feeling,
reactions, and self-presentation by interacting with other people.

Since the initial experiment had seemed an unqualified success, I decided to go ahead cautiously with my own experiments with group therapy. During the balance of 1963 and throughout 1964, my group practice gradually enlarged. For all my patients, the number of private sessions was decreased and the number of groups increased. Patients who had formerly come in three or four times a week for private analysis now saw me alone only once or twice a week and attended two or three group sessions.

# Anger and Love

"Encountering" was the motif in those early groups. My patients faced accusations I could never have offered. They confronted each other about behavior and attitudes, often with more anger than anyone deserved. They were screamed at for being emotionally dishonest; told they were boring when they rambled with facts, not feelings; loudly admonished when they withdrew emotionally from the group. And they were challenged to give up their destructive symptoms. For the most part, these patients made faster progress toward emotional health than they had on a strictly analytical schedule. In a few cases, I saw no real improvement. (But these were cases in which I had not seen improvement in private sessions, either.) In no instances did I perceive that the group sessions were doing any damage to my patients.

Initially, I led all groups myself, with a paid catalyst also in attendance. Then, as time went on, I saw that my catalysts could express anger more spontaneously than I could. My professional training had stressed that I avoid anger in relationships with patients, and in those early groups I found it almost impossible to scream angrily at them. I began to wonder if I had to be—or should be—in the groups all the time. Perhaps one of my leaders should take over occasionally.

In one of those early groups, something else important happened that had nothing to do with anger. One day, a woman named Elizabeth sat in her chair, crying uncontrollably. Moved by her pain, the group catalyst and another woman rose spontaneously from their chairs, pulled Elizabeth to her feet, and embraced her. The action startled me. I was moved by Elizabeth's tears, but my training and my position as an authority in the group prevented me from doing what the catalyst and the other group member had done. Yet this incident was an absolutely pivotal moment in the development of my process. The embrace proved vitally important to Elizabeth. It made her realize how much she had needed love all her life. Even more significantly, it caused the entire group to become emotionally exhilarated. Group members freely hugged each other, many of them crying with both pleasure and pain. Elizabeth finally turned to me for an embrace. Should I follow my human impulses, or stick rigidly to my professional training? I was tense, but I hugged her. The group burst out in laughter and "bravos." The reaction was threatening, yet I felt deeply warmed by the experience.

My psychiatric training and experience had taught me to avoid touching anyone in a professional relationship. There also were ways in which my training had conditioned me to remain neutral and nonresponsive. Clearly, without the impediments of the psychiatric education I had experienced, my catalysts—and my patients—were freer to get involved and interact with others.

By this time, Dave Deitch, the Synanon director at Westport, had replaced one of my catalysts. I decided to experiment by having him and the other catalyst each run a group, without me in attendance. (I sat in on the group at the beginning, then left the room.) The reactions of group members were good. Some people reached a more intense anger than they ever had with me in the group, and I saw the value of these breakthroughs in subsequent private sessions. Clearly, experienced peer group leaders were able to do a lot on their own, so I asked the two men to continue to lead groups in which I did not participate. I sat in on these groups frequently, taped all groups, ran groups myself, and continued to work privately with all patients.

During the first six months my groups contained only patients whom I also saw individually. But group members began to talk to other people about what was going on in their groups. Soon people came to me who "just wanted to be in groups," not in private treatment with me. To agree to such requests violated my idea of psychotherapeutic technique. I still felt individual treatment was necessary, so I turned down the first requests. But the queries increased. Most people asking to attend "group only" were in treatment elsewhere. Finally I agreed to let several of them into group, without the requirement that they be in private treatment with me, as long as their therapist agreed. Within a few months, I realized that the experiment was extraordinarily effective. Later I relaxed the rules so that individual sessions were not a prerequisite. Exposed finally *only* to group sessions with me, some new patients were making emotional breakthroughs and gaining insights I would not have believed possible in so short a time.

As time went on, groups gradually became the core of my practice. In the meantime, I had become cofounder, psychiatric director, and medical superintendent of Daytop Village, a therapeutic community for drug addicts much larger in scale than Daytop Lodge. It was the first of the therapeutic communities fashioned after Synanon, but it was supported with government funds. It has served as the model for a score of other communities. Daytop now has a total of five hundred beds in five facilities. Many of its graduates have become active in other drug-addiction therapeutic communities, such as New York's Phoenix House; Chicago's Gateway; Miami's Concept House; the Marathon Houses in Rhode Island, Massachusetts, and Connecticut; and Gardenzia Houses in Pennsylvania.

Dave Deitch became executive director of Daytop. (He also continued to run some groups for me.) Daytop provided an ideal human laboratory for group therapy techniques. Working together, Dave and I modified and redefined the behaviorally based process of Synanon. We added new techniques as we learned them. We introduced into Daytop techniques developed in my private practice and vice versa. We brought ex-addicts from Daytop to sit in on some of my private groups, and we sent some of my patients to Daytop groups.

The groups in my private practice evolved into something different from what they had started out to be. The attack-encounter discipline melded into something else. Anger was still important. But so was love.

Two factors contributed significantly to this change. One was the freedom felt by my group catalysts (and many patients), who were not psychiatrists or psychologists, to express their loving feelings openly to other group members. The other was our experimentation with an extended group, called a "marathon." At the time, both approaches were somewhat controversial. Today, the marathon is widely accepted as a valuable tool of group psychotherapy. The use of laymen as group leaders remains in question.

# Introduction of the Marathon

I had a hunch during those early groups that running a session for several hours without stop would prove particularly effective with character-disordered personalities. This is a category into which most of the ex-addicts at Daytop would readily fit, but most of my patients were character-disordered, too. They were people who suffered from what I call "anesthetized feelings." Though they might be in touch with superficial, defensive feelings, they were really out of contact with their deepest emotions.

My private groups, which lasted an hour and a half or even two hours, did not give the dynamic a chance to work on severely character-disordered people. Just as things got going the time would be up, and these people could walk out the door to retrench their defenses. A longer group might well get to these individuals. What I read and heard about the extended time groups being run by George A. Bach and Frederick Stoller on the West Coast made the technique seem very interesting.

Dave agreed to let a Daytop group run as long into the night as the group was willing to continue. He came to me the next day, aglow. Something beautiful had happened, he said. The group kept going all through the night with the usual shouting and yelling, and about five in the morning the dynamic changed. One of the toughest former addicts broke down in tears, and suddenly everyone was holding him and crying, too. The entire group was filled with love and a new feeling of closeness. "It was like a rebirth for all of us," Dave said. "We felt like brothers— like one person all together."

This was the beginning of regular marathons at Daytop. We took the name (but not the process) from the West Coast experiments being run by Bach and Stoller. From the beginning, we sought the experience of love and community in our marathons. The sessions ran for thirty hours and allowed the group member not more than four hours of sleep. We found marathons unusually effective in breaking down tough lifetime defenses and in opening up people emotionally to new tender feelings. The fatigue of staying awake for many hours had much to do with these emotional breakthroughs, but we did everything we could during the marathon—and in the "post-marathon" groups following it—to reinforce the feelings and insights group members had gained. (Today, our techniques have developed to the point that we don't need thirty-hour marathons. Most of our extended-time groups last only sixteen hours and have twice the number of participants as the early twelve-man marathons. There is more emotionality expressed in thirty minutes of our current marathon than was expressed in the thirty hours of the original variety! Now almost all participants have a very significant emotional experience.)

# Screaming

As my group practice grew, I began to use some of my more advanced patients as catalysts, then to train them to conduct groups themselves under my supervision. Like my earlier catalyst/leaders, these new leaders added much to my understanding of emotional interaction. Some were remarkable instruments of human feeling—intuitively aware of what was going on with themselves and with other group members, and emotionally free enough to express what they felt.

Often these leaders helped group members find more effective ways to express feelings. In one group, a woman began to talk about her fear. As she went on for one tension-filled minute after another, the anxiety in the room became almost unbearable. People shuffled restlessly, coughed, glanced toward me and the catalyst. The group leader interrupted with a question: "Are you afraid?" Annoyed, the woman glared at the leader/catalyst. "Yes, I'm afraid," she yelled. Tears came to her eyes, as her surface anger turned to fear. Then, she began to shout: "I'm afraid! I'm afraid! I'm afraid!" The shouts led to screams and shrieks. It was a significant emotional experience, not only for the woman, but also for others in the room.

Through such one-at-a-time occurrences, it became clear that *words alone* were often a defense which insulated many persons from actually experiencing the emotions they were talking about. At another time, a henpecked man named Tom was explaining why he was irritated with his wife. "You don't *sound* angry," I told him. The group agreed, and their agreement visibly annoyed Tom. Suddenly, he leapt to his feet. "I *am* angry," he screamed. "I'm ANGRY! . . . I'm ANGRY! . . . I'm ANGRY!" His screams continued, getting louder and louder, until he had reached an intense rage. This suddenly turned to pleasure. His shoulders squared back, and he began to grin as he shouted. I felt his deep-level anger, and so did everyone else. After his anger had been expressed, Tom sounded more free and assertive.

"Now, Tom, what were you saying about your reasons for being angry toward your wife?" I asked.

He laughed. "Reasons, hell," he said. "I'm angry. I'm going to tell her to *stop* it. That's all there is to it." (Tom's complaint was that his wife interrupted him in public and corrected the details of his stories.)

"Pretend Margie is your wife," I told him, gesturing toward a group member. "Tell *her* to stop it."

Tom began to shout "stop it" at Margie. It sounded a bit artificial at first, but then became increasingly vigorous. The power of his assertion was contagious. The group enjoyed it and gave him the homework assignment of making the assertion to his wife.

The following week, Tom reported that he had made the assertion.

"*Did* she say she would stop it, Tom?" a group member demanded to know.

"No," he admitted, ashamedly. "She told me she interrupted only when my facts are wrong."

"Didn't that make you angry?" A member of the group asked.

"No," Tom replied with obvious discomfort. "She's right, I guess. Sometimes my facts aren't right." Then he added: "But I don't like it." The group, which had enjoyed Tom's anger of the previous week, got him to his feet again to shout "I'm ANGRY." Then they asked him to voice his assertion again, and asked him to report back the following week on a second confrontation with his wife.

It took three weeks before Tom was able to report he *had* got angry at his wife, and that his wife had agreed to try to stop interrupting him. (The group's next assignment to Tom: Bring your wife into the group, as a regular member.)

The use of mats on the floor was introduced quite by accident about three-and-one-half years ago. Rick, a rather sullen, withdrawn social worker, was expressing anger. We encouraged him to express it louder and louder and louder. In the course of the anger exercise, he was hit by what we now associate with "identity pain." He screamed out this pain again and again, suddenly clutched his stomach saying, "Oh, my God, it's unbearable!" and fell off his chair onto the floor. At this moment the quality of his pain changed. You could hear the difference in the sounds, see the difference on his face. It was no longer the pain of the here and now, but rather the pain of a historic moment early in his life. The total feeling of helplessness while lying on his back, no longer a peer sitting amongst us, apparently brought back the historical feeling buried in his unconscious. I got other people in Rick's group to get down on the floor right away. Immediately, the quality of their feelings changed, too.

This tremendous abreaction of historical feelings has proved to be extremely therapeutic in helping the person become aware of current feelings, attitudes, and behavior. Today we use mats and makeshift pillows for historical emotional exercises in all marathons. Often several people will be on the floor at once. Two or three group members will cluster around each one, occasionally holding the person's hands, stroking his arms, massaging his clenched belly, all to encourage him to express the sounds of his historical feelings. In advanced groups lasting only two or three hours we also resort to mats on many occasions. In this way advanced patients are able to get to their deep feelings rapidly, then sit back and connect the experience with fascinating insight into their present-day problems.

Thus effective techniques developed, one step at a time, through the dynamic of the group process. Group leaders, as well as group members, helped devise techniques for aiding individuals in expressing deeply-felt emotions. Then, as time went on, the techniques became "exercises" which many group members and leaders were familiar with. In the largest sense, my group leaders and I saw that confrontation was not the only way. We saw that deep feelings required expression just for themselves. Group members were encouraged to scream out their anger or fear or pain "full measure," at the top of their lungs. We also found that holding people who were screaming gave them extra emotional support and so made the painful or frightening feelings a bit easier to experience.

# AREBA

The AREBA program was an outgrowth of the Daytop methods, enriched and extensively modified by my emotional group process. AREBA (Accelerated Re-education of the Emotions, Behavior, and Attitudes) is a therapeutic community which combines a rigid structure and discipline with encounter and other techniques, and is designed specifically for the rehabilitation of middle-class youngsters who are drug addicts or suffer other severe problems which keep them from functioning.

As my group practice developed, I saw that drug addiction continued to be a serious problem. Several parents in my groups were having problems with children who had become addicted to hard drugs. These youths needed more than even the most intensive of psychotherapy regimens. They needed a program of intensive care that would teach them how to function.

The AREBA program consists of three phases spread over a period of twelve months or so. In the first phase, young people live and "work" at the AREBA headquarters, which are on the top four floors of the Casriel Institute building. During this phase, the AREBA residents are under intensive control from the moment they get up until the time they go to bed. They all have specific projects and jobs for which they are responsible within the AREBA community. In the second phase, the youngsters continue to live at AREBA but are permitted to go to school or to take an outside job. In the third phase, they are permitted to live outside the building as well as to work or go to school, but they must return for groups and other therapy.

Throughout the program, the youngsters take part in groups consisting exclusively of AREBA members and in groups at the Institute which contain middle-class patients as well as AREBA residents. In addition, there are special groups consisting only of AREBA young people and their parents.

At this time, 80 percent of the eighty youngsters who entered AREBA during the past twenty-five months are still in the program or have completed it. Twenty-four of the twenty-five who have graduated have stayed healthy. Of the sixteen who left without graduation, four were withdrawn because of financial reasons, and twelve left on their own and did not return. However, half of these "splitees" are functioning today without drugs.

# Human Needs in a Sick Culture

Despite the material wealth of America, a sense of dissatisfaction prevails among the people. Scores of millions feel unfulfilled, unhappy, aimless. An increasing number of people seem to grasp for the thrill of the moment in order to dull a lifelong feeling of deprivation. More and more Americans numb themselves with alcohol, canned entertainment, drugs, compulsive work, nonfeeling compulsive sex, spectator sports. More and more human beings find that, though they may not be *un*happy, they are not *happy*—without knowing *why* they are not happy, or what to do about it.

A vast number of Americans seriously suffer from "anesthetized feelings." In psychiatric terminology, these are "character-disordered personalities." They are angry, afraid, in pain, or in need. But they *don't feel* the anger, fear, pain, or need—except, perhaps, superficially or sporadically. These symptoms are typical of the addicts at Synanon, Daytop, AREBA, and of the majority of my middle-class patients at the Institute. They are actually encapsulated from their gut-level feelings. Their capacity to relate to other people with trust and to give and receive love is critically impaired. Often, they "act out" destructively on the basis of deep feelings from which they are insulated. They keep on doing the same thing day after day, without knowing why they do it or what it is all about.

As individuals, many of us tend to function in terms of the socially accepted values and images of our particular subculture, rather than out of a sense of our own worth. The institutions and mores in our pluralistic society even reward us for lack of conviction. Millions are role-playing: In our jobs, as we light the boss's cigarettes. With our neighbors, as we pretend to be cordial hosts. With our children, as we attempt to be "pals." With our mates, as we pore over texts on sexual techniques and strive mechanistically to be good lovers. We repress our honest feelings as we strive to do the socially appropriate or admired thing. "Don't get involved." "Don't make waves." "Don't get angry." "Don't be afraid." Or, in the phrase of youth, "Cool it."

The motif of the entire tableau is an Emotional Turn-Off. In order to play out their roles, a vast number of Americans must insulate themselves from their gut feelings. Otherwise, they would feel the painful confusion and humiliation which their roles exact. We are taught at a very early age to repress gut-level feelings—feelings which have meant survival to animals and indeed to other human beings in much earlier times.

What we're left with is some contact with superficial feelings, most often defensive ones designed to ward off those deeper feelings which our culture forbids. And we are left with a symptom-ridden world. People are often actively destructive to themselves and to others. At best, they feel a discomforting malaise, a sense that something is not right.

My groups did not start with a theory about the needs of people in contemporary society. They evolved, one step at a time, through trial and error. Only after I had observed the group dynamic working successfully did I begin to search for a theoretical structure that would explain what was going on, and explain why nonverbal techniques were proving therapeutic for so many patients.

Most basically, I saw that we were learning to deal simultaneously with all three sides of what I call "Triangular Man"—his *behavior, feelings,* and *attitudes.* When successful, we could bring about basic personality changes. The nature of these changes have led me to call the process "the New Identity Groups."

I saw further that, in addition to helping neurotics, we were getting at a defensive mechanism specific to the character-disordered personality. It is a mechanism different from the classic responses of "flight" or "fight" which I had learned about in my psychiatric training. I believe this new defensive mechanism—which I call "freeze"—has not heretofore been discussed in medical literature.

Despite the theoretical structure of my groups, I feel it is the process itself which is most important. The process involves more than sensitivity groups, more than encounters. I occasionally try new exercises and techniques, experiment with different group formats, add to the theoretical basis of the process new insights and crystalizations of old ones. Our group method is constantly changing. The stress is on exercising and improving those things which appear to be of greater value and eliminating those which appear to be of lesser value. By its nature, it is a *dynamic* process.

As effective as the techniques used in my practice have been, the Casriel Institute and AREBA meet with their share of failures. We have not been able to help every alcoholic, every emotionally infantile person, every drug addict, or even every mild neurotic. Some people have come to a few groups, then departed. There is no real chance to treat them. Others stay for dozens of groups, and leave when the pressure to change mounts. But we have helped many with symptoms similar to those who leave. A primary reason, I believe, is that the New Identity Process is a therapeutic method which can get *beyond the symptom* very quickly—beyond the symptom to the feelings and attitudes that are its genesis. It is with these deeper facets of Triangular Man that an individual must grapple in order to change his life significantly.

Such change can only take place and become permanent if the group experience occurs within a specific, demanding structure to which the individual is fully committed. *My groups involve a process of education. There is no magic.* Group therapy is not meant to provide an escape from struggle, a hiding place from the outside world, a promise of instant cure. It is, rather, an educational program aimed at helping patients by rehumanizing them. Group therapy helps emotionally disturbed people identify the problems that they have in relating to others. It can help eliminate destructive behavior, feelings, and attitudes. It can begin to reprogram people toward greater pleasure, toward greater genuine productivity.

# CHAPTER 4 | *Emotional Health*

To be free to choose, one must first be free to feel, free to think, and free to act.

How do we recognize such freedom? How do we achieve it? What, really, *is* emotional health?

In a world where symptoms of emotional sickness are rampant, do we have any real criterion of what people would be like if they were not emotionally "sick?" What would be there in place of symptoms?

There is pitifully little psychiatric terminology to describe health. After all, we psychiatrists devote ourselves to treating varying stages of emotional discomfort and self-defeat. We are really unfamiliar with emotional health. Our preoccupation is with symptoms. Even our professional diagnoses are essentially labels for maladaptive feelings, attitudes, or behavior.

Remove the overt, observable symptoms, and we too often call the patient "healthy." But few of us have attempted to define the nature of emotional health. We have not struggled to be precise about the goal our profession supposedly points to!

You do not have to be a psychiatrist or a psychologist to know that some people are emotionally disturbed. You *know,* for example, that one friend is too rigid in his views. That another

66

cannot laugh at himself and is often a bit pompous. Perhaps you know a woman you do not trust because she is "too nice." If you are like most of us, you have friends or acquaintances who are too argumentative, too talkative, too gossip-prone, too quick to take offense, too quiet, too bossy, too something. A list of the "human excesses" of *others* can seem virtually endless.

Even so, you probably think a lot of your friends have reasonably good mental health. *All* of them are not getting divorces, underachieving on their jobs, suffering from ulcers, drinking too much, eating their way to obesity, taking drugs, overtly messing up communications with children (or parents), or constantly quarreling with co-workers and relatives. *Some* of the people you know are living their lives productively and responsibly without seeming to be in a constant state of despair. And most of these people are okay to have as friends, neighbors, co-workers, parents, children, and relatives.

Or are they? How do you gauge the mental health of a friend or neighbor? Is it so hard to be emotionally healthy that nobody makes the grade? How do you gauge your own emotional health?

To answer these questions, in my judgment, you have to look at all three parts of "Triangular Man." You must look at behavior, feelings, and attitudes.

Straightforward facts about behavior are not by themselves enough to indicate health. Quite simply, some emotionally disturbed persons "act out" destructively and others do not. Of course, whether or not they act out destructively, disturbed people "leak" bad feelings, such as hostility. A man may be under tremendous inner pressure, yet appear to be functioning normally. If you don't know him well, or if for any reason you are insensitive to the "signals" he emits, you may think him quite healthy emotionally. You would be wrong, as those who love the man will tell you if you talk to them intimately about him.

The person who appears to be behaving so responsibly may be a character-disordered personality, out of contact with his feelings. Compulsive persons often act responsibly—toward everyone but themselves. The world is better off, generally, because they exist. But compulsive persons do not get the pleasure they are entitled to have. And neither do their mates, their offspring, or their employees.

Obviously, outward behavior alone cannot be the standard for emotional health. It is necessary to know how an individual *feels* about his life, and how those closest to him feel about their relationship with him. The feelings beneath the façade of social conventions must be ascertained. Otherwise, unless you are extremely sensitive to human "signals," you can be fooled.

Attitudes are the third criterion. In emotionally distressed people, you can sense self-destructive attitudes. You hear them manifested in words. You see them in glances. Or in withdrawals from human contact. Attitudes are the residual value systems we all carry with us, and are based on the experiences we have had. In emotionally disturbed people, a great number of viewpoints are self-defeating.

I have a patient who carries around the attitude that women are less intelligent, less competent, and less trustworthy than men. A lonely bachelor in his thirties, he is heterosexual, dates girls, and sometimes sleeps with them. But no relationship with a girl lasts more than a few months. The women he dates find him physically attractive, but they seem to get bored with him rapidly. Undoubtedly, they "feel" the attitude he has toward them as well as the fear and aggression tied up with his antifemale outlook. This man was an only child in a household without women. His widowed father bore a grudge against women. And the son adopted this attitude. During therapy sessions, the son complains in genuine bewilderment about his failure to sustain a lasting relationship with a woman.

One of my first group patients had difficulty experiencing pleasure. His attitude was that pleasurable experiences have to be paid for with subsequent pain. Over a period of three years, he gave up his symptoms of depression and acute alcoholism, worked through his anger toward his mother and father, moved into a girl's apartment, and finally married her. Yet throughout this period, and afterwards, he has had to struggle with his pain-follows-pleasure attitude. For a while he enjoys being with his wife and with other friends. Then he becomes engulfed in a shroud of depression, mingled with pain.

This story illustrates why I call attitudes "residual." Long after a person has forsaken his "symptoms," worked his way through core feelings in his belly, and begun to behave as he should, the multitude of destructive attitudes programmed into him in child-hood still affect his feelings. And his actions, if he lets them. Attitudes are, after all, structured patterns of thinking which have taken a lifetime to develop. Though they are specific, they are adaptable and come with infinite variations. They can be subtle and therefore difficult to identify. They can permeate all areas of an individual's life. Attitudes are not easy to change. If a maladaptive attitude is not uncovered, it may remain with a basically healthy individual for life.

We consider all three sides of Triangular Man when inter-viewing new patients at the Casriel Institute. The system of evaluation we use in this initial interview will give you an idea of what I believe the nature of emotional health to be.

First of all, we ask: *What are the person's symptoms? What brought him to seek therapy?* Is he an alcoholic who has trouble holding a job? A homosexual? A high-I.Q. student who is flunk-ing out of school? An overweight girl who never goes out with boys? Is he alienated and lonely or unable to maintain significant heterosexual peer relationships?

Spotting the symptoms matters a great deal, because my ap-proach to therapy requires a patient to give up destructive symptoms from the start.

Some of our initial history-related questions are also aimed at determining whether or not an individual may have suicidal or homicidal tendencies. Has he ever attempted suicide? Has a parent or relative? If depression exists, how severe is it? How prolonged has it been? Does the patient use sleeping pills? Why? Has he ever taken too many by accident? What were the years before age six like? How deprived was the individual of the emotional nourishment he needed? How *angry* does the person get? What makes him angry? Has he ever tried to maim or kill anyone? If so, why? How often has he been involved in physical violence? Does he feel anyone is "against him"? Who? And why?

Questions like these are attempts to identify persons who should be specially supervised in a group situation. Certain kinds of answers indicate a need to examine the person carefully before he is admitted to a group.

Our second question: *Is the individual open or closed?* An

open person shows his feelings on his face and expresses with his voice the feelings he is talking about. If he is talking about fear, I *hear* fear in his voice. And, chances are, I experience some of his fear in my belly. The emotions the person is feeling and showing are communicated to me (or to any open, knowledgeable listener). I am able to empathize and understand.

A closed individual, when talking about emotions, frequently transmits no feelings whatsoever. A closed individual may be talking about how he was rejected in a love relationship. His words may be crisp, chilly, matter-of-fact, boringly modulated. One hears his words, droning on like a computer recording in a science fiction movie. At a feeling level, a listener experiences tension and anxiety, with sporadic "leaks" of hostility, fear, hate, and so on. These are "leaks" only because he cannot show his feelings openly. You are bored quickly when you listen to a closed personality. And you want to switch off the confusion. It's as though the video and audio on a television set were not aligned. You want to turn off either the audio or the video. Or *both.* Trying to concentrate on everything going on is tension-producing, discomforting, and unrewarding.

Most closed people do not know they are closed. Often, they are aware that "something's missing" in their lives. They feel lonely and out of contact with other people. But they are oblivious to the fact that they fail to transmit real feelings to other people.

Most open people can show anger, but closed people exert a tremendous amount of control, leaking hostility rather than expressing anger. Open people also can show fear; closed people withdraw instead.

Our third question attempts to evaluate the emotional, attitudinal and behavioral maturity of the person. We ask: *Is the person an infant? A child? An adolescent? Or an adult?*\*

It is not always easy to put someone into one of four classifications. Some individuals sit right on the line between childhood and adolescence or between adolescence and adulthood. Often the new patient is an adult in some ways, a child in others. But

---

\*Although these classifications sound similar to the "parent," "child," and "adult" of Eric Berne's transactional analysis, they are not the same.

we do try to pinpoint some distinctions in our initial interview. We make the diagnosis on the basis of what we see and hear during that interview. We gauge emotional maturity by the feelings, behavior, and attitudes of the individual. These are some of the guidelines:

Adults realize that they cannot have their cake and eat it, too. They are responsible on their jobs and in their personal lives. You can rely on them, because they do what they say they will do. They accept the responsibility for their own lives, are aware of choices, and realize there may be prices to pay for certain choices.

Adolescents want to eat their cake and blame their parents because the cake is gone. They are angry at Mommy *or* Daddy, at *both* Mommy and Daddy, and often at brothers and sisters, too. They seldom know it, but they are shifting the responsibility for their own lives to Mommy and Daddy. Often, the behavior of an emotional adolescent (who chronologically may be fifty-five years old) entails destructive acting out. Rebellion is the motif. Teachers, professors, college presidents, bosses, mates—all can represent authority symbols against whom they must act out. Emotional adolescents are hard to please and quick to find fault. (Embarrassingly, their insights can prove altogether too accurate!) Their difficulty is that they seldom solve their basic problems. Like grasshoppers, they hop from one set of problems to a new set of difficulties, which turn out to be similar to the ones they have left. Emotional adolescents demand the freedom to act, but do not accept responsibility for their behavior. They become angry if you insist that they must accept the responsibility.

Emotional children differ from emotional adolescents in that they are not in rebellion. Instead, they act out essentially seductive roles with mates, bosses, offspring. An emotional child "converts" a significant person into Mommy or Daddy, and then performs to get love or approval. A child wants to have his cake and eat it, too. In therapy, the difficulty is that he quickly turns his therapist into Daddy or Mommy, and says, in effect: "Just tell me what to do, and I'll do it. I'll be a good little girl, and then you'll be nice to me and make me well and I'll love you forever, Daddy."

Emotional infants want their cakes to be magically hand-fed to them, for ever and ever. When emotional infants arrive at my office, invariably a spouse, parent, or someone in authority brings them in. During the initial interview, the emotional infant demands instant magic. Most drug addicts fall into this category. Their attitudes say: "Cure me immediately and painlessly, Dr. Casriel. Lay the magic wand upon me, and then I'll worship you as God." Emotional infants are self-centered and demanding babies, incapable of relating to the feelings and needs of others. If you have a modicum of perception, they are easy to spot.

Our fourth set of questions is as follows: *Is the individual able to maintain an intimate and meaningful relationship with at least one peer? If so, does the relationship appear to be mutually rewarding? If not, what appears to be in the way of his forming such relationships?*

It takes greater emotional maturity to maintain a satisfactory relationship with someone than it does to live an emotionally separate existence. Often problems which seemed tiny when an individual was alone begin to loom much larger under the stress of a close relationship.

The word "peer" is important. A person who relates only to those who are not his intellectual, social, and economic equals isn't taking many risks. He is living in a "sheltered workshop!" Also, of course, relationships should be mutually rewarding, or something unhealthy is going on.

Our fifth question has to do with the three diagnostic labels used by most people in psychiatry today: *Is the person neurotic, character-disordered, or psychotic?*

In psychiatric terms today, the three classic divisions of emotionally distressed people are the psychotic, neurotic, and character-disordered. (I discuss them at length in Chapter 8.)

The people in my practice today are either character-disordered or neurotic. Although I have occasionally put psychotics—all borderline schizophrenics whose conditions were offset by medication—into groups, I have found the experience was not really beneficial to the schizophrenic or to the group. I no longer accept schizophrenics into my practice.

For the character-disordered and neurotic personalities, there are some important distinctions. Basically, the character-disordered person (about 80 percent of my patients) defends himself by anesthetizing his feelings. He really cuts himself off completely from his basic feelings so that he is in a state of emotional isolation. He reinforces this withdrawal by acting out his symptom: He may shoot dope, get drunk, work sixteen hours a day, over-eat, or clean house with the compulsion of a perfectionist; whatever the symptom, it is a means of neutralizing his deep feelings before he has to face them at a conscious level. He uses a defense mechanism which I call "freeze."

The character-disordered personality represses most of his feelings so that he does not feel them at a conscious level. The neurotic suppresses his feelings—especially the basic survival feelings of fear (which prompts the defensive mechanism of "flight") and anger (which prompts the response of "fight"). Yet these suppressed feelings constantly reappear in distorted, emotionally painful ways. The neurotic is in pain most of the time, whether it comes from severe anxiety, depression, a particular phobia, or other neurotic symptoms.

The distinction between neurotics and character-disordered people rapidly disappears once they get into the group process. However, it is important for me and my group leaders to understand at the start which defensive mechanism the individual employs.

Our sixth question attempts to categorize the person as one of two types: *Is he an Acceptor or Rejector?*

At this point the terms will seem a bit jargonistic. The concept is explained fully in Chapter 11, so I shall only touch upon the highlights here.

In the Acceptor/Rejector diagnosis, my concern is with how the individual basically reacts to others. What does he expect from relationships with other people?

In childhood, a response pattern is established which becomes fundamental to a person's life. The child either accepts or rejects the significant authority/love relationship with the person who provides for him or gives to him. Unconsciously made, the decision is a result of many factors, both biological and environmental. Once made, however, the decision is not changed. It becomes pivotal to the individual's personality development.

Our diagnosis of Acceptor or Rejector grows out of the facts we learn, as well as the dynamics of the initial interview. An Acceptor has been conditioned to pay a high price in pain for love and approval. He expects to pay for any love and is what Freud misunderstandingly called a masochist. A better word would be Dr. Sandor Rado's "pain-dependent." An Acceptor expects and even searches out pain in a love relationship because that is what he is accustomed to. An Acceptor will frequently be involved in a bad marriage or love affair and will be paying a terribly high price for a meager ration of love. Although he finds such a situation painful, he will tend to take the continuing hurt for granted. An Acceptor will often be immobilized by fear and have only modest access to anger toward people important to him. Typically, Acceptors have deep-seated identity problems. They unconsciously fear they actually cannot exist without a significant loved other. Thus they are willing to pay any price, no matter how unfair. They frequently do not respect the loved one in the relationship *unless* the price they pay for love is painfully great.

The Rejector, on the other hand, has a far stronger sense of his own identity, but is a great deal less trusting toward significant human relationships. He has learned to "suck his own thumb"—to do for himself—rather than to trust others for love. He has been programmed to have only a modest tolerance for pain, and he consistently "turns off" pain in himself and others. He tends to react with distrust. If he is a neurotic, his response is often anger, physical and aggressive. (This is Freud's mistaken concept of a sadist, which arose from observing Rejectors who react with anger when threatened by love from a loved object.) If he is character-disordered, his response may be tight-lipped control. A neurotic Rejector may also react with fear; a character disorder, with overt or covert withdrawal. The Rejector keeps to himself his innermost needs for love. Even in a marriage he considers good, a Rejector often feels lonely and isolated. He cannot accept love from others because he unconsciously feels that the price he may have to pay in pain is too great.

The Acceptor, although he suffers pain in a human relationship, does enjoy love when it is offered. The Rejector, on the other hand, does not take the chance to get involved. He suffers no pain, but he feels no love. He feels instead a loneliness and isolation and, finally, put-upon and burdened, as though he is contributing more to the relationship than he is getting out. This, of course, is true, but he doesn't realize the situation is of his own making.

Our seventh question asks: *Is the person productive in terms of his background and potential? Is he potentially a first-class citizen, although he is operating comfortably as a second-class citizen?*

Something is wrong if a Yale graduate takes a permanent job as a shipping clerk. Or if a girl with a master's degree in philosophy spends her free social time dating high school drop-outs. Something is amiss when an intelligent, educated, and capable housewife and mother allows herself to become so bogged down in day-to-day chores that her conversation and attitudes bore her husband and neighbors. Something is wrong if a youngster with outstanding art and design talent takes a job doing mechanical paste-ups, and continues to do paste-ups, without striving to better his lot.

Potential is different in every individual. Potential depends upon intelligence, physical health, creativity, specific talents, physical appearance, education, social status, and even the things that money can buy, good food, medicine, education, and leisure. A healthy person works productively toward his potential. He takes time from work for relaxation, pleasurable activities, contemplation. But, centrally, he finds challenge and stimulation in stretching his abilities productively.

The final set of questions attempts to gauge *how the individual deals with anger and love,* the two feelings least understood and most distorted in our society. Here, actually, four questions are involved:

1. *How is he at receiving love?*
2. *How is he at giving anger?*
3. *How is he at receiving anger?*
4. *How is he at giving love?*

Giving and receiving love and anger are quite different things. A Rejector, for instance, can be good at giving love. But taking in love is terribly hard for him. He knows that he is entitled to be loved, but he feels that the price is too great. He has no problem being an individual; he has a strong identity. But he feels he cannot—will not—be part of an emotional couple. It will cost him too much pain. To take in love, the Rejector must abandon the façade of pride and self-sufficiency behind which he has hidden fo᠆ most of his life. He must openly admit his *need* to be loved. The admission makes him feel dangerously vulnerable. When a Rejector truly takes in love (as opposed to pretending socially to take it in), tears of historic pain fill his eyes. Acceptors can usually take in love more easily. Expecting to pay a price in pain for it, they show the pain more readily. They are programmed that way. But if there is not enough pain, they may negate or downgrade the love, or even reject the person who gives the love. An Acceptor's subjective pain is not as unbearable as the Rejector's subjective feeling of pain.

In our culture, almost everyone has some trouble giving and receiving anger. It is a constantly stifled feeling. Yet psychologically it is impossible to love someone without feeling angry at him quite frequently. If the anger is not shown, it has to be bottled up. And bottled-up anger leaks out as hostility, boredom, depression.

An Acceptor especially fears anger because he feels he would lose the loved object. That is why he is willing to pay such a large price for love and why he feels he is not entitled to love without paying that price. He has no problem being the inferior partner of an emotional couple because he feels he cannot survive as an individual without the relationship. He is dependent upon the loved object to survive, to give him identity. He must keep the relationship even if the partner says he does not love him. He does not show his anger, but depression is a frequent symptom.

Our groups focus right away on love and anger because they are the easiest basic feelings to observe and project in a therapeutic situation. But *pain* is just as basic. How an individual relates to pain tells us how he has been programmed. For one thing, people react to anticipated pain (called "danger") with fear or anger or emotional isolation, depending upon their emotional upbringing.

I find that the feeling of pain has been greatly misunderstood by many psychotherapists. One reason may be that psychotherapists tend to be Rejectors and isolate themselves emotionally from the intense pleasure/pain of human relationships. Because they personally have so much difficulty in feeling and expressing their pain, they have evaded and ignored its significance. Some have even called pain a physical feeling and not an emotion. Conversely, they have called depression (really covered-up anger or loss of love) a feeling. Depression to our groups is a symptom and is dealt with as are all symptoms. We try to push beyond the symptom to the feelings underneath.

The fourth basic feeling—fear—is especially distorted for men in our culture. From early childhood, they are presented with the enculturated attitude that "men are not afraid." They spend their entire lives trying to deny or disguise what is actually a basic survival feeling. (Many women are taught that anger is "unwomanly." The connotation of "bitchiness" is female, and bitchiness is really anger which has had to come out indirectly.) I have also seen that both sexes frequently associate fear with helplessness, a state unconsciously "remembered" from infancy, when the individual actually was helpless against danger. In groups, it is often this feeling of helplessness which patients fear, not the feeling of fear itself.

The fifth basic feeling is pleasure—the feeling of having one's needs met by others and one's self. (Love is the anticipation of pleasure, both through relationships with others and through self-esteem, or self-love.) Most likely, the individual being diagnosed hasn't much of a capacity for pleasure at that point. We will get some idea of his capacity when we ask about significant relationships in his life and about his own productivity. A basic aim of therapy, of course, is to recondition the individual so that life can be more pleasurable.

The eight diagnostic statements that follow suggest the profile of emotional health:

1. *Psychologically healthy people are free from self-destructive behavioral patterns.* They treat their bodies and their minds with respect, because they respect themselves. They are not victims of drugs, alcohol, overeating, late-night carousing, or other damaging habits. Motivated toward maximum pleasure (not pain),

they do what is best for *them*—unless doing so brings harm to others. They don't isolate themselves needlessly. Unlike Saul Bellow's Herzog, they don't subsist on canned foods when they can eat steak. They are able to enjoy their sensuality and sexuality fully—without shame. In every area of life, a psychologically healthy individual maintains *maximum choice*. He uses insight and feelings to control his activities. He doesn't estrange himself from peers unless he has a goal-oriented, reality-based reason for doing so.

2. *Psychologically healthy people are able to be emotionally open, when they choose to be.* An emotionally healthy person is "turned on" to the feelings of others, *and* to his own gut feelings. His emotions link directly to his perceptions. His words and actions don't override the feelings of others. Because he has continuing access to his own emotions, he is able to be less rigid, more spontaneous, more productive, than those who are emotionally blocked. Yet he isn't compelled to be open all the time. In some situations, such as when someone is trying to manipulate or take advantage of him, or when being open will expose him to needless hurt, a healthy person can stay emotionally closed.

3. *Psychologically healthy people are emotional adults.* They're aware that if they eat their cake, the cake will be gone. They choose pleasure over pain. But they know that with freedom comes responsibility, and that they (not Mommy or Daddy) are responsible for their own lives. A healthy person arranges things so that he generally has a lot of choices in any situation. He knows he is responsible for making the choices, and that he must pay the prices for his choices.

4. *Psychologically healthy people are able to initiate and maintain close and meaningful relationships, with others. They can also terminate relationships, if the price proves too much to pay.* Healthy persons do not stay isolated. They get into contact with others. If a job takes a psychologically healthy person to a new community, he is able to reach out to others and start new relationships. He is like a pedestrian who, halfway across a busy street, encounters too much traffic. He is aware that he can: (a) continue to the other side; (b) go back to the side from which he

started; or (c) stay where he is. In a love affair or marriage, if the price is too high, a healthy person can break off. When necessary, an emotionally healthy person can cut off a relationship with anyone—a spouse, parent, grown child, relative, boss, lover, employee, or political leader.

5. *Psychologically healthy people have maximum choice in how they defend themselves from danger.* Depending upon the situation, they can use the mechanism of "flight" or "fight" when they experience the healthy, undistorted survival feelings of fear or anger. In some situations, when appropriate, they can subdue their feelings.

6. *Psychologically healthy people have insight into their emotional programming. They use their self-knowledge to control, expose, or withhold their feelings, behavior, and attitudes.* Healthy persons know where their conditioning has been maladaptive. They fight distorted emotions, separate attitudinal maps from the actual territory, and appreciate the consequences of their own actions. Rejectors learn to get at buried pain, so that they can accept another's love. Acceptors get at buried anger so that they can accept an identity, independent of others, without fear. Rejectors learn to fight the conditioned tendency to say "no" to significant human contacts. Acceptors fight the tendency to say "yes" at any price. People programmed to be jealous struggle with the feeling. Those who, for historic reasons, are extra-angry struggle not to act out their anger against people who have not earned it. People immobilized by fear fight their fear and take whatever actions are called for despite it.

7. *Psychologically healthy people function productively in relation to their potential.* They choose personally satisfying careers and behave like first-class workmen entitled to job recognition and approval. Free of twisted needs and defenses, they are free to focus energy on being productive. But they are not compelled to "perform" for the approval of supervisors. They are sufficiently secure to seek out peers and to enjoy equality in personal and work relationships. They are sufficiently secure to hear constructive criticism, to test its validity for themselves, and to act on the basis of what they understand to be best.

Psychologically healthy people who are in a position of authority use the best available information at their disposal to make decisions. They do not procrastinate out of fear of failure. When the decision is wrong, they are the first to admit and correct it. They do not defend or hide mistakes.

8. *Psychologically healthy people are capable of showing their basic emotions full measure.* They can explode with identity anger—their self-knowledge tells them, "I've been hurt. It wasn't fair. I'm not going to let that happen to me again!" They can openly display the tender affection of love, show uninhibited fear, or moan with excruciating pain. The choice and the range of feelings belongs to them. They are fun to be around, seldom boring, full of life. Because they are able to focus anger on loved objects, they do not leak hostility. They "take in" the anger of loved ones as concern. They appreciate that anger from a loved one is a form of love—that is, concern. They permit the expressions on their faces to change in relation to changing stimuli. By showing their need for love, emotionally healthy people make the persons they love feel more important. The way in which they give love and affection provides comfort and support, not smothering pressure, to those they care about.

From these points we conclude that emotionally healthy people select pleasure over pain. They control what they are able to control and relinquish to others the things they truly cannot control. They maintain emotional contact with people they love. Linked to their own feelings, they are able to be spontaneous and creative in their approach to living. At every step, healthy persons preserve access to a maximum number of choices.

*The crucial point is that psychologically healthy people anticipate pleasurable success, not painful or fearful failure.* They enter into a new relationship or job with pleasurable, joyous expectation, not a debilitating dread of being hurt. Healthy people realize that you can get pleasure without pain, and that pain is not a normal state of human existence. However, while pain is to be avoided, where possible, they accept it as a natural feeling that is part of the price for living, because pain protects us from more pain, destruction, and death.

In our confused and demanding society, emotional health is not easy to achieve. It requires staying emotionally open when, in many instances, being closed would be less painful and less fearful. To be emotionally healthy means struggling with distorted feelings, adapting behavior patterns to new circumstances, and fighting against outmoded attitudes which don't work.

Emotional health gives you maximum choice, maximum range, maximum use of your abilities, maximum emotional contact with others, maximum opportunity for fulfillment. The opportunity for fulfillment means you are offered the best chance for sustained pleasure, for happiness and joy, for the pulsating, energetic, *turned-on* exhilaration of being alive and staying alive.

# CHAPTER 5 | *Beyond the Symptom*

IN THE MOST BASIC SENSE, this book is concerned with going *beyond* symptoms. By symptoms (in medicine, they're called "signs"), I mean the observable, behavior-based labels so frequently used to characterize emotionally disturbed people. We say, "Joe is a homosexual," or "Pete is an alcoholic." We call John a "drug addict," Susie a "kleptomaniac," and Harvey an "incessant eater." Tom is "unreliable." Henry is a "compulsive worker." Sophie is "promiscuous," Nancy is "withdrawn," Al is an "underachiever." Betty is "depressed," Bill "uptight," Jack "smokes too much."

Symptoms entail observable behavior, what people do or how they appear to be. Symptoms involve actions which are destructive to oneself or to others. Frequently, when society disapproves of a symptom, we tag the "sickness" with a label that is emotionally weighted and damaging. Branding anyone a homosexual in our culture, for example, can cause the person substantial social and economic harm.

On the other hand, there is no social or economic disaster if the symptom is one which society sanctions. Consider a figure familiar to all of us: the businessman with compulsive work habits. A patient of mine named Harry was typical. He spent ten or twelve hours a day at his office, and a couple more hours getting to and from the office. He made a good living. But he was able to show his wife and children few real feelings. When his teenage son brought home good grades from school, Harry would look them over without a display of pleasure, even though he was secretly proud of the boy. If Harry was upset about something at the office, he would insist that nothing was wrong when his wife asked what was bothering him. His attitude: fear is something men do not give in to or admit to. For Harry, sex ended with ejaculation. There was no closeness or tender cuddling afterwards. Real feelings of pleasure, from his own accomplishments or from a close relationship, were never allowed full expression.

Harry's wife enjoyed a lot of advantages—a lovely home in a nice neighborhood, jewelry, beautiful clothes, her own car, membership in a country club. Yet these benefits did not compensate her for the lack of affection within her home, or for the aridity of an existence devoid of the emotionality she craved. Her sex life was not good. Even when physically it was all right, something vital was missing. The children went to the best schools, dressed well, had all the material goods they could want. But they never had the chance to feel close to their father, to speak their minds with any hope that their thoughts and needs would be understood. The members of Harry's family felt they were not important in his eyes because he would not trust any of them with his feelings.

In human terms, a "symptom" like Harry's can be almost as destructive as one with a more emotionally-charged label, such as alcoholism. The wife of a man like Harry flounders on the edge of despair. A son may be deeply involved with drugs, a daughter underachieving in school and promiscuous besides. But our society is not too harsh in its criticism of Harry. Despite the role his symptoms play in bringing pain to the household, compulsive overwork is recognized as having obvious social value. Neighbors, associates, and friends make allowances for the husband. "That's Harry's way," they'll say. Even when Harry's wife despairs, friends tell her how lucky she is to have such a capable and thoughtful provider. Yet her isolation and emptiness are real—and perhaps as great as those of a woman whose husband gets drunk every night.

Fortunately for Harry and his family, groups were able to help. Harry's son, Tommy, had originally come to me, and he finally convinced his father to participate in a group. When, after several sessions, Tommy was able to scream out his anger and his need for his father, Harry became defensively angry, and then began to cry. He tried to hide his tears, but the group gently prodded him to express his fear of love by saying over and over, "I'm afraid, I'm afraid." Before long, he was screaming out the words, and suddenly they changed to an agonized, "I need! I *need!*" and he was able to accept his son's tearful embrace. Gradually, through groups and some hard work with his family (his wife and daughter also came into groups), Harry learned to accept his fearfulness as a normal feeling and to show his need for love, as well as his capacity for pleasure.

Any general discussion of individual symptoms of emotional disturbance runs into difficulty for several reasons. For one thing, hundreds of discernable symptoms exist. For another, no symptom is acted out individually; it exists in combination with other symptoms. Third, any culture tends to view symptoms within the framework of its attitudinal value structure: what is sexual promiscuity in one culture, for instance, can be sexual health in another.

Such complications make it risky for professionals to devise broad-spectrum generalizations about human behavior. If we define symptoms as *destructive* behavioral and attitudinal patterns, we are confronted with the task of distinguishing between what is "destructive" and what is "nondestructive." Most of us agree on what is obviously destructive: drug addiction, alcoholism, criminality, perhaps homosexuality, and so forth. But what about the forms of emotional detachment which society views as less damaging to its structure? What about a reasonably attractive woman who goes through life a virgin, without having tried to establish any meaningful relationships with men? She may serve as the town librarian and provide necessary and useful help to dozens of people every day. Yet she has stifled her potential to be a full and vital woman. How do we judge a hard-working factory foreman who holds down two jobs in order to "provide" for his family, yet must escape to television or the bowling alley as soon as he gets home? What about a brilliant surgeon who saves hundreds of lives, but cannot make emotional contact with his patients, his staff, his friends or his family? How about an overweight housewife whose conversation is limited to what her children do or say each day, or what she sees on television? Although society may not suffer dramatically from the symptoms of these people, the toll in human life is great. For that matter, the loss to society may be great as well. When individual productivity is stunted, even though the symptoms are not socially destructive, the accompanying emotional disturbance will of necessity waste a vast amount of human energy.

## The Symptoms of a Sick Society

The symptoms of emotional disturbance today have many faces, many forms. Here are the underachievers, the unhappily married, the drop-outs, the job-drifters, the chronically disorganized, the perpetually unemployed. The price in human heartache and misery is impossible to measure. The problem is significant to business, significant to government, significant to taxpayers, significant to all thoughtful Americans.

In America's urban centers, drug addicts constitute a giant portion of all criminals. Every day they are responsible for a frightening number of burglaries, larcenies, muggings, frauds, acts of prostitution and physical violence. The motivation is to obtain the hard cash for a strictly COD drug transaction. Experts estimate that, on the *average,* it may cost an addict as much as $36,000 a year to support his habit. Although it is impossible to discover exact figures, the educated guess is that drug addiction—as it involves financial loss to crime victims, the police and other preventive expenditures, research, education, treatment and rehabilitation—costs the country more than $2 billion every year. The federal budget for treatment and rehabilitation alone for the fiscal year of 1972 was about $200.2 million, and that does not begin to take into account local expenditures. New York City, for example, received no federal funds.

Nor is the drug problem just the province of the big cities. More and more suburbs and small towns are waking up to the horrors of overdose deaths, open drugs transactions in brand new schoolyards, thefts within the home to pay for drugs.

The United States Department of Health, Education and Welfare estimates that there are between nine and ten million alcoholics among our nation's drinkers. Often, these alcoholics appear to be "social drinkers." It is not always easy to diagnose the symptom. But employers see it, in absenteeism, tardiness, irresponsibility on the job, and human-relations problems with co-workers. And loved ones *feel* it, in day-to-day destruction and pain.

About one out of twenty American men is believed to be a practicing homosexual, and about one out of fifty women. Many of these have virtually dropped out of a productive heterosexual society, preferring to live in a homosexual subculture. They often work at jobs far beneath their potential, waiting on tables or bartending in order to remain in seemingly safe surroundings. But there is always the pain of alienation, the fear of police raids, the moment-to-moment wrench of promiscuity that usually becomes part of that way of life. Families reject them, most members of society scorn them. If an active homosexual has chosen to work in the "straight" world, he faces the constant fear of exposure or even blackmail.

Overweight is another symptom of emotional disturbance. According to the American Medical Association, one out of five adult Americans is at least 10 percent above his ideal weight. It is easy to sense unhappiness in compulsive eaters who stuff themselves to obesity. According to a medical criterion, anyone who is over 20 percent above his ideal weight is obese. By this standard, then, about one in ten adults is obese. But what of the millions of others who have let their weight go up without showing a strong compulsion to eat? Consider the young girl who devours a box of candy because she is unhappy about not having dates, or the buffoon whose chubbiness is part of a jovial image. To be sure, food is abundant—for some—and work-saving devices take their toll in unburned calories. The cost of overweight is high. According to the recent, authoritative Framingham Study, when a person's weight goes 25 percent above the ideal, there is a sharp increase in other concommitant disorders, and the mortality rate from cardio-vascular problems increases, too. Certainly for anyone significantly overweight there is a loss of energy and, consequently, productivity. And often for overweight people, there is the lonely pain of being unattractive and unwanted.

Another widely prevalent symptom in our world is passivity. There is a kind of "let-George-do-it" attitude when it comes to taking hold and struggling with the day-to-day problems of who and what one is to be and how to go about becoming it. I asked one sixteen-year-old who had left his Westchester home to grow long hair and don love beads in the East Village what he proposed to live on. He looked at me in disbelief. "Why, man?" he said, in all sincerity, "Bread *is*." His attitude was that food and all other basics will somehow be there. He had left behind a comfortable home; the privacy provided by a bedroom of his own; continuing access to a car; enough money to pay for cigarettes, movie tickets, late-night suppers with friends. But some important ingredients surely were missing. Otherwise, this youngster, and thousands like him, would not have dropped out of school to search out a whole new world. True, our affluent world breeds spoiled children. And I can well understand why many of these youngsters have tried to reject the trappings of affluence which their parents showered upon them. Yet I see genuine bewilderment and pain in many of my young patients. They just do not know how to grow in a world whose values seem like tinsel on a dried-up Christmas tree.

The average American family is estimated to invest over 42 hours a week watching television. Though television has provided some excellent, enriching entertainment and information, most programming offers only mindless escapism. It is difficult to develop the skills of communication when one-way entertainment is so readily at hand. No effort is required to communicate in return. The average teenager listens to 13½ hours of radio a week. Many cannot do their homework without the radio blaring, or walk down the street without a transistor squawking into their ears. It's as though they need the distraction to lessen the task at hand. Or perhaps the noise provides reassurance that they are not living in a void.

Many people simply cannot function in our society without chemicals of some sort to help reduce the pain of awareness, the pain of everyday functioning. A housewife in Indiana takes pills to reduce the tension of her day-to-day life. She cannot run out of the house, she cannot fight her life's confusion, so she just removes herself through a chemical prescription—Milltown, Librium, Equinol, dexedrine, barbiturates, or any of the others that have made the drug companies into billion-dollar businesses. Obviously, when living is constantly painful, something is wrong. But taking a chemical to remove the pain does not remove the cause. Soon more pills must be taken to reduce the pain. Still it does not go away because the unfulfilled needs behind the pain remain untouched.

Many women use marriage as a means to avoid the struggle of fulfilling their human potential. Research will never be able to pinpoint the figure accurately, but I would guess that millions of women suffer this kind of second-class citizenship. I cannot help but sympathize with their lot. Our culture puts extreme pressure upon women to be married and, at least by implication, to gain identity through marriage. The woman who is an old maid is usually pitied and even ridiculed. The man who "escapes" marriage often is considered a hero. It's understandable that many women seek self-fulfillment through marriage, but too many believe that the institution provides the identity, and not the chance to be who they are and who they can become. The fact remains that many women, angry at the secondary role they have accepted (without knowing why they are unhappy), are really avoiding the struggle and the satisfaction of developing as individual personalities.

Take Ellen, a patient similar to several others in my groups. After college, she took a job at a public relations firm which she didn't particularly like. She found the struggle of working and trying to support herself difficult and unrewarding. She made little effort to advance at work because she expected, sooner or later, to get married. In the meantime, Ellen was having a great time in the singles' scene in Manhattan's Upper East Side. In her mid-twenties, she met a man whom she didn't find especially objectionable, he proposed, they married and had children. Their relationship fell into a pattern. There was adequate money, but inadequate love or empathy in the marriage. As a competent, intelligent woman, Ellen had little trouble running her suburban household and managing her young children. But she was bored and unchallenged. She frequently drank too much; she took tranquillizers to sleep, diet pills to reduce. Stuck at home, she would look to her husband to bring into the household the challenge and excitement lacking in her own life. She hated him for not bringing it to her. In reality, Ellen had used her marriage to avoid her own identity struggle. She had not used life to find out who she was, what she liked, what she wanted.

Then there is Janie, who rushed into marriage right out of high school for fear that she wouldn't get married otherwise. She, too, got no chance to explore her potential. Her identity had been pegged to a romantic image of the marriage bed and housekeeping. The dream soon dissolved, as babies came and her young husband dragged himself home each night, bewildered and frightened by the hard business of supporting a family. In the beginning, Janie got pleasure out of washing her husband's socks and putting his neatly ironed clothes away. Before long that pleasure changed to drudgery. She would get angry at him because there was no excitement in their lives, and they always had to worry about money. But the truth was, Janie was depending upon the magic of marriage to make her happy. She was really a child wanting to play a game. She had not chanced growing up and discovering what kind of woman she was.

The "alimony junkies" whom I see in my groups are also symptom bearers. Again, our culture is largely the villain; alimony really relegates women to another form of second-class citizenship. Many divorcées use alimony to live parasitically off their former husbands. It is a way to avoid coming to grips with the essential problems of their lives as adult, responsible women. While child support is unquestionably necessary in most cases, there are many instances where the children would be better off if their mother did not get alimony. Her life should be oriented outward into the world and require increased personal productivity. With that would come increased self-esteem. Invariably, the divorcée would feel better about herself if she mastered a skill and became part of productive society. Moreover, as a productive member of society who feels good about her accomplishments, this woman would stand a greater chance of meeting and becoming involved with a more adequate man.

There are many kinds of underachievers in our country. You find high-IQ children performing poorly in school. Graduate engineers doing maintenance or assembly line work in a factory. Lawyers working as counter clerks. Here, however, a distinction must be made between underachievement and dropping out. Many people who "drop out" of society do so because they have decided after serious thought to reject society and its standards. Such a move may well be an assertion of their independent identity and value system. They have made an observation of the world and their own abilities, understood the prices they must pay to drop out, and often have been successful in creating a healthy, productive life for themselves on their own terms. Some have cultivated self-sustaining farms, for instance, or supported themselves through handicrafts which give them great pleasure, rather than using sterile skills for which they were highly trained. By the same token, a brilliant advertising executive may choose to become a school teacher because he gets much more satisfaction in that role. Or a medical student may prefer research to a practice as a doctor.

Certainly one's goal should not be just to make more money or to gain recognition on someone else's terms. Productivity is a sign of health, and it is for each person to struggle to discover what his potential is and how he can fulfill it best within a realistic appraisal of life's demands and the world he lives in. To underachieve on a permanent basis—whether by "dropping out" or by choosing to work at a level far below one's abilities—is often mere avoidance of the struggle to realize one's growth potential. For the youngster who angrily refuses to work in school, the reality remains that his performance there could be important to the rest of his life. For the man who settles for less money and prestige in his job than he is capable of obtaining, the pain of "playing it safe" is as great as the pain he might experience by risking vulnerability in trying to move ahead. Though that struggle involves strain and discomfort, it can lead to satisfactory recognition. That pleasure can engender even more productive energy—not just at work, but in all phases of his life—and that creates, in turn, more pleasure.

Business suffers in many ways from emotional disturbance.

Ernie, an intelligent, educated group member in his early thirties, has held five jobs in the last twelve years, most of them in business offices. There he would receive a certain amount of management training, start to function at a fairly responsible level, then quit because he could not get along with his boss, was bored with the job, or did not like his fellow workers. The reality, of course, was that he was bringing the same set of problems to each job. The son of an authoritative father, Ernie could not tolerate being told what to do. Before he got into therapy he had no insight into the distortions with which he would view his boss or any co-worker who competed with him. It took a lot of work in groups for Ernie to learn to express the deep anger he felt against anyone in a position of power over him.

From doing anger exercises, Ernie also learned to feel what I call the "fourth stage of anger." This is really a positive feeling of self-assertion, strengthened by the sense that, although he has been hurt, he will not be devastated by such hurt. He has the capacity to seek what he wants and succeed in getting it. Ernie has also had to examine the negative attitudes he held about men in authority and see how these attitudes have interfered with his pleasure and success in work. And he has had to struggle hard right on the job to try to behave in new ways. Recently, he switched from office work to sales in a big company. So far, he is pleased and excited about his job and is doing well, even though the sales manager is demanding and the other salesmen are highly skilled.

There are many Ernies in this world, men who leave their jobs because of human-relations problems or constant restlessness—problems they could grapple with, if given the right insights into their emotional make-up. Certainly such people cost business a great deal of money. Consider, too, how much business suffers because of faulty decisions made by executives as a result of communications problems that could have been corrected. Also, how often do "office politics" interfere with the operation of an efficient and profitable business?

And on and on—millions of people plagued one way or another by the symptoms of a sick society, but with little hope of changing things and even less awareness of how life can be pleasurable and fulfilling. But my purpose is not to dwell upon symptoms—rather, to go beyond them, as we attempt to do in our groups.

# The Classical Treatment of Symptoms

In classically-oriented approaches to one-to-one therapy, a patient's behavior is virtually ignored, except as something he reports upon however he chooses. Often the patient will ramble on about how he has acted out his various symptoms. Sometimes the psychiatrist or psychologist may ask the patient why he doesn't stop. More directive therapists may even *tell* the patient to stop acting out. But usually changes in behavior are not demanded. The therapist is probing instead for underlying motivations. Someone who is overweight can continue to eat too much. A homosexual may go on seeking sexual contact with those of his own sex. An alcoholic can continue to drink, then report his actions with great remorse, complain about his hangover, agonize over his guilt at hitting his wife or failing to show up at his job.

Take the symptom of homosexuality, for example. Psychoanalysis usually cannot cope with homosexuality because the one-to-one, analytic approach cannot begin by enforcing cessation of the homosexual behavior. Here, for example, is what happened when Jim, a male homosexual, came to see me while I was practicing analysis. Jim was deeply depressed because Johnny, his lover for two years, had left him. I asked Jim to tell me about the relationship. He described what a lovely man Johnny was, how sensitive and perceptive he had been. Jim narrated the nuances of their sex acts, described what fun they had had because they liked the same things. They had understood each other so well. And so on. A few sessions of this helped relieve some of the emotional pressure in Jim. Then we moved on to his early life. He told me his mother was a castrating bitch and that his father was never around. He had been picked up by a homosexual when he was twelve and had been introduced to sex by the man. He had been scared, but found he liked it. That's how it started, and this was the kind of homosexual Jim was when he came to see me. With every signal, he was telling me how painful it was to be alone.

The analytic process went on for about three months. In talking about his childhood, Jim hinted at his anxieties and insecurities, his anger and pain, his need for love. Then, before transference had begun (transference is the key to successful psychoanalysis), Jim came in happily one morning to inform me he had just met Harvey. He told me about Harvey's charm, good looks, intelligence and sensitivity. Inevitably, he and Harvey had made love. After a few more sessions, Jim terminated his treatment. "You've helped me so much, Dr. Casriel," he said. "My depression is over. I feel loved and secure." Jim left therapy, and I never saw him again. His affliction had caused him some pain. His treatment under the classic method had relieved a bit of the pain. But the feelings which had caused him to act out homosexually were never truly touched.

# The New Identity Group Approach to Symptoms

In the groups in my practice, this is *not* the pattern. Instead, a homosexual (as well as everyone else) is told immediately to stop acting out his obvious symptoms. He is encouraged by other members who have undergone the same struggle, or a similar one, but the demand is firm: "Act as if you're *not* homosexual. Date girls. Don't go to gay bars. Try not to fantasize about attractive men you meet. Then come in and tell the group what you're feeling." If he slips up, he may tell the group that he has acted out. They'll usually know by his signals anyway. But he is not allowed to dwell upon how he has acted out, or even upon his remorse (if he feels any). My work with drug addicts and later with patients exhibiting other symptoms taught me that most often when a patient talked about his symptom, it was a way of coddling it. He could relieve his anxiety about his behavior without taking any responsibility about how he would act from then on. In our groups, we tell someone who has acted out not to describe what he has done, but to express what he is feeling right then. Usually it will be anger at the struggle the group is forcing upon him. Often pain and fear emerge as well, and he will begin to show the helplessness he truly feels when stripped of the symptom.

The reason for this approach is basic: The homosexual's major symptom, for example, has insulated him from struggling with his feelings. He was denied the expression of his deep emotional needs as he grew up. Probably, his father was physically or emotionally absent. Sometimes a superior sibling stood in his way. Invariably, his mother was too demanding, too threatening, or too seductive. Whatever the combined factors in his life, his homosexuality developed as a defense against having his needs denied.

When he drops the symptom—even temporarily—and tries to behave in a new way, the feelings which have been buried so deeply will start to emerge. Then his emotions can be dealt with in groups.

# Survival-Based Feelings

Fear, anger, pain, pleasure, and the need to give and receive love are deep, survival-based feelings. Repeatedly, in group therapy, I have seen these basic feelings underlying not only homosexuality, but also a vast range of other symptoms. (Symptoms such as guilt or anxiety have proved to have one of the primary feelings—or a combination of them—at their core.) Symptoms are surface behavior. Deep down, underneath the symptoms, the dynamics of scream exercises reveal an astonishing similarity in human feelings and human needs.

In my groups, it is not unusual to hear shrieks of fear turn into screams of anger, to observe angry screams become pained sobs and then delight when the person doing the exercise breaks into joyful laughter. This exercise may take place in only five or ten minutes. Yet the entire group will share the open exhilaration of the person who has worked. Love and joy fill the room. Tenderness and acceptance are everywhere.

In fact, human emotions today are pretty much as they were half a million years ago, whereas the nature of culture has geometrically multiplied the complexities of our civilization. As civilization becomes ever more dehumanized, the individual becomes more isolated, alienated from a world that appears to require him to anesthetize himself from his most deeply-felt emotional needs. (We call these "gut-level" or "belly feelings" because their intense expression involves the whole body and it feels as though they are physiologically centered in the belly.)

Today, this thought has been stated so frequently that it is a cliché: The demands of civilization are at odds with man's vital emotional needs.

Forced to repress the expression of these needs, the alienated person either retreats behind a socially acceptable façade or behaves in a distorted, often destructive way that temporarily relieves some of the pressure of his buried needs. Neither "solution" really works; neither is a direct expression of that person's emotional core. An important part of the individual is denied expression. He is alienated from himself and from the world in which he exists.

The alternative is emotionally honest interaction, a dynamic which is not easy to explain to someone who has never taken part in an encounter group. At the outset, attention tends to be drawn to the drama of angry confrontations. Yet something more significant takes place. It is the expression of pain and pleasure, the giving and receiving of love, and the open display of fear. When I have recorded group sessions on videotape and replayed the tapes, viewers who had never been in group therapy have been able to understand and empathize with the emotions being shown. These viewers have recognized the honesty of what was going on. They were able to respond with empathy and insight based on their own feelings and emotions.

In emotionally honest interaction, each individual feels sufficiently secure not only to feel and show genuine emotions, but also to experience the emotions of other people. The result is mutual vulnerability and meaningful emotional contact. It cuts through the façade of pride and the psychological distance with which we try to protect ourselves. Emotional honesty establishes responsible concern, and leaves you feeling warm inside.

Symptoms are acted-out camouflage, designed to protect the hurt inside an emotionally disturbed person. Beyond the symptoms there is a soft core of vulnerability and need in each of us. Despite surface differences, despite antisocial behavior patterns, despite defensive hostilities, despite words and rationalizations, despite socio-economic distinctions, despite achievements and awards, there is an astonishing similarity to the emotional needs we share. We all require self-esteem (which is really love of ourselves). And we want to to be loved by others.

CHAPTER 6 | *The Human Need for Bondedness*

PSYCHIATRISTS have a lot to learn from other disciplines about man and his culture. Anthropologists, ethnologists, archaeologists, primatologists—all consistently and constantly contribute new information about man. So do their counterparts in other disciplines.

Psychiatric thinking has been affected only modestly by this wealth of new information. It is true that some theories which evolved as breakaways from Freud attempted to account for the effect of culture upon human beings. But these therapy systems have not caught up with today's information about how human beings behave, think, and feel.

Recent findings in these various disciplines suggest many reasons why there is such a restless search throughout the country today for group interaction, whether hippie, sensitivity, encounter, body movement, love-ins, pot parties, mass demonstrations, youth music festivals, therapeutic communities. The information pouring forth from the behavioral sciences certainly sheds light on why various group therapy systems have been effective.

Today, we know a great deal about the nature of culture which Freud could not know. Ethnologists have made extensive studies of other human societies. The evidence shows that there are *many* ways to be "human."

We also know more about man's beginnings, thanks to studies of fossil records, even though archaeology and human paleontology have begun literally only to scratch the surface of the mysteries involved.

All of this objective evidence provides substantial information about man. Yet psychiatric literature has made only a modest attempt to incorporate the information into the mainstream of theory and methodology.

Why this lack? For one thing, few psychiatrists and psychologists truly understand the nature of culture and the immense implications of its effect on every human being. Certainly Freud did not undertand. He saw society as a static force, developed to control man's instincts. The only change which took place in the course of centuries, Freud thought, was that society became more efficient in controlling our instincts. Freud believed that man gained civilization at a price: the renunciation of his instinctive satisfactions. Freud thought that all that is creative in man, all that is cooperative, is paid for by denying instinctive drives.

In 1913, Freud published *Totem and Taboo*. He based it on the miniscule anthropological material then available (chiefly Frazer), conjectures of Darwin, data gleaned from patients, and Robertson Smith's totem theory. The book transports the Oedipus story to prehistoric times. Freud saw the leader of man's primal horde as an autocratic father who subjected other males to his will, and who kept the available women for himself. According to this theory, sons were forced to live without sexual contact with women—until they killed and ate their father/leader. However, having killed the father, the brothers began to fear each other. The risk was that one of them would now assume the dead father's role. Hence they denied their sisters to themselves and established a within-the-tribe taboo against killing anyone. Incest became taboo, and males had to go to another tribe to find women.

As poetic insight, this is not bad. But it is not in accord with what is known about Homo sapiens. It projects Freud's view of Victorian Europe backwards to prehistory. In the language of anthropologists, the theory is "culture-bound." Although ethnology is still in its infancy, sufficient evidence now exists to show that man does *not* universally conform to the pattern described by Freud. Many variations in man's character can be traced to cultural differences. It seems clear that Freud greatly underestimated the influence of culture.

Consider how culture-bound the Oedipal theory is. There are, for example, societies where the word "mother" does not exist. Women of the same age span are (for want of a better term) "aunts," and all children are "brothers" and "sisters." Freud's Oedipal theory flounders in the face of these relationships.

Since Freud's day, ethnologists have reported an astonishing number of ways to be human. One study of a culture where men greatly outnumbered women showed that *females* occupied the position of power. Many human societies are significantly less aggressive than ours. Sex is never the same kind of problem in a culture which doesn't inhibit or degrade it the way our culture has. And so on. The variety of behavior patterns among human cultures is vastly greater than most people raised in one society even imagine.

This variety is built into the nature and definition of culture. *Culture is what man has and no other species possesses.* It is different from the term "society," which requires only the existence of an organized social structure. Bees and ants have societies, but *not* culture. They can't do what man is able to do—*pass along knowledge from generation to generation.*

The ability to transmit knowledge from one generation to another is of pivotal importance. Starting with knowledge from the previous generation, each new generation is able to accumulate still more knowledge, then pass the accumulated knowledge to the next generation, and so on. The process evolves geometrically. Especially at the technical level, information generates more information at an accelerated rate. Every decade generates more information than all the previous generations put together. (Today, some communicators are calling our next era the "Information Revolution," predicting that it will change western civilization more rapidly and radically than the Industrial Revolution.)

*Communication* lies at the core of man's ability to transmit learning. And, in an important sense, genuine communication is what my group therapy process is concerned with. My groups try to teach people to communicate better emotionally, to show themselves more directly, and see others more clearly in order to achieve maximum understanding. To understand culture—as well as much of what goes on in my groups—it is essential to take a closer look at the nature of communication.

There are three basic ways in which to communicate. Only man has all three:

First, there is communication by means of *signs*. All animals use signs as a way of teaching. Signs involve acted-out examples. A mother cat, for example, teaches her kittens to urinate through example. The mother cat squats, urinates, and scratches dirt over the urine. Then, she nudges her kittens (a sign) in order to transmit the command: "Do it the way I do it." Eventually, through replication of behavior, the kittens learn to urinate in the tidy manner of the mother. The key point: signs utilize movements, sounds, or gestures which actually involve, or are similar to, specific actions. All animals, including man, communicate through signs. (What we commonly call "signs"—traffic signs, store signs, and so forth—are really "symbols," as you will see in what follows.)

The second means of communication is through *signals*. This vital form of communication has almost never been adequately treated in psychiatric literature. A signal communicates meaning, of and by itself, without necessarily involving an example. Humans use hand gestures, body postures, eye movements, tones of voice, hundreds of other mannerisms as signals. Julius Fast has written a book about human signaling called *Body Language*. The volume shows, for example, how the positioning of arms, legs, torso, and so on, indicate important information about an individual's feelings and state of mind. All animals signal constantly. If a monkey sees a lion, he emits a cry that means "danger—lion," and other monkeys in the troop scamper for trees. Birds sing songs which represent warning signals, mating calls, anger, and so on. In our groups (and in most human interaction), interpreting signals accurately has a great deal to do with the communication of feelings and whether or not we trust those we are hearing.

Third, it is possible to communicate by means of *symbols*. Symboling involves assigning an *arbitrary* meaning to communication. Human language, both spoken and written, arithmetic, and art forms are examples of symboling. *Only man symbols. And symboling is the basis of culture.* Symboling provides the means of transmitting information at a geometric rate; thus culture can be expected to change at an accelerating rate. But symboling can also get in the way of communicating human feelings. Sometimes, people let words stand for feelings too much, and expression of the feeling itself is lost.

Once you understand the importance of symboling, you *begin* to understand the nature of culture. Through the unique ability to symbol, human societies develop a superstructure which envelops and conditions every individual from birth to death. A newborn baby enters the world with basic physical and emotional needs. From there on, the process of enculturation goes to work.

Culture has been compared to a giant cloud that envelops man. An infant inherits the cloud from preceding generations, is controlled by it for his entire lifespan, and during the process makes additions to the cultural "cloud" he has inherited.

Culture really has a life of its own. It evolves the way life-forms do. According to anthropologists, cultural conditioning determines far more about man than has even been suspected. It affects man's attitudes, his beliefs, his behavior, and his interpersonal relationships. Culture even governs the ways in which man tries to fulfill his basic biological needs. The examples which follow illustrate what I mean.

What we all consider "food" is deeply enculturated and not always propitious for survival. When World War II was over, the skeletons of two American airmen were found on an atoll. Evidence told a grim story about enculturated attitudes toward food. When their plane crashed, the men abandoned it, taking partial survival equipment. There was ample fresh water on the island. The problem for survival was how to keep from starving. The shoals and cliffs surrounding the island made fishing almost impossible. The men had a government-issued survival manual with them, and the manual indicated that the grubs in a particular tree contained sufficient nourishment to keep alive. The evidence showed that the men peeled off the bark from trees, found the grubs, and swallowed the "food." But their enculturated digestive systems wouldn't keep the food down. They vomited the grubs repeatedly. Slowly and painfully, the men starved to death. That's how enculturated man's ideas about "food" can be!

Another example: A man once told me a story about a friend of his who, while recuperating from minor surgery in a large hospital, complained of "starving." The man who had been operated on was a Ph.D., well-known in his specialized field. He was also a Chinese who had spent his earliest years in China and had been raised on traditional Chinese food. Investigation revealed that the hospital served steak, mashed potatoes, pork chops, a profusion of desserts, and so forth—but *no rice*. Without rice at every meal, the man felt hungry.

Put yourself to the test. Is rattlesnake meat "food" to you? (Those who enjoy it say it tastes like chicken.) How about grasshoppers, squid, octopus, ants, dog and horse meat? In some parts of the world, human beings eat and enjoy these foods, with an enculturated idea that they are food. Yet you would probably have trouble keeping some of these foods in your stomach, and so would I.

Or take a look at the vital role culture plays in determining how man behaves sexually.

When Western Man first came to Tahiti, he found a sexual paradise. Beautiful young girls had intercourse with men freely and easily without shame or embarrassment. Following a few carefree teenage years of such dalliance, these girls each mated to one male, and were more or less faithful. At this point, they had children and raised them. Other cultures, in Polynesia and Africa, have developed similar patterns. No value is given to virginity. And it is recognized that youth, physically and emotionally, is a time for responsibility-free acting out of sexuality. This pattern of sexually-free behavior is *as human* as the Victorian European behavior with which Freud dealt. Many of the emotional problems we see in my groups stem from the changing attitudes toward sex in America today. The new freedom brings behavioral and emotional stress to people who are enculturated with older values.

In some cultures, sexual behavior is generally constrained, but there are "Mardi gras"-type sexual orgies during which males and females have intercourse with whomever they desire. During this prescribed period, no shame or embarrassment is connected with "indiscriminate" sex.

Among some Alaskan Indians, sex was culturally separated from fatherhood and child-rearing. The totem was part of the tribe's religion, and *one* of the heads on the totem pole was always considered the father of a child. Having children was thus related to ideology. But *sex* was for fun. Females mated permanently with males for socio-economic reasons—to have someone to hunt and gather for themselves and their children. Socioeconomic matings did involve continuing sex. But (since sex was for pleasure) sexual activity could be freely enjoyed with a variety of individuals in the group, whenever spontaneous desire was felt for it.

There are thousands of ways to be "human." Quite simply, any "truths" about human psychology run the risk of being culturebound, as were Freud's theories, which reflected the existing society in Victorian Europe.

Herein lies the problem. Although Freud underestimated culture and was inaccurate about the biological nature of man, he was intuitively right: *The nature of civilization is not attuned to man's survival-based emotional needs. Nor, many times, to his biological needs.*

The accumulating fossil and ethnological evidence about man indicates that Freud's intuition was on target. Too many of man's biological-based emotional needs are stifled continually by the requirements of civilization.

What are these needs? Why describe them as "survival-based"?

Human beings have been around a long time. Some of the records of man's past are available for inspection. Depending upon which authority you select, Homo sapiens is at least 75,000 years old. Perhaps he is a lot older than 350,000 years.

Carleton Coon, a foremost archaeologist, has classified the European-found Swanscome and Steinheim bones as Homo sapiens, and this would date man as being at least 350,000 years old. Coon also calls Neanderthal "Homo Neandertalensis sapiens," which moves "man" back to where he is about 500,000 years old.

Archaeologists L. S. B. and Mary Leakey have discovered bones which they call Zinjanthropus, dated through a potassium-argon technique as *1,750,000 years old.* While physical anthropologists are still arguing about exactly what Zinjanthropus is, most experts agree that Zinjanthropus is "hominid"—meaning a man-like primate. Today, the Leakeys say they have found specimen bones of a hominid *older* than Zinjanthropus.

As far as is known, Homo sapiens and his hominid ancestors lived in *primate survival groups.*

An examination of primate behavior and survival needs is fundamental to understanding man. The roots of what man is, physically and emotionally, are to be found in primate physical and emotional characteristics.

Primatology is a discipline barely more than two decades old. Primatologists do exactly what the term implies. They study primates. But *not* the primates in zoos, because most primates in zoos are very neurotic. Primatologists study primates under natural conditions. They go into the jungle, find an ape or monkey troop, then live as members of the troop for a considerable period of time—perhaps a year and a half.

To be accepted into the troop, primatologists must avoid direct, prolonged eye contact with primate members. Eye contact signals a challenge. Primate troops are arranged in hierarchies, and less dominant members avoid trouble by turning their eyes away from more dominant members. After a few days of only brief eye confrontations with all the members of a primate troop, when it has become established that the primatologists are the *least dominant members,* there is no more trouble. The people are free to wander about and observe.

To understand primate behavior, let us look at a baboon troop. Typically, it contains about thirty to forty individuals. The troop eats together, travels as a unit to a water source, and encounters an enemy as a survival unit. Baboons do not stray from the troop.

The troop is a highly structured organization, with an established social hierarchy. Dominance marks one of the keystones of the social organization. A dominant male enjoys special privileges, but also assumes special responsibilities. When a female is estrous, for example, he mounts her repeatedly; a less dominant male mounts her only when the backs of more dominant males are turned. But if a lion attacks the troop, the dominant males fight the lion, while the rest of the troop flees.

The structure of a baboon troop has enormous survival value.

Baboons spend their nights in jungle trees, but feed in savannahs, which are treeless. African savannahs provide a fine food supply. But, in a savannah, the baboons are in constant danger of attack by wild cats and other carnivores. Frequently, the troop is three miles or so from the safety of the jungle. A single baboon would not last long in this setting. However, four or five dominant males—all of whom have large, sharp teeth—can fight a lion with considerable success, even though one or more baboons may be killed or wounded.

While feeding, the troop disperses in an organized way, with dominant males at each end, and the least-dominant males, females, and infants in the middle. At the signal of danger, baby baboons jump under their mothers' necks, and the mothers run in the opposite direction from which the signal has come. The whole troop runs away as fast as it can as a unit, leaving the dominant male "scouts" to cover the retreat.

When the troop perches safely in trees, dominant males also serve as "babysitters" for the adolescents in the group. The "games" the young play are rough: running, jumping, wrestling, biting, and so on. Such games have the obvious survival value of conditioning the young for the adult rigors of being a baboon. But when biting or wrestling games get too risky, the dominant male will signal "stop." If the too-rough game does not stop immediately, the adult baboon will clout a youngster so hard that he may sail several feet through the trees. In a baboon troop, *no fighting among members is permitted if it risks serious wounds or danger to life.*

Dominance, once established between individual baboons, is not challenged again. The less dominant baboons avoid prolonged eye contact and turn away. The hierarchy in a baboon troop thus remains a firmly established ranking. Only adolescents must confront the existing situation, in order to determine their position as adults among the already adult baboons. A dominant female can have a higher place in the hierarchy than a male who is low in dominance. Acceptance of this social system within a group avoids struggles. It establishes a system which works. It minimizes disagreements within a troop. In fact, without such a system, there would be serious fights over estrous females.

New troops are formed by dominant males, with the agreement of others in the troop, when a troop increases its members to about fifty baboons. It seems understood that this will happen. Some twenty baboons will go away to a different territory; and, somehow, everybody seems to be able to decide whether to be in the old group, or the new group, without traumatic indecision.

Everything considered, the social system evolved by a baboon troop works extremely well. The fossil record bears out this success. In their present form, baboons have been around for more than two million years. There is no proof, but physical anthropologists believe the baboon social system has remained the same for a similar period of time.

Each of the primate species has a different pattern of behavior. These patterns are called "species specific" and are important to the survival of that particular species. Still, the social pattern of a baboon troop illustrates the *kind* of pattern which applies to all nonenculturated primates and which was familiar to man's primate ancestors (who were savannah dwellers, also). Individual members live in groups, within a well-defined structure. They do not try to live alone, or with only a mate and offspring. There is a programmed tendency not to stray very far from the others in the group. The primate pattern of gregariousness prevails; primates continually need others of the same species. They want to be together when eating. They need sex, physical touching, "grooming," and cuddling during sleep. (Significantly, the need to touch and hug shows up all the time in my group therapy dynamic.)

Primate behavioral patterns are very different from those of other mammals. Members of the cat family, for instance, hunt alone. A mating pair of cats generally lies a few yards from one another and when they sleep they don't need to cuddle. A male lion will stay with his mate and her cubs until the cubs are old enough to run fairly fast, then he will start taking prolonged treks to other areas. The lioness and cubs are left more or less on their own. Once the cubs are adults, they will go away from their mother, to roam in a solitary manner. Quite simply, groups are *not* part of a survival pattern for cats.

But groups *are* part of a survival pattern for human beings.

They are important to meeting human biological needs. And emotional needs, which are survival-based. To comprehend the importance of the concept of group survival to man, it is necessary to take a closer look at man's past.

There have been four known glacial periods, the first of which ended approximately 550,000 years ago. During each glacial period, large portions of the world became inhospitable to warm-blooded mammals such as primates. But in the inter-glacial periods, when ice retreated toward both poles, the weather became more temperate in vast-sized areas.

During the first three glacial periods, large numbers of mammals retreated from the advancing ice toward warmer climates. Hominids retreated with the food supply, finding new and warmer areas in which to live. Somehow, during the fourth and most recent glacial period, Homo sapiens did something he had not done before. The fossil record shows that many groups of men stayed in the cold areas, and through intelligence developed means of surviving in the cold. These men invented snow shoes, skis, fur garments, and a host of other survival-value techniques for controlling their environment, including building better and warmer shelters.

Why man suddenly became so creative during the last glacial period, no one knows. It just happened, possibly because a few creative individuals made accidental discoveries, possibly for other reasons. At any rate, it is clear that Neolithic man had the ability to symbol, and thus transmit the knowledge he developed to the following generations. With this ability, man was set apart from other animals. Man alone had what we now call "culture." When the last ice age ended about twenty thousand years ago, encultured man was pretty smart. He could pass along to his offspring all the significant information he had acquired. Now he had the method for *leaping forward* technologically at a geometric pace!

About 10,000 years ago, man made two incredibly significant discoveries. He learned how to domesticate animals and how to domesticate plants. These discoveries were the foundation of civilization.

From an ethnological viewpoint, the story of hominids can be divided into two parts. Everything *before* the invention of animal and plant domestication falls on one side. Everything that happened *afterwards* falls on the other side.

Prior to domestication, man lived as a hunter and gatherer. He hunted wild animals for his meat supply; he picked berries and fruit for his other food. Thus he was a nomad who followed his food supply.

All hunting and gathering cultures which have been studied share a number of significant traits:

In a hunting and gathering society, *there is no specialization—except by age and sex.* All adult males do the same things each day; so do all adult females—but these are a different group of tasks than the males perform. And children see before them an example of what being a male or female is.

All hunting and gathering societies live in "bands." The band (or group) is structured with behavioral rules. A group has a territory in which it hunts and gathers; so do other groups. Although one group will occasionally make a "raid" into another group's territory, this leads to rapid retaliation. And it is a sporadic occurrence, *not* a warlike pattern.

In all hunting and gathering cultures, there are *ritualized patterns which relate to food.* When one individual eats, *everyone* in the group eats. In a hunting and gathering culture, it is taboo for a hunter to kill an animal, then to bring it back for *only* his mate and children to eat. *He must share the food with the entire group*—generally, in a ritualistically-determined way.

Also, among human hunters and gatherers, there is no individual ownership of natural strategic resources. Everyone in the group "owns" a lake, a beach, a stream, or a forest.

Such a social structure is vastly closer to general primate behavior than is the structure that has developed in the 10,000 years of technological advance following the discovery of domestication. The hunting-and-gathering pattern lasted 1,750,000 years. Undoubtedly, Zinjanthropus lived in a group much the way present-day hunters and gatherers do. Actually, the hunting and gathering cultures existing today follow a way of life far closer to the social structure of a baboon troop than to the crazy-quilt structure of most of Western civilization.

In terms of fulfilling man's basic survival-based emotional

needs, I believe hunting-and-gathering cultures were the "Garden of Eden." Developed over a period of hundreds of thousands of years, hunting and gathering societies provided the bonded group which enabled its individual members to stay alive. Hunting-and-gathering societies fulfilled man's biological-based requirements for emotional bonding to his fellows.

Civilization stands on the foundation of animal and plant domestication. Once domestication of animals and plants was discovered, some men were able to stop roaming and settle in one place. The concept of land ownership was developed. Bartering came into practice. Villages were born. Some villagers began to specialize—for example, some became makers of footwear or clothing. Villages slowly grew larger and developed into small cities. With the city came the beginning of civilization as we know it today—and its problems. (Studies of rats and monkeys, for example, suggest that overcrowding by itself produces neurotic and psychotic reactions.) Certainly a civilized society, which all of us take for granted, differs radically from a hunting-and-gathering society.

Civilization has advanced incredibly since the first domestication of plants and animals. Yet man's biologically-based emotional needs have not caught up with his technology. Our bodies are a minimum of fifty thousand years out of date. Consider that emotional reactions are actually physical responses to stimuli. Then look at one of the five basic feelings—anger.

Man's anger, called "aggression" by many anthropologists, involves chemical responses to stimuli. Adrenalin rushes into the blood, affecting the circulatory system. The heart beats faster. Extra blood goes from the skin and viscera to the brain and muscles. Blood pressure rises. More red blood corpuscles are produced. Blood will clot faster. The processes of digesting and storing food come to a stop. Stomach movements, the secretion of gastric juices, and the peristaltic movements of the intestines are reduced. Hair stands on end. And there is a tendency to sweat. The rectum and bladder won't empty as easily as when anger does not exist. Carbohydrate that has been stored leaves the liver, putting additional sugar into the blood. Breathing becomes deeper and quicker.

All of these body activities have enormous survival value for man. The extra blood in the brain is for quick thinking; the extra blood in the muscles is a preparation for strenuous action. The additional blood sugar helps muscles be more efficient. Hair erection and sweating help cool the body, thus preventing over-heating from exertion. The speed-up in coagulation reduces the blood that might be lost in the event of injury. The changes in respiration permit faster intake of oxygen and elimination of carbon dioxide—a process which might be vital in a life-or-death struggle.

These physical changes in man's body that result from anger demand to be expressed. When they are not expressed in some form or other, a person "feels bad" for a considerable period of time thereafter.

Man's pain also demands expression for emotional health. Pain in animals is a warning to avoid more pain and, ultimately, death. In addition, man's pain most probably is a deep-rooted way of getting into emotional contact with other people in order to receive comfort or help from them. Its survival value is evident.

Pleasure is the fulfillment of one's survival-based needs, some of them modified by cultural conditioning.

Perhaps most important, love is a basic need in man. Love involves the anticipation of having one's needs met. It encompass-es the need to "feel bonded" to others, an essential element of group survival. Love also involves the need to touch, the desire and need to give concern to others, and the need to let *their* concern penetrate into one's own emotional awareness. And, of course, love involves man's sexual drives.

In *The Naked Ape*, Desmond Morris makes an interesting conjecture about man's sexuality: Intense sexual pleasure for females was an evolutionary creation of Homo sapiens. Such an invention was necessary, says Morris, in order to bond a female to a particular male, since a male had to spend so much of his time on hunting expeditions. The bonding of a male and female, he believes, was essential in order to permit the raising of children over a prolonged number of years during which the children could not survive on their own.

But this is not in accord with the majority of professional belief. Most qualified experts feel that hominid males simply were not designed to be monogamous. Today's scholars seem to think male hormones signal him to fornicate with his mother, his sisters, and his daughters, just as other primates do. Furthermore, they think he feels almost as strong an *emotional* affinity for a male friend as he does for his wife. This vision of man emerged during the past decade from the work of many behavioral scientists in such diverse fields as genetics, neurophysiology, and primatology. The picture is alarmingly out of alignment with the demands of civilized society.

The broadest way to state the viewpoint of modern behavioral scientists is this: *Culture has a biological basis.* Says anthropologist Robin Fox, of Rutgers University: "It is highly probable that the species is predisposed to behave in certain ways and that these ways are probably more numerous and specific than has been thought."

Such a behavior-based view differs radically from the orientation of most contemporary psychiatrists. We are only beginning to have a glimmering of the implications. It is dazzling to imagine what will be revealed when we study behavior as carefully and thoroughly as we have studied the physiology of the human body all these years.

In the light of recent evidence, for example, most anthropologists view the subject of man's sexuality in a markedly different way today than just a few years ago.

Primatologists report that least-dominant baboon males almost never have an opportunity to mount a female when she is in heat. To do so, nondominant males must hop a female when no more-dominant male is looking. This sexual activity of least-dominant males has enormous survival value: They have fewest opportunities to transmit their genes to the troop's gene pool. Therefore, the qualities of low-dominant males are less likely to be passed along to subsequent generations.

Modern anthropologists think that a sexual pattern similar to that of the baboons prevailed among hominids for over a million years. Robin Fox, with Berkeley's Sherwood Washburn and Michael Chance of England, developed theories to explain how nondominant, peripheral males acquired "equilibrium," which also helped the gene pool. "Equilibrium" is the ability to hold off immediate gratification of needs. In other words, by understanding in advance the consequences of one's actions, one can control or time responses so that adverse results are unlikely to occur. Foolish nondominant males, obeying their hormone drives, invaded the female domains of dominant males and were killed or banished from the troop. But intelligent, nondominant males successfully controlled their impulses and bided their time for the right moment. Eventually, they invented mother-brother-sister relationships, with attendant survival-value "bonding" functions, to make access to females more equitable. This view is quite different from the one presented by Freud in *Totem and Taboo*, the "anthropological" foundation of his Oedipal theory.

In short, man's brain and his cunning have been vitally important in evolving the primate form we are today. We are a generalized creature, who has developed the need to be fearful, pained, loving, group-oriented, angry, and (relative to other species) *intelligent*. How does this fit into a highly civilized, technological world?

Sherwood Washburn says: "It is not only our bodies that are primitive, but also our customs. They are not adapted to the crowded, technical world, dominated by a fantastic acceleration of scientific knowledge. There is a fundamental difficulty in the fact that contemporary human groups are led by primates whose evolutionary history dictates a strong desire to dominate. Attempts to build personal or international relations on the wishful basis that people will not be aggressive is as futile as it would be to try to build the institution of banking with no auditing on the basis that all employees will be honest."

What does happen to aggression in such a world as ours? The biological basis for aggression is the chemical-generated reaction which I call anger in my group process. It is a survival-based feeling, requiring expression in some form. In many dangerous situations, an angry reaction is physiologically inevitable. Human beings can be programmed to bury the feeling, to not feel it at a conscious level. But they cannot avoid feeling it *unconsciously*. *The feeling of anger is in their blood.* When it is not expressed overtly, the chemistry is not resolved totally. The anger is internalized, and a person carries it around in his belly along with the remnants of other anger he has denied expression. Expressing this buried anger plays an especially significant part in my groups.

The other feeling which our culture distorts especially severely is love. As a primate, man requires love in many forms. Sex is a big part of it, of course. But as love becomes enculturated, as human groups become bonded, love also involves recognition and approval. And it involves the need to give—and receive—affection in a bonded way.

Fundamentally, love is connected with *trust*. There appears to be a primate need to extend trust to others, and to have it extended to himself in return. Within a trusting emotional atmosphere, man can feel secure to express his inner feelings more freely and more honestly—even though he cannot *act* on all his feelings.

All known words for tribes translate into "The People." Eskimo, Navaho, Zuni, Arapesh, Bantu, Banshi—all mean "The People." On the other side of the coin is the fact that *other* human beings are "*non*people"—*or enemies who cannot be trusted.*

*The trouble with civilized life, the way most of us live it, is that it is structured with "nonpeople" whom we do not trust with our biological-based feelings. Even family members often become "nonpeople."*

Zoologist Morris points out that if you examine the personal phone directory of a contemporary urban man who is not a salesman or other kind of "human engineer," you will find the phone numbers of about thirty or forty friends and associates. This is approximately the number of group members in many primate groups.

An important reason, in a basic sense, why my groups are effective involves man's need to establish an emotional bond with a group of other people. It is a need with ample hominid precedent, but a need which civilization often denies. Man needs to find a trusting atmosphere where he can show the biological-based feelings he keeps pent up against the actions of "nonpeople."

In a crucial sense, herein lies the fundamental problem of achieving emotional health in our twentieth-century world. Deprived by our early programming of a sense of bonded trust, we are unable to develop the trust we need in order to express our emotions honestly to others and to let the feelings of others penetrate our deepest awareness.

We suffer from loneliness and alienation because we are deprived of the emotional contact we crave with other human beings. Emotional contact is what takes place after trust is established. The need for meaningful emotional contact is an important reason for the emergence not only of group therapy, but also of the entire human potential movement.

An important need thwarted by civilization's regimen is the desire to touch. Unless we are lovers, we are conditioned not to touch each other—except through the process of a ritualistic handshake. This is because civilized man does not trust enough to risk touching. It might prove offensive and be rejected. Therefore it is better to control the need to touch—to pretend it does not even exist. Yet the need to touch openly and frequently is a part of all primate behavior. Jane Van Lawick-Goodall, who reports her observations of Tanzania chimpanzees in her volume *In the Shadow of Man,* reports that, "when a chimpanzee is suddenly frightened he frequently reaches to touch or embrace a chimpanzee nearby, rather as a girl watching a horror film might seize her companion's hand." She continues: "This comfort, which chimpanzees and humans alike appear to derive from physical contact with another, probably originates during the years of infancy, when for so long the touch of the mother, or the contact with her body, serves to calm the frights and soothe the anxieties of both ape and human infants. So, when the child grows older and his mother is not always at hand, he seeks the next best thing—close physical contact with another individual."

Exercises aimed at developing a greater sense of trust, expressions of deeply-felt emotions, attempts at honest emotional interaction, expanded sensitivity, techniques for developing better awareness of oneself and others—all are aspects of the human potential movement. And whatever the ultimate judgment about the techniques and theories that are involved, one fact seems clear: The human potential movement arises out of a deeply-felt human need. I believe it is the struggle to express biologically-based survival feelings which society causes us to stifle.

Every patient I see is a product of our society, and I cannot help thinking deeply about this society. The sickness of our culture shows itself in the emotional stress my patients feel. We see the manifestations almost everywhere—in the newspapers, on television, in magazines and books; at the office and on the streets; in our homes and schools; with friends, families, and relatives; with acquaintances; and with strangers. America today is demanding, pluralistic, and complex. To the individual, life seems almost out of control. There is poverty amidst plenty. A costly war in Southeast Asia is hard to understand. The threat of racial warfare in our streets hangs over our heads. The fear of instant nuclear annihilation is all too real. Our cities are blighted, and our suburbs soon will be. Our air and waters are choked with the by-products of technology. The society in which we live is changing rapidly. There are dropouts, turn-ons, turn-offs. A sexual revolution is under way, but who knows where it's going? Young people are rejecting establishment values and conspicuous consumption, but for what? You can choose your form of escape: drugs, alcohol, mindless television, promiscuous sex, compulsive overwork, out-of-the-world vacation trips.

The patterns of emotional disturbance are different from those of Freud's day, when conduct was modulated and values were fixed. The growth of group therapy is no accident. It is true that many more persons need help today and that groups can treat a far greater number of people than any form of individual therapy. It is also true that group therapy is expanding because it costs less than one-to-one treatment. But there is another reason, too. Group therapy fulfills a vital requirement: The need for human beings to be bonded to others by showing their honest emotions and empathizing with the honest feelings of others. Individual psychotherapy—which involves an essentially private, one-person-to-one-person relationship—cannot fill this human need.

The nature of our culture has created a population which, in varying degrees, is emotionally disturbed. The theme of individual alienation is a twentieth-century cliché, an ever-present part of our existence. People are alienated because they cannot trust others enough to show them their authentic, human feelings. When repressed, these survival-based feelings give rise to various types of "sicknesses" which show up symptomatically in the form of damaging emotions, behavior, and attitudes.

Fundamentally, *people need other people*. Man, the primate, requires continuing emotional contact with other human beings.

The need is firmly rooted in the survival-based nature of a creature that is at least 1,750,000 years old. Compared with so much time, the ten thousand years comprising the span of civilization is but a thin veneer.

Group therapy says that any feeling *you* have is one that other human beings have had and can share with you. Emotionally-oriented groups stand in contradiction to the inhibitive culture in which we live. They provide a safe and trusting atmosphere in which you can express any emotion openly to others. Groups can promote a bondedness that becomes the basis for learning to trust. Through groups it is possible to develop the capacity to relate to significant persons as trusted intimates, rather than as "nonpeople" who are not to be trusted.

When an individual in a group screams out a basic emotion, most of those present *feel* as well as *hear* the emotion. Such feelings are communicated at a signal level. That is, a feeling can be separate from the verbal (or symbolic) communication the individual attempts to convey. For example, a woman's words may concern facts about how she was punished at age five by her mother. If her face and body show the fear and pain she experienced when she was five, most group members will sense and empathize with her feelings. *Half* of the process of emotional contact will have been effected. The other half depends upon the woman's ability to empathize with the emotions of the other group members. This means she will allow herself to feel the impact of others' feelings and respond to them with her own honest feelings.

If this woman fails to show feelings with which others can identify, she will not be able to involve their emotions as she tells her story. She will merely communicate facts. She will be what members of my groups call "turned-off"—that is, out of contact with her "gut feelings." Real emotional contact with others won't exist. After a while group members will become anxious and restless. Then if the woman continues to talk without genuine affect, she will usually be interrupted with suggestions and criticisms. She may be hurt or angry that no one wants to listen to her. Even though she is cut off from her own deep feelings at a conscious level, she has suffered from discomfort for years. She may not understand why others won't respond to "how she feels," when in reality she is not sharing that feeling. Group members often will understand her feeling "by proxy." They have had similar experiences, and being open to their own feelings about that experience, they can know how she is feeling. But until she can dare to show the feeling to others, there can be no true emotional contact of the sort which human beings need.

A major first step in my group process is to train such a woman to be sensitive to her own feelings, and then to show her emotions in her signals (her body posture and tone of voice) as well as in her words. It is one thing to say matter-of-factly, "I was scared when my mother hit me," then (usually belligerently), "Wouldn't you be?" It is quite another to scream out the terror, "Momma! Don't hit me! Stop! Please stop!" Until that real fear is released experientially, it can affect her entire life in the present. Her efforts to avoid feeling the fear may lead her to distorted perceptions about situations which realistically are not so fearful. The defensive energy required to repress the feeling will interfere with the quality and naturalness of her emotionality as an adult. And it will impede her chances for honest emotional contact with other human beings.

Feelings are the medium in which emotional contact must be effected. When such contact is lacking, we communicate like computers. At a verbal level, it is possible to convey facts, figures, abstractions. The transmission of such information is essential in any human civilized society; but computers are not human.

Human beings require emotional communication with other humans. Without using *your* experience to feel the emotions of another human being, you cannot be truly concerned about him. Unless you can show the feeling which his feeling evokes in you, you cannot get back the emotional response you really need. Yet our civilization requires that we "cool" our feelings in personal interactions (usually reserving them for society's sanctioned outlets, such as the football stadiums or sentimental movies). Our civilization also frowns upon much physical touching between individuals. This, too, is a basic need that has been smothered. It is a need which can be met in an emotionally satisfying way only through the trusting exchange of honest feelings.

Such are the core elements of human bondedness which unfold in my group process, as well as in other processes which have arisen in the human potential movement. The dynamic of my groups may sound complicated; yet when someone sees it at work, it is understandable. Some people have run from the room because the emotional intensity has been threatening. But their need is great, and most come back. Others have been set shouting against the group, suspicious, like animals caught in a corner. These people, too, finally reveal their need to be a part of the human whole, rather than to stand opposed to it, in angry isolation.

Then there is the familiar, verbally-oriented person who uses words to defend himself against a community of emotional closeness. I remember five or six highly verbal persons whom groups confronted in similar ways. After a number of groups, the verbalizers began to be given affection and love, with no dialectic or verbal explanations. They were puzzled, but they liked the warmth they experienced. One man I remember especially well was a lawyer named Don, a brilliant public speaker who came into therapy because of a wretchedly unhappy private life. After a few groups, when he began to talk, someone would say: "Cut the crap, Don. We love you *without* all those words." After a while, when this refrain took place, you could see tears of historic pain in Don's eyes as he let the love and concern of the group into his awareness. With a few months of group therapy and after a couple of marathons, Don began each group by standing up and vulnerably asking for love. He would turn to someone, look the person in the eye, and say, "Sally, I need love," or, "Dick, I need you to love me," then reach for a mechanistic embrace. Gradually, as he learned to experience the pleasure of such contact, Don's use of dialectic almost disappeared in group. He became intuitive, emotional, empathetic. Significantly, he found it the beginning of a richer, more satisfying life for him.

As individuals learn to express their feelings and entrust themselves to other group members, inevitably a joyous sense of vitality emerges. I have seen people laugh aloud in childlike wonder and glee as they sense the new choices that are available to them as open human beings who are in contact with their deep feelings and capable of reaching out to others.

Ours is also a dynamic which draws people into a circle of love, arms flung around each other, eyes peacefully shut, contented sighs and hums rising up like some forgotten campfire song which everyone somehow knows.

It is a very human dynamic, and it is far older than civilization.

# CHAPTER 7
# *A Character-Disordered Society*

As a psychiatrist, I make no attempt to understand the full range of social forces which have shaped the culture we live in. I leave extended comments to sociologists, ethnologists, and other social scientists who are better equipped to deal with the subject. Here I will try only to highlight what I find to be our transition from a nation of neurotics to a society of character-disordered personalities.

The differences between neurotics and character disorders tend to be subtle, because so many people exhibit characteristics of both types. In a psychiatric framework, it is the predominant characteristics which determine the category into which a person fits.

A neurotic has distorted feelings, and suffers from the feelings. He experiences his pain. A character-disordered personality, on the other hand, can be alienated and lonely, but he does not know he is suffering. Someone who is character disordered cannot be responsive to his own emotions, because he does not really know what he feels. To a large degree, genuine affect is missing from his existence. At an early age, to avoid the pain, he encapsulated his deepest emotions from his conscious awareness.

A person who is character disordered cannot express his innermost feelings; they are too deeply buried. Failing to create or sustain meaningful emotional contact with others, he inevitably has difficulty in trusting. How can he trust the emotions of others when his own feelings are so tenuous and untrustworthy? Frequently, he can function quite effectively (as opposed to the neurotic, whose maladaptive feelings usually militate against patterns of success). But even when accomplishment achieves success and recognition, a character-disordered person has isolated and lonely feelings. Approval, money, and possessions are not substitutes for the love he craves but does not know how to take in.

Lacking access to his deepest-level emotions, the character-disordered personality is to some degree untrustworthy. He is most particularly the victim of his unconscious. As the pressure of unexpressed emotions builds up, he will act out in destructive ways—perhaps through sexual promiscuity, overeating, antisocial withdrawal, overspending, or physical violence. For the most part, character-disordered persons have been considered "untreatable" by psychologists and psychiatrists. This is different from neurotic persons, who are easier to help with traditional psychotherapeutic methods.

Based on what I observe in my practice, there has been in the United States a tremendous increase in personalities who are predominantly character disordered. The society that Freud wrote about was very different. Rigid value systems held behavior under control, and neurosis was the prevalent personality type. Today, attitudes toward behavior are enormously more permissive. And significant changes have taken place in the fabric of our society.

For several years, 80 percent of my patients at initial interviews have been character-disordered personalities. Approximately 15 percent have been neurotic, and 1 to 2 percent have been schizophrenic. The balance (3 or 4 percent) have been basically healthy, despite emotional stress growing out of a specific reality or emotional problem. This pattern is confirmed in discussions I have had with professional colleagues, who have been encountering severe problems with the character-disordered personalities they find themselves attempting to help.

A pivotal factor in the transition from a neurotic to a character-disordered society, in my judgment, has been the demise of the extended family. In the United States, a young male and female who are attracted to each other begin to live together—in urban centers, with or without marriage. They want privacy from parents and relatives, time away from what they perceive as the prying eyes and confining attitudes of older people. No longer are grandparents, maiden aunts, and an unmarried uncle or two part of the scene. Gone are the differing viewpoints and varying degrees of emotionality provided by the many individuals in an extended family.

A newly-married couple quite literally locks itself into an apartment or house and begins—generally in a quite symbiotic way—to set up barriers between "us" (the new two-person family unit) and "them" (everyone else). The new twosome purchases dishes, silverware, draperies, furniture, a hi-fi. They furnish their new abode, defining themselves in terms of life style and taste. They entertain friends from their respective pasts, attempting (as they do so) to determine what friends they are going to retain as a couple. There seems to be precious little bondedness involved. Friends of ten years can be dropped quickly if a new mate objects to seeing them. Then, when children come, the offspring are exposed, basically, to only the two sets of symptoms of their parents, in a psychologically compressed situation.

The sense of structure provided by a patriarchal family has vanished. There is no longer the defined role for each individual in a family that there used to be. In 1940, the majority of Americans still lived in farming country. But World War II brought large-scale migration to the cities and a loss of population in rural counties which was to become permanent. Despite the population increases in America, dozens of rural counties have been losing population, according to the last three decennial censuses. Today in over a dozen major nations, agriculture employs fewer than 15 percent of the economically active population. In our country, where farms feed over 205 million Americans plus an estimated 160 million other people around the world, the number is below 6 percent and is shrinking rapidly. The reason lies in the increased efficiency of agricultural equipment; machines do what individuals used to do.

The important fact is that children on a farm could see, understand, and respect the skills their fathers used to support the family. Today, in a city, it is an unusual child who understands or respects the skills his father utilizes. On a farm, a new infant was a potential economic asset, whether it was a boy or a girl. After a few years, he or she could do chores—feed the chickens, chop wood, get vegetables from the truck garden, help milk cows, help with the planting and harvesting, and so forth. In a city, however, children are economic liabilities who require food, shelter, clothes, and education. Inevitably, parental attitudes toward children reflect this economic fact of urban life. In my practice, for example, I know many married couples who are in violent disagreement about whether or not to have children. In a typical case, the man is divorced and responsible for the support of children from his previous marriage. But the woman— who has not been married before—is childless and wants to bear the children of the man she loves. To the man, the central problem is economic. As one man raged about the problem recently in a group, "Why should *anyone* want a child these days? I figure the two kids I've already got will cost me about $50,000 each by the time I get them through college. That's $100,000—a hell of a lot of money. What do I get for it? My boy's hair is longer than my girl's. They're both on pot—if not something stronger. Neither one of them wants to communicate with me. They're embarrassed about what I do to make a living. All I'm good for is to shell out money. . . . " Similarly, I know several women with children from their first marriage who do not want to "go through the problem" of having more in their second marriage, even though their new husbands want children.

A strong view about children? Certainly. But it is held by a lot of men these days—and women, too. Any children born to parents who hold such a view must sense it.

The nature of the work men do has a great deal to do with this attitude. Most jobs have little intrinsic value. For most people, working is a way of earning money to fulfil other needs and wants. How much satisfaction can a man or woman experience on an automobile assembly line? Selling mass-produced items behind the counter of a large retail store? Mailing out billing records? Working as a filing clerk?

Even when a specific job involves activities which are meaningful and understandable, chances are the objectives of the corporation itself are depersonalized, three-times-removed, and hard to relate to.

To compound the problem, many wives are cloistered in bedroom suburbs, removed from their husbands' ways of making a living. They do not fully understand the struggles or humiliations he must face each day in a depersonalized work world. *Her* world is filled with children, boredom, household drudgery, lack of stimulation. Much of a couple's life is, in fact, not shared at all. Communication becomes difficult. Then home life can disintegrate even further when a mother leaves her children to go to an outside job.

The truth is, whether married or not, no single human being can meet the full-time needs of another. Emotionally, each of us needs to be bonded to a number of other people. We need friends, relatives, teammates, partners, co-workers, whom we can trust. Yet the competitive urban society in which we live makes bonded relationships increasingly difficult to develop and maintain. Twenty-two percent of all U.S. families move annually, a figure that translates into untold anxiety and isolation. For moving means new work associates, new friends, new neighbors, new schools, new clubs and associations. Many begin to study the art of mobility at universities. Right now, an estimated 750,000 college students are living away from home, learning how to cultivate transient friendships and sex relationships.

When an executive is transferred to a new location, his initial contacts are inevitably people from his company. However, whatever capacity he and his wife have to establish meaningful relationships with these people is limited by the socio-economic restrictions of business. In some corporations, unwritten laws about executive conduct prevail. One buys a house in the appropriate part of town, lives in a dwelling that is smaller than that of his immediate superior, and entertains subordinates only in a circumscribed way. In *Future Shock*, Alvin Toffler quotes an executive: "A wife can be downright dangerous if she insists on keeping close friendships with the wives of her husband's subordinates. Her friendships will rub off on him, color his judgment about the people under him, jeopardize his job."

While many people stay with one company for a prolonged period, job turnover is becoming the motif of our era. Of the seventy-one million workers in the U.S. labor force in 1969, the average man had held his current job only 4.2 years. This is radically different from the time of Freud, or from Japan and other countries today, where a job is likely to be synonymous with a career.

As a society, we seem to have lost the ability to do what my group members call "hang in." Why take the trouble to confront a neighbor with whom you are angry? Why bother to tell off a friend who has been gossiping behind your back? It's easier to sever the relationships and avoid the turmoil of confrontations.

Our mobile society takes another toll: People no longer remain under the stress of a particular household situation. Rather than struggle with an emotional problem—and perhaps grow in the struggle—one can simply go away from it. Women leave husbands. Adolescents leave parents. Husbands abandon wives and children. Fear and anger, the classic defensive reactions to stress and danger, now take second or even third place. Isolation and withdrawal—mechanisms that are the defense of the character-disordered personality—provide much easier methods of eliminating discomfort.

When emotional problems erupt, it is often easier to leave the scene than stay and work through the situation. This is the pattern of our times in mobile America, circa 1972.

To fulfill themselves better and to help pay the bills, many women work. In the 1970 census, two out of every five women in the United States were part of the labor force. A job can be an excellent solution for both the husband and wife, but in too many instances today it means a woman is withdrawing from the emotional stresses of building a better relationship with her husband and children. So often, when an emotional problem is growing worse, it seems expedient to focus time on *another activity* (such as a job) rather than to face up to the difficult-to-work-through problems of human relationships. When it comes to raising children or relating to a spouse, it is the *quality* of time that is important, not necessarily the *amount* of time.

Urban life is complex and confusing. In order to preserve a kind of equilibrium, city dwellers insulate themselves against the stimuli bombarding their psyches. Georg Simmel has pointed out that if an urbanite reacted emotionally to each and every person with whom he came into contact, or cluttered his mind with information about them, he would be "completely atomized internally and would fall into an unthinkable mental condition."

Examples of the depersonalization of city life are plentiful. I know of a woman, for example, who fainted while standing up on a crowded Manhattan subway. The doors opened at Forty-second Street, and the rush-hour crowd surged out. Woozy and half unconscious, the woman was pushed through the doors and onto the subway platform—where she fell down, amidst rolled-up candy wrappers, gum, and spittle. Until she became sufficiently conscious to pull herself to her knees, literally thousands of people stepped over her, wanting to avoid involvement. Probably they thought she was drunk. But, even so, it is an example of callous urban inhumanity.

Urban man is bombarded by more than 1500 advertising impressions a day. He cannot absorb all these impressions or react to all the stimuli. To stay sane, he must click off some of his awareness—not only of "impressions," but also of the multitude of human lives that cross his path. But how does he go about numbing himself to *some* confusing stimuli, without beginning a process which goes further and deeper than he wants it to go?

If one day you shut your eyes to the sight of a drunken derelict passed out on a street corner, the next day you will find it easier to walk past another man (who might be a heart-attack victim) lying on the street. Then, if you can pass by an unconscious *man* who needs help, why not a child? Why not a newborn infant? Where do numbness and insensitivity stop? Where does common humanity *start*?

Ironically, we tend to fuzz reality and bring nonreality into sharp focus. The flesh-and-blood reality of the streets is too painful and too threatening, so we block it from our awareness. Then, for insight and information about the rest of the world, we rely upon the edited-for-significance and organized-for-comprehension presentations which the media put before us. Wars become movies, with a voice-over. Catastrophes telescope into interviews with eyewitnesses. On election nights, computers predict the final outcome soon after the polls close. The typical metropolitan daily paper may receive approximately 8 million words of copy a day from its staff, wire services, feature syndicates, correspondents, and special writers. Out of this mass of verbiage, only about 100,000 words will be printed.

So much of our day-to-day knowledge of the world depends upon what others have decided we should see and hear. For several years, for example, we have observed the war in Vietnam as a drama on our television screens. We have seen soldiers wounded and killed, towns bombed, shells bursting, huts burning, refugees clogging roads. Even though we also read newspapers and magazines, our sense of the war has derived from the television screen.

The dependence upon third-hand, edited-and-processed information can generate distrust. In 1969, when two astronauts landed on the moon, the event seemed so unlikely that a friend of mine found himself wondering if it could really be taking place. "Could this be a propaganda stunt?" he asked. Suppose two actors were strolling around a sound stage dressed up in silly-looking padded suits? How could he tell it wasn't an Orwellian prank? How could *anyone* tell?

Is it any wonder that young people are skeptical about what they see and hear? Politicians and leaders can manipulate ideas, distort and oversimplify facts. How can the truth be sorted out from what isn't true?

Once upon a time, man's reality was as immediate and personal as the fingers on his two hands. It comprised the people he lived with and the trees and bushes and animals he saw each day. News did not come to him through a mechanized process, edited and organized for speedy understanding. An individual relied on what he himself saw or heard. Or he obtained news from a person he knew and trusted—someone he could count on to have seen or heard what he was reporting on. Today, conversation at a dinner party frequently involves information originated by depersonalizing media. There is a kinetic quality to information in the United States—fast, always moving, always to be updated.

The next time you go to a dinner party, observe the reaction when someone says, "I had the most incredible experience today

. . ." and launches into a highly personal anecdote about something which *actually happened to her*. You can believe in the story, enjoy it, and laugh openly with the teller.

In initial interviews in my practice, I frequently meet character-disordered personalities who seem more like robots than human beings. Their talk is depersonalized, without affect, without humor. They transmit facts without feelings. And what is worse, their attitudes seem to have been obtained from media to which we all have access—*Time, Newsweek, Harper's, The New York Times Magazine,* and so on. Truth to tell, such people are incredibly boring to listen to. Interviews with them fill me with anxiety. Invariably, it is a relief to meet the individual several months later, after he has been in groups for a while. There is emotion and affect in the voice, sensitivity and responsiveness in the way he looks at you.

I remember a man, Humphrey, who sounded like a sociology text. He came to me because his wife (who was in a private analysis with another psychiatrist, as well as in my group system) wanted a divorce. Humphrey reported the story without expression or change of inflection: "When Marlene asked me for a divorce, I was aware that one out of three marriages ends in divorce. So I told her, yes, she could have the divorce. After all, it isn't shameful to join a third of our population in solving our society's most difficult relationship in this manner. . . ."

"Was her request a surprise to you, Humphrey?" I asked.

"Many husbands are surprised by a request for divorce. I read a book last week which said. . . ."

"No, Humphrey. I want to know about *your* reactions. Had you sensed something was going on? Did your marriage seem good to you?"

"Marriage today is a most difficult relationship, Dr. Casriel. I have read that in one county in California, the divorce rate is over fifty percent. The problems of marriage are inherent in. . . ."

"But, Humphrey," I interrupted again, "I want to know yes or no. Did you *know* she was going to ask you for a divorce?"

Humphrey looked at me for a full ten seconds. "No, Dr. Casriel," he replied, smiling mechanically as he said it. "I did not expect such a request. I thought we had an excellent marriage—relatively speaking, that is."

Months later, after a program of three groups a week and three intensive marathons, I saw Humphrey sob out his pain about the impending divorce on the shoulders of every member of a fifteen-person group. He loved his wife very much.

I am pleased to report that there was a happy ending to this story. Delighted (although also scared) by her husband's new-found emotionality, Marlene decided that she didn't want a divorce. She and Humphrey are living together, working through emotional problems in a mature and sensitive way that is bonding them closer together.

Humphrey had turned off his feelings early in life in order to avoid pain that seemed unbearable to him. But by avoiding the pain, he also avoided feelings of pleasure. And he was boring—frustrating to listen to, impossible to relate to, unsatisfying to attempt to respond to. The tragedy is that Humphrey is a dramatic example of what is prevalent today throughout our character-disordered society.

Manifestations of anaesthetized emotions and the inability to relate can be found everywhere—in our high divorce rate; in the depersonalization of sex (both within marriage and out); in the complaints about isolation and alienation which are the signs of our times; in mechanized or ritualized actions performed without meaning or feeling; and in the massive identity struggle which all of us experience. Our character-disordered society is not an easy one to live in.

The report of the Joint Commission on the Mental Health of Children, headed by Dr. Peter Neubauer, calls the emotional health of children the number one public health problem of our day. The Commission's estimate is that 25 percent of the nation's children need emotional help, and that "emotional ill health is of epidemic proportions in our land." Dr. Neubauer, who is head of the Child Development Center in New York, says: "We see preschool children with problems of a nature that lead us to believe that their appropriate development has already been interfered with. There are the children with extended sleep disorders who cannot fall asleep because of the specter of nightmares. There are children with fears so great that they interfere with function. We see speech problems and bed-wetting problems and temper tantrums. We see over-dependency of such magnitude that a child cannot go on to next steps, next growth. We see hyperactivity prolonged past its normal time so that a child cannot be still enough to learn. We see children who are obsessively orderly, too long and too fearfully dependent on ritual. We see children with consistently low tolerance toward any kind of frustration. With all these children, behavior that might be appropriate to one stage of development has lasted far longer than it should and this spells trouble."

The symptoms of emotional ill health to which Dr. Neubauer refers will become more pronounced as the children get older, and the problem will become vaster in scale.

The truth is that we live in a country in which most people have only limited access to their own deep-level emotions.

We are born to parents who have turned off *their* emotions. We fail to experience what Eric Fromm calls "milk and honey"— the accepting love and warmth of an emotionally responsive mother. Then, as we grow up, we are conditioned to contend with hostility (instead of anger); depression (instead of anger or pain); lectures and attitudinal attacks (often camouflaging a parent's fear and lack of knowledge); endless criticism (instead of a meaningful holding to account); martyrdom (instead of healthy, mutually freeing self-interest); and destructive patterns of behavior (instead of healthy patterns, to use as role models).

Then we go to school to obtain facts from teachers who have also opted for the emotional turn-off. But studying the story of George Washington and the cherry tree does not help a boy find his own identity. The geography of anger is not on schoolroom maps. And multiplication tables do not teach a child what to do about the pain inside him, which he doesn't know how to express.

We are introduced to the joys of sex—but too often without love. We learn how to use sex, somewhat mechanically, as a creative tool kit. It provides a pleasurable way of gaining access to our feelings, for a brief period of time.

Later, many of us go to college, where we become more adept at locating, organizing, and manipulating specialized information. In the process, we somehow acquire a skill which is translatable into money. We get a job and move out of the nuclear home.

Then we choose a mate, marry, and form a nuclear home of our own. Chances are, whether or not it ends in divorce, the marriage will be bad. How can it be good, given the role-models we have observed and the conditioning and education we have received? Insulated from our deepest-level feelings, we will re-enact the same scene with our children that our parents enacted with *us*. Probably, we will enact the scene less healthily than they did, because we have had worse conditioning.

This is the basic pattern of our character-disordered society. It is very different from the Victorian society in which Freud made his profoundly important discoveries. Freud's era tended to produce neurotics.

What is the difference between a character-disordered personality and a neurotic? The distinction is important in terms of my process, which is centrally designed to bring patients into contact with intense, long-repressed emotions. Let us take a closer look at the distinction in the next chapter.

# CHAPTER 8
# *Neurosis and Character Disorder*

IMAGINE THIS SCENE on television: Three men in their thirties are conversing over cocktails in a fashionably modern living room. The conversation is low-keyed, the tones pleasant. Suddenly one man jumps up angrily and tells the others that they are fools and have no right to talk to him "that way." Then he stomps out of the room, slamming the door.

One man looks quizzically at the other. "Don't you think Hank is getting a bit neurotic?" he asks. The question is immediately understandable to anyone looking on.

Suppose instead he were to ask: "Don't you think Hank is getting a bit *character-disordered?*" The term sounds so ludicrously clinical that an audience would laugh.

When it comes to the communication of popular culture, "neurotic" wins hands-down over "character-disordered"— despite my belief that a vast majority of the people in our culture are character-disordered. Clearly, the concept of "character disorder" will not soon replace "neurosis" in the cocktail-party parlance of the post-college crowd. For one thing, the word "neurosis" has a devilish, somewhat interesting connotation, rather like some of the movie roles played so ably by Tony Randall. In contrast, "character disorder" sounds like a moral judgment handed down by a jury of George Apley, Grant Wood, Calvin Coolidge, Hester Prynne, Daniel Webster, and William Jennings Bryan. Secondly, there have been decades of education about Freud, Adler, Jung, Pavlov, and others. Literate adults in the U.S. know what neurosis is. In urban centers like Manhattan, it's fashionable to admit to a bit of neurotic behavior (provided the behavior is interesting enough).

Do those who use the term "neurotic" know its meaning? Generally speaking, yes. They have a good common-sense understanding of it. They might run into trouble when the need arises to distinguish between neurotic and nonneurotic symptoms—but that's a task which can be difficult even for a psychiatrist. Similarly, most people have a fairly good idea of what they mean by "psychotic" behavior, although they of course do not have the professional training to make an accurate clinical diagnosis of psychosis.

# The Problems of Diagnostic Labels

Almost everyone can be classified in psychiatric terms as basically one of three personality types: *psychotic, neurotic,* or *character-disordered.* These three categories form the diagnostic platform for most professionals practicing psychotherapy today. The only exceptions, in my opinion, are people with organic brain damage caused by disease, birth or congenital defects, infection, poison, tumor, or physical injury. There are also a few Americans whom I would call "emotionally healthy" by the standards discussed in Chapter 3.

While I am generally critical of psychiatric labels, I find their general distinctions important. I believe there is an important difference between the psychic dynamics of character-disordered and neurotic personalities. This difference may shed light on the failure of much of psychiatry to deal successfully with character-disordered personalities. Psychoanalysis and many other forms of one-to-one therapy have been successful only in treating neurotics. Group psychotherapy, on the other hand, when it works with basic feelings, can be effective in treating both neurotics and character-disordered personalities.

Nevertheless, it is important to remember that psychiatric classifications are reference tools, not hard-line realities. Like most labels dealing with human behavior, they serve as guidelines. If a patient is a neurotic with anxiety reaction, we have some idea of how he might handle the loss of his job, or why he might have lost it in the first place. We also are provided with some valuable clues about how to understand him, how to get through his defenses, and so forth. But these are suggestions only, drawn from observation and clinical experience. They are not clearly defined facts.

Too often, beginning with the initial diagnosis, psychiatrists stamp human beings with the traits of a basic personality type. From then on, a patient is viewed in terms of his prototype and its characteristics, not in terms of individual personality. His feelings, his special pain or confusion, and his deepest needs are pushed into a stereotype for the convenience of the therapist. The patient's humanity is sacrificed. The label becomes the patient.

Anyone is bound to suffer from such superficial judgment. I frequently see the danger of this in my work with drug addicts in AREBA. Classically, most addicts are diagnosed as severe character disorders. Until very recently, there has been little success in treating them. For want of a better understanding, many professionals automatically assume that severe character disorders are "untreatable." Worse, they "treat" the "untreatable" accordingly. I am sure that much of the punitive, restrictive handling of addicts results from this attitude. Yet our group process has had considerable success with addicts, especially in a therapeutic community.

"Untreatable" simply does not seem to be the permanent condition of the character-disordered drug addict. (Early in Daytop history, over half of those admitted had been diagnosed elsewhere as psychotic. But these diagnoses were wrong. In reality, most had severe character disorders, and many responded well to the Daytop dynamic.)

Clearly, you cannot pigeonhole people too tightly within the confines of a diagnostic label. No one falls absolutely within one category or another. I have never seen a character disorder without some neurotic symptoms or a neurotic without some signs of character disorder. Also, though only a small percentage of the population would be clinically diagnosed as psychotic, in theory everyone has the potential of becoming psychotic, given severe, prolonged environmental stress coupled with insufficient sleep, food, and human contact. Diagnostic labels really refer to the predominant theme within a particular person at a particular time.

Another problem lies in the concept of "sickness." I find that the majority of psychotics are medically ill. Like many clinicians, I believe that a chemical imbalance in the psychotic's metabolism interferes with his reality-testing and his thinking processes. The disease does not mean, however, that all psychotics are necessarily "sicker" (as we usually mean in the context of emotional imbalance) than other people. Psychotics generally have problems in functioning that are more serious than most character-disordered or neurotic persons. Yet many neurotics and character-disordered people are as mixed up and destructive to themselves or others as psychotics.

Furthermore, the severity of problems varies within each personality profile. Some neurotics have more disturbing feelings than other neurotics. Some character-disordered persons are more cut off from their basic feelings than others. Some people are dangerous, some highly responsible. Also, the degree of "health" within an individual changes at different times.

At least 80 percent of my patients are character-disordered when they come to me. The others are basically neurotic. With a very few exceptions, I have not put people with mental deficiencies or severe physical handicaps, such as blindness or paraplegia, into my groups. It has just been too difficult for other group members to grasp the situation of the handicapped person, even though scream exercises have helped some physically handicapped people cope with their feelings.

I have, however, put a few psychotics—all borderline schizophrenics whose conditions were compensated by medication—into some carefully chosen groups. In view of the increasing numbers of groups throughout the country and the lack of responsible controls over many groups, it is important to discuss psychosis briefly before exploring the two diagnostic profiles which embrace my patients—neurosis and character disorder.

# Psychosis

My records indicate that fewer than 2 percent of the people who come to me are psychotic. From a technical viewpoint, there are two kinds of psychotics: those with organic, demonstrable brain damage, and those without. Organic psychotics show brain damage resulting from one of a variety of causes, such as alcoholism, trauma, injury, or poison. The damage is observable with a microscope. In chronic cases, it cannot be helped with chemicals. Damaged tissue *is* damaged tissue. In nonorganic psychosis, no microscopic brain damage can be found. About 80 to 90 percent of such cases are schizophrenics or manic depressives, with the vast majority being schizophrenic. Many clinicians find schizophrenia to be primarily a physical illness caused by specific metabolic enzymatic-genetic imbalances. Often medication can help. My clinical experience concurs with this metabolic view. I no longer accept schizophrenics into my practice, but those who remain from before seem to respond to medication.

At this time, I am not prepared to evaluate the possibilities of our group method for the treatment of schizophrenics. The little clinical evidence I gathered suggests that, though some schizophrenics can be warmed by the process, none can make real progress. Some schizophrenics may cause undue disruption in groups. They can interfere with the process, and nobody benefits.

There also can be some real danger to having schizophrenics in groups. The intensity of the process may cause deterioration of a compensated schizophrenic condition. What's more, the histories of some schizophrenics indicate they could be homicidal in such a setting.

A danger here deserves stress. Since groups are increasingly in vogue these days, many people are joining them with little knowledge of the qualifications of those running their groups or of the stability of other group members. In one case a schizophrenic who was, like many schizophrenics, quite charismatic, ran an ad in a New York newspaper and got about forty people to join groups which he led. His basic problems soon emerged, and he was rehospitalized at Bellevue. The people abandoned his groups. But who knows what damage was done in the meantime to susceptible group members?

A great deal more remains to be discovered about group therapy for psychotics. Psychiatrists in a special program in New Haven recently reported some success. It is my personal belief that such people can find help in groups, but undoubtedly the place to experiment is in groups comprised of other psychotics. I gather this is what is being done in the therapeutic community of Dr. R. D. Laing in England. His enormously interesting book, *The Divided Self,* teaches that diagnostic labels can be vicious, and he gives great insight into individual psychotics. But we must still wait to learn what his group therapy is like.

It is essential at this time to weed out schizophrenics from groups for neurotics and character-disordered persons. The screening process takes professional skill. That is one important reason for having a trained psychiatrist or psychologist in charge of any group therapy system.

# Neurotic Personalities

Psychiatrists describe neurotics in terms of "reactions." All are "ego-alien." The reactions entail continual emotional discomfort, often severe, from which the neurotic has little escape. Despite their decreasing proportion in the general population, neurotics remain the bread and butter of psychoanalysts.

Anxiety is the *bête noir* of all neurotics. The feeling can be very unpleasant. Often, we refer to anxiety as "butterflies in the stomach." In my view, anxiety is disguised fear which is not appropriate to the reality situation. Thus it is "maladaptive." The manner of disguise makes it ineffective and frequently quite painful. The feeling of fear is, of course, a basic emotional mechanism to defend the individual against pain or the anticipation of pain, which we call "danger." With fear, the adrenal system is activated, enabling the individual to run faster and better avoid the threats that confront him. But anxiety chokes off the valuable use of fear, and when anxiety is severe, it is very painful. The threat is internal, the danger often unidentifiable. Most people can usually curtail impulses and feelings that would raise severe anxiety. They develop behavior patterns to meet their needs, both internal and external, without getting into anxiety-provoking situations. But the neurotic cannot do this successfully. His anxiety builds up like a pressure cooker, and he subconsciously tries to release the pressure through some psychological device.

The form taken by a neurotic's particular defensive device constitutes his neurotic symptom, or reaction. There are six basic categories. In addition, there is the category of "undifferentiated," which is a typical catch-all phrase to accommodate all those neurotics who do not fit well into the six standard categories. For each, scream exercises help free the neurotic from his symptomatic pain by cutting through to the deep-down feelings he has been disguising.

1. The neurotic with *anxiety reaction* releases the tension in an overt way. Usually a sort of free-floating, uncontrolled anxiety is his primary symptom. If the anxiety is chronic, he emits jittery signals most of the time. At the slightest stress—in reality, often not threatening—his heart will beat faster, his palms sweat, and he may even burst into panic and hysteria. A more moderate condition is not so obvious under day-to-day circumstances, but pressure situations still evoke overwhelming feelings of helplessness, near life-panic, and often an urge to run.

I have found that people are not necessarily afraid of fear. But many associate fear with helplessness, a state unconsciously "remembered" from infancy. Once a person confuses this fear with helplessness, he is paralyzed by the resulting anxiety. In reality, fear does not make one helpless. Fear is a demonstration that one is *not* helpless. Fear can be an appropriate survival feeling, allowing one to escape real danger. The treatment problem in our groups is to lead these people to see that the feeling of fear lying under their anxiety is not magical. We encourage group members to express fear by screaming, by telling each group member that "I'm scared," and by other exercises. When the words sound like those of a helpless child, the group prods the person to try not to sound so helpless, to take responsibility for his feeling instead, by expressing it with assertion. The ominous, malevolent magic of fear begins to fall away as these people feel the strength and freedom of being able to express fear without becoming helpless. Gradually, they learn to understand, at both a feeling and intellectual level, that fear need not render them helpless. They learn that it is possible to feel and express fear—and still function effectively.

2. *Depressive reactions* are typical of about three-quarters of all neurotics whom psychiatrists see. The classical explanation is that chronic depression stems from one or more of three situations: repressed or suppressed anger which one cannot express; a lowered self-esteem; the loss of a significant loved object (either person or possessions, such as money).

In my groups, I find one reason basic to all depression: the fear of expressing one's pain. Our dynamic rapidly cuts through depression (often in just a few groups, or even less) to its cause—pain. Sophie, a tiny-framed bookkeeper in her late fifties, had had a severe depressive decline since the death of her sister six months earlier. She had been unable to function at all, and she was on her way to the hospital for electric shock treatment when her daughter persuaded her to see me first. In our conference, Sophie was very withdrawn, barely spoke, and sat rocking back and forth in the throes of her depression. From her daughter, I learned that Sophie had loved her sister very much. Sophie's husband had died six years before, and her children had grown.

After deciding that Sophie was not victim to an organic or psychotic depression, I put her into a group. (I gave her no medication.) She sat like a stone, almost catatonically, through the first hour. Then I saw her look up briefly at a woman who was saying, "I am lovable." Gently, I turned to Sophie and said, "You're lovable, too." She looked at me to see if I was talking to her. I nodded. "Say it." For the first time in over an hour, she uttered a word: "I'm lovable?" It was a question, not a statement. I asked her to repeat it several times, telling each person in the room. Always, it was a question. "I'm lovable?" But she began to see that the group members were responding to her, nodding, smiling, reinforcing the thought that she was, indeed, lovable. We got her to say it louder and louder. She stood up, and suddenly that tiny frame was bellowing, "I'm *LOVABLE!* I'm lovable."

The screams ended in a wail of pain. She started to collapse physically, and another woman grabbed her and held her, standing, while Sophie sobbed uncontrollably, mumbling the words,

"I am lovable," again and again. Four or five other group members gathered around her, touched her, stroked her until her tears quieted.

Those five minutes told the whole story, which she then talked about. She had never loved anybody but her sister and, to a degree, her husband. When he died, she leaned totally on her sister, who was slowly wasting away of cancer. Throughout her life, Sophie had felt unlovable, but she had accepted her sister's love. Now her sister's death meant that the last person on earth who loved her had died. She felt nobody else, including her children and grandchildren, loved her.

As Sophie talked, she again became emotionally aware that she was lovable, and she broke out in a tremendous rage at the deprivation of all those years. The rage turned into deep pain, but it was a pain pure and simple which she intuitively understood and accepted. Her depression lifted in that group. She went back to work and has functioned happily ever since.

When the depressed neurotic feels secure in groups, he learns to express the suppressed feeling which caused his pain. If he is someone who feels the pain of low self-esteem, he does exercises asserting that he is lovable and entitled to love, and he begins to feel that way. He learns to expect and take in the love of others. If depression over a loss is his problem, he becomes aware in groups that he can develop more love, additional love. The group supports him in his grief over his loss. When he knows he can replace his loss because he is lovable, when he trusts new love will come in, he is free to show his pain at the previous loss. If repressed anger out of fear of rejection and the resulting helplessness is the cause, we encourage expression of the anger and of the fear associated with it. If the person can do this while taking in the acceptance and love of the group, the depression will dissipate in a few minutes. As he exercises his feelings of fear, anger, love, pain, and pleasure in groups, he learns to combat the depression as soon as it starts to descend upon him.

3. The classical literature describes *obsessive-compulsive* symptoms this way: "A defensive regression of the psychic apparatus to the pre-Oedipal, anal-sadistic phase, with the consequent emergence of early modes of functioning of the ego, superego and id. These factors, along with the employment of

specific ego defenses, combine to produce the chronic symptoms of obsessions, compulsions, and compulsive acts." Sandor Rado simplified this concept by stating that the obsessive-compulsive is caught on the seesaw of fear and anger: "I want to . . . I'm afraid to . . . ." Rarely can this kind of neurotic make a decision one way or the other. As tension mounts within him, he becomes obsessed with a particular thought or with some compulsive act.

Our group process has led me to see the obsessive-compulsive as one who has a very weak conceptualization of himself. He really has an identity problem. In effect, the obsessive-compulsive does not know who he is. Is he himself? Or is he an appendage of Mommy or Daddy? When he performs an act or thinks of a situation, he is emotionally bound to his early, infantile life, and he is unable to distinguish what is right and what is wrong for him. What would Mommy want? Then he is angry at Mommy for having that power over him. On the one hand, he wants to please; on the other, he is furious at having to please. He is both afraid to do it wrong and prompted to do it wrong, in order to show Mommy up. In this conflict, he is never sure whether he is thinking or doing something to please his parental figure or doing it for himself. When he switches to the opposite tack in a particular situation, again he is confused: Is this opposite tack an expression of him or of his parental figure?

This explanation of obsession-compulsion makes special sense when you consider that adolescents are typically compulsive. They are, after all, going through a traumatic crisis. They are making the physiological change from childhood to adulthood. And they are preparing psychologically and behaviorally for independence, when they will be acting on their own, following rules of their own choosing, not of their parents' selection.

I have found that we can break through obsessive preoccupations or compulsive states by making the person scream out such assertions as, "I am *me!* I'm entitled to my own feelings! Fuck you, Mommy! I am ME." By daring to denounce his parents this way and to assert his identity independently of them, he gains a tremendous sense of freedom and his obsessive symptoms begin to drop away.

Part of learning to accept his feelings as his own also comes from acknowledging the fact that the individual may hold contradictory feelings. One woman in our groups, for instance, had a handwashing compulsion. She would rush to the sink and scrub her hands dozens of times a day. She would frantically wash off her purse if she dropped it even on a clean rug. She was able to hold a low-level government job, but every other minute of her time had been centered around her hand-washing compulsion. She had no social life. All her money above baseline living needs was spent on treatment. Jean was sixty years old when she came to me, and she had spent forty years in private therapy.

In her second group with us, Jean lost her compulsion permanently. She had been "raped" by her boyfriend when she was seventeen. (All her therapists had known of this incident, of course.) She had been humiliated; yet she also had felt pleasure. She did feel some anger at having been violated, but it was anger which her parents' and society's teachings told her she *ought* to feel. Every time she felt angry about what had happened to her, she also felt guilty because of the mixed-in pleasure she remembered unconsciously, pleasure which her parents would have detested. Her hand-washing was an expression of this conflict. Was she to feel anger or pleasure? She felt guilty feeling angry, and she felt guilty feeling pleasure. Thus her anger never came out straight or forcefully. Nor could her pleasure.

The group showed Jean that they could accept her ambivalent feelings about the rape. They encouraged her anger, saying she had a right to it—for herself. They also encouraged her pleasure. When she accepted this insight, she began, with group prompting, to express her anger. First, it was a kind of exercise, not really hooked up to her true feelings. But all of a sudden it turned into explosive, foot-stomping, fist-clenched screams of, "I'm ANGRY!" She let out the tremendous fury which her guilty feelings had muffled up until then. Then she started to express the fact that she had enjoyed being raped. "I enjoyed it, I enjoyed it!" she screamed, gaining greater and greater pleasure. She finally admitted emotionally to the full measure of pleasure she had received.

Her compulsion started to dissolve—right in that group. She has not washed her hands compulsively again. Of course, the precipitating trauma of the rape and her confusion about it was superimposed on a very severe pathology evolved from infancy and childhood. She still had much of this past to work out after she dropped the symptom of her compulsion, and she stayed in treatment for about a year after that. Last summer, after a lifetime of paying psychiatric bills, Jean had saved enough money to make her first trip to Europe. The compulsion which she had suffered from age twenty to age sixty had disappeared. Her hands are no longer red and raw from scrubbing. Now going on sixty-two, Jean is enjoying life more than ever before. She accepted and enjoyed a love affair for the first time in her life. She accepts the freedom of having two opposite emotions coexisting side by side. They are *her* feelings.

4. A *phobic reaction* symbolically represents a frightening situation or object from the patient's past. It may be a fear of closed spaces, for instance, and cause the victim to rush choking from the subway or to avoid subways altogether. This kind of neurosis depends upon fear, the fear of being controlled or helpless. When you work one out with a patient, you are bound to find severe hostility against Mommy or Daddy, whoever put the fear there in the first place. Sometimes the phobia is a fear of one's own hostility. But the real fear has to do with pain: the fear of being exposed to the pain of parental supercontrol, or the pain of an unfulfilled need for the parent's love, which the person is helpless to do anything about.

Phobias are overcome in our group process by enabling the person to get to his basic anger so he can feel the security of being mobile and not have to cater to anyone's control. There may be a dramatic breakthrough to this realization in group, but it takes a lot of work and a redoing of the basic exercises for months longer before the phobia completely disappears. Currently, John, a young man about thirty-two, is in group. Successful in business, he had developed a severe phobia against elevators. Considering that he had to visit offices in tall Manhattan buildings, John's phobia was seriously affecting his ability to function.

When he first joined the group, John parried everything with verbalizations. He had a deep sense of the ridiculous and often laughed at himself and others. And he had to be a big shot—in business and in the group. In reality, John had tremendous unconscious feelings of inadequacy and rage. His father had been a successful businessman who gave him little affection, but some approval for good performance in the world. Anger was not allowed, and John prided himself on being "a nice guy" who never got angry.

He did not do well in groups until we got him into a marathon. After almost everyone else had worked out on the mats, John stretched out on the floor, too. He had become sufficiently attuned to the emotional intensity built during the marathon, and before long a simple anger exercise turned into a screaming, kicking temper tantrum. John was so shocked at his own anger that he wanted to deny the whole experience. So we made him get down on the floor again. He had another tantrum. And this time he accepted the responsibility for his feelings. He realized that he had tremendous hostility toward his father and that he had never faced it. Furthermore, John had been consumed recently by the fear that he would kill his children. This was displaced anger that he really felt toward his wife (his current "Daddy," in the role she played) and his historical father. His murderous impulses against his kids were greatly reduced after that marathon. He also began to tackle his fear of elevators. With great trepidation—and courage—he rode a couple of elevators during the next week. And two weeks later, he came into group with a broad grin and an announcement: "I got all the way up to the thirty-fourth floor in an elevator today." A couple of weeks after that, however, John came into group very frightened. He had started to feel the phobia again. We pointed out that he had to do the same emotional exercises in groups over and over again to reinforce their effect against the phobia. One burst of emotional understanding and a subsequent intellectual awareness of what has happened cannot undue the damage of thirty years. It takes time and hard work to overcome such defenses.

5. A *conversion reaction* shows up as a physical malady. The person translates his anxiety into paralysis, for example, or blindness. The unconscious purpose of a conversion reaction is to relieve the patient of psychological pressure. Often the conversion will reflect something the patient is afraid of in himself. He may have buried tremendous anger and deep down fear that he may kill someone. He cannot possibly act out the impulse if

he is paralyzed, so he becomes paralyzed, literally. The conversion reaction very simply releases him from the emotional conflict. Such symptoms also may help him avoid some responsibility, while giving him an outward excuse for failing.

In Okinawa during the Korean War, a soldier was carried in to me by his buddies, his legs paralyzed. With sodium pentathol I managed to convince him that he could walk. A few days later, he came in again—walking—but he couldn't see. I got him through that hysterical conversion. Then he came back deaf. And then dumb. I finally sent him back to the States. (I'm still not sure that he wasn't smarter than I was all along.)

Conversion reactions are rarer today because people are more sophisticated. They will be found still in less psychologically aware cultures—among the New York Puerto Ricans, for example. But if I see the syndrome in a culturally sophisticated person, I seriously consider schizophrenia.

6. The *dissociative reaction* involves ways that a person can remove himself from conscious awareness of unpleasant data or conflicts. Amnesia and somnambulism fall into this category. This reaction is sometimes associated with temporal lobe epilepsy. I have never seen the most dramatic syndrome—the multiple personality—except in *The Three Faces of Eve*. I have, however, seen dissociation on a different level, in terms of feelings, not personality. One pretty young girl—Helen—who had been in group for quite a time really could not accept any feelings of pleasure. There was always a rain cloud over her head. In a marathon, she finally took in the loving feelings of other group members. Then she felt wonderful—smiling, alive, bubbling with good feelings. Yet thirty minutes later she was back in a funk. All her good feelings, and those of the group, hadn't happened. She really could not remember them. She could not accept that she had accepted the love of others and had responded happily to it.

The group worked with Helen. She got back to the good feelings. Then, a half hour later, she was denying them again. We became furious at her. We thought she was playing some kind of game. But then I realized that she really could not accept the good feelings. It was as though they had never happened. The experience had been frightening to her, so she could not allow it to exist. Unconsciously, she was compelled to deny that it had ever happened.

Helen was so deeply conditioned to believe that pleasure leads to pain that she gave up her memory of the experience of pleasure. The expectation of pain that she was emotionally programmed to expect after any pleasure was too frightening. Helen had come to me mistakenly diagnosed as a schizophrenic. Now, after several months in the group process, she has learned to accept love with infinitely greater emotional security.

All people feel emotional pain in one way or another. The searing tension of experiencing such pain actively can tie us up in knots. So does the fearful anticipation of pain, our sense of "danger." Whatever the symptomatic reaction, it is usually either an attempt to resolve pain or an anticipation of pain.

A neurotic person feels he cannot cope with the pain. He may be extremely anxious or angry. He may further bury his anxiety or anger under depression. He may feel jittery and fearful, obsessed by guilty feelings, crippled physically, alienated in defensive anger. All are ways of avoiding deeper pain. Caught between two pulls, the neurotic will do anything to avoid the emotional pain that he fears. This attitude/feeling is an excruciating one with which to live. Yet a neurotic's attempt to escape the pain limits his capacity to function. It is sometimes more painful to be helpless and hysterical, and the neurotic does not like that feeling any better than the pain he is trying to escape. He consciously feels he wants to get rid of it, and often he will seek professional help. Unconsciously, of course, his symptom is a fearful defense against greater pain, also unconscious. Scream exercises help free him from his symptomatic pain by leading him to the deep-down feelings he has been disguising.

# Character-Disordered Personalities

The term "character-disordered" is really a self-serving label for psychiatrists and psychologists. They often use the phrase to categorize a wide variety of personality types who prove "untreatable" (or difficult to treat, depending on the viewpoint) under traditional techniques of psychotherapy.

The implication is that a serious, permanent flaw exists in the character-disordered personality. The label suggests an impairment which makes normal human relationships and values impossible to sustain.

In order to understand what is meant by a character-disordered personality, it is necessary first to explore what we mean by both "personality" and "character." "Personality" refers to the entire structure of the individual—the most characteristic integration of the ways he acts, his interests, intelligence and other aptitudes, his attitudes, his modes of emotionality. I say *most characteristic* integration because no one behaves in the same way in all situations. Personality has to do with those traits which we view as more or less permanent. If someone is generally calm, for instance, but occasionally explodes with rage when severely provoked, we think of him as having a calm personality, not an angry one.

The word "personality" probably comes from "persona," the mask worn by actors in ancient times to indicate what roles they were playing so that the audience could expect certain traits in the character portrayed. There are any number of traits which we would consider traits of personality. One study found about 1,800 trait names in various dictionaries—intelligence, emotionality, pugnacity, dominance, sociability, introversion, and so forth. Many words evidently overlapped and referred to the same trait; still, the variety is enormous.

"Personality" has a strongly social connotation—how we appear to other people and behave in reaction to them. Physical appearance is a key here. For instance, people react to how we look, and we react in turn to their reaction. The social aspects of personality are especially evident in such judgments as "He has no personality at all" or "He has a great personality." Everybody has some sort of personality, of course. Describing someone in terms of little or lots of personality merely reveals the describer's likes or dislikes.

"Character" generally refers to those aspects of personality which are viewed from an ethical or moral standpoint. Is the person honest, reliable, thoughtful, honorable, trusting? Most basically, character involves "responsibility" and "relationship." Is the person responsible to himself, emotionally and physically, so that he may develop to his greatest potential? Is he self-destructive? Can he be relied upon to be responsible and do what he says he will do? Can he honestly say he will *not* do something? Does he trust other people? Can he be trusted? Does he have empathy? Can he show his feelings honestly and sustain emotionally healthy relationships with other people?

All of these questions have moral implications, but they also have survival implications in our society. A psychiatrist, as a scientist, might claim to be morally neutral about "character." But even he could not deny the survival/adaptability implications of these questions. In our inter-related society, self-destructive behavior and behavior which pushes others away are not conducive to the survival and growth of the organism. Hence the suggestion of serious flaw and impairment in the diagnostic label "character-disordered personality."

Most drug addicts are character-disordered personalities. They are emotionally immature, self-centered, low in empathy for all except those who share their own emotional orientation. The majority of hardline addicts will lie, steal, cheat, do almost anything, to obtain the means to buy drugs. In any conventional view, a sense of right or wrong is not part of an addict's way of life. In psychiatric terms, something is clearly wrong. The term "character disorder" is used to express what is wrong.

Most, although not all, alcoholics are character-disordered. Capable of deceptive charm when they are not drinking (and sometimes when they are), alcoholics can lie, cheat, steal, betray anybody in order to obtain liquor.

The character-disordered list does not stop with people who act out obviously antisocial symptoms. It includes most homosexuals. An untold number of obsessive businessmen. Many compulsive housewives. Often, youngsters underachieving in school.

The key to the character-disordered syndrome is behavior. The symptoms often are blatantly destructive, although many have positive *social* value (if not human value), such as those of the hard-working executive I mentioned in Chapter 5.

Many housewives also typify a kind of socially acceptable character-disordered personality. There is one in group now. When Mary first came to see me, she devoured all sorts of "ups" and "downs" just to get through each day. Yet she kept an immaculate suburban home. Everything had its place. The floors glistened from daily scrubbings. Her children went off to school in perfectly pressed clothes. The problem was that Mary's obsession dominated her family's life. She never allowed a child to leave a toy out. She couldn't put leftovers in the refrigerator; they had to be thrown away. When she gave a dinner party, everything was perfect.

Mary had chronic headaches. She was also so tired by the end of the day that she would fall asleep after dinner, even though her husband wanted companionship or sex. She came to me finally when she discovered that her husband was having an affair. She couldn't understand why he was being unfaithful: she was a dedicated mother and homemaker.

The shock of discovering her husband's affair caused Mary pain. Otherwise, I doubt that she would have sought psychiatric help, even though her teenage son couldn't wait to leave home and her youngest daughter suffered from asthma. Today, Mary is painfully gaining insights into her conduct. Group exercises such as, "I'm lovable even if I'm not perfect" and "Shove your approval up your ass, I'm lovable!" help resolve her tension. At the same time, group members tell her to stop being so compulsive about the neatness of her household. They tell her to forget about "things" and concentrate on human considerations. In one recent session, the group gave her the homework assignment of having sexual relations with her husband at least twice before the next group meeting. She did her homework (and enjoyed the assignment).

Mary faces a lot of work. In group exercises, she must continue to dig into the deep anger she feels against her domineering mother (long since dead), as well as into the terrible fear she felt as a child if she did not live up to her mother's expectations (Her mother gave her approval—not love.) Mary also must continue to do "act as if" behavior assignments—make herself let the dishes wait occasionally, or let an ashtray stay dirty, and relate to her family members differently. In groups and out, she must examine all her attitudes about being "a good mother and homemaker." What happens if she does not perform according to the rigid standards that she held (standards that are really her mother's)? What does perfection mean to her? How about making mistakes? Mary's distorted explanation of her behavior was that "mothers and homemakers should keep a neat house." This is typical of how character-disordered persons operate. They'll find all sorts of ways to rationalize their behavior and hunt for "realities" to explain why they behave the way they do.

George, an alcoholic, would tell my groups that he felt entitled to a drink or two for "a little relaxation." He would excuse his cruelty to his wife by saying he was "a little high."

Sam, a top clothing executive, used to explain his working late at the office by citing all the problems that had to be solved. In reality, he needed to learn how to delegate work to others and develop a better relationship with his co-workers.

Isabel, a recently divorced mother of two children, was sleeping with a different man every week. She would insist that her friends listen to all her escapades so they could share "how happy" she was. She actually believed it, despite the frozen smile that made everyone uneasy.

Jimmy was a plant foreman who worked overtime every week because his family needed the money. Yet, in fact, he was on a conspicuous consumption kick, triggered in part by a lifelong rivalry with an older brother who had always outperformed him and, as an adult, was making quite a bit more money. Jimmy had plunged deeply into debt by buying a new color television set and a flashy car that his family did not need. He was working so hard that he rarely had time to enjoy his purchases or his family. And his anxiety about money laid a heavy burden on the household.

All of these people were out of touch with their deepest feelings—most specifically, pain. Their various modes of destructive conduct were ways of avoiding feeling that pain.

A character-disordered person is like someone with a rotting tooth. He does not feel the pain, even though the cavity may be deepening. If on any occasion the tooth does cause pain, the character disorder may seek professional help. But he probably will stay only as long as the stress continues. He will not acknowledge or attempt to deal with the underlying problem that could cause him pain again. (A neurotic, in contrast, is like someone with a chronic toothache. He is more likely to seek help and stay in therapy until the cause of the pain is removed. He knows what pain feels like, and he wants to rid himself of it once and for all.)

Character-disordered personalities actually can go through years of one-to-one therapy without making real progress. They'll talk about their symptoms, paint verbal pictures of their lives past and present, rationalize, defend, parry with the therapist. But rarely will their deepest feelings be touched.

When drug addicts seek treatment at Daytop or AREBA, we don't ask what painful feelings have brought the addict to our door. Instead, we ask, "Who's on your tail?" Perhaps they have been given the choice of going to jail or Daytop. Many AREBA youngsters are dragged in by their parents. Some addicts come to us in physical pain. Some are weary of the life they must lead to maintain their habit. (We always get many more Daytop applicants in the winter. They have hocked their coats and everything else, and it is cold outside. In the summertime, addicts are all up on the rooftops shooting dope. Who needs help then?)

You'll find the same lack of motivation to get well in most homosexuals. (Remember the story of the classic analysis of a homosexual in Chapter 5.) Usually he comes for help because of a broken love affair. Or perhaps he has recently been scared by the police or by a threat of exposure at work. As soon as a new friend appears or the police back off or the job changes, the patient leaves therapy. His momentary pain has been relieved. The feelings that caused him to act out homosexually are never truly touched. The homosexual is adept at protecting and defending his symptom.

So is the addict. That is why an addict entering Daytop must undergo a grueling session with former addicts before he is admitted. These addicts know all the tricks. Every man has been there himself. If the applicant minimizes the extent of his habit, they'll pounce on him: "Bullshit! We can see you shot up just before you came here. Why can't you be honest, man?" If he brags about his habit (a typical urge), they will belittle him, call him stupid. If he says he is there because he wants help, they will denigrate that, too. Ex-addicts know better. What they want from the newcomer during this session is a genuine plea for help. Eventually, they will have him screaming for help. He may start screaming just to mollify them, but usually that scream connects—

if only for a flash—to the first genuine feeling of need the addict has experienced since infancy. It is the addict's first move beyond the symptom to a glimpse of emotional health.

We discount a character-disordered person's symptoms from the start at the Casriel Institute. I no longer listen to stories of love affairs or of vicious mothers when a male homosexual is interviewed. Instead, I ask him, "Do you want to feel, think, and act like a heterosexual? Do you want to enjoy the feeling of a heterosexual man—and even dream about women?" Most often he will fence with me, responding, "Can't I do both?" If I can get him to commit himself to two weeks of intensive groups, to stop acting out homosexually and act as if he were a heterosexual by dating women, there is a chance that he will begin the painful probe to the feelings behind the symptom.

A character-disordered personality must begin as soon as possible to unlock the deeply-buried feelings from which he has protected himself so long and so thoroughly. Our scream exercises start him down that path.

## "Fight" . . . "Flight" . . . or "Freeze"

As my groups developed, I began to see that there was a basic difference between the psychic dynamics of the neurotic and the character-disordered personality. This observation grew in part out of my earlier training in Adaptational Psychodynamics, developed by Sandor Rado and Abram Kardiner at Columbia. This school of psychotherapy, like others that arose during and after World War II, came about through dissatisfaction with Freud's libido theory. Freud's ideas were in essence a biological explanation of human evolution and personality development. The dissident schools stressed—and, when they could, put into theoretical formulation—the impact of cultural involvement upon the human organism. They felt that personality entails more than the fixed, instinctual course of development of the libido. They wanted to account for the roles of people and culture on an individual's personality. Thus the Horney, Sullivan-White, and Rado-Kardiner schools of psychodynamics evolved. Horney and Rado-Kardiner developed theories which conformed with their clinical observations. The Sullivan-White school, despite their original contributions, did not evolve a comprehensive theory.

Rado and Kardiner attempted to fuse the factors of biological growth and development with existing knowledge about neurophysiology and culture. They sought to explain human thought, emotions, and behavior in the language of the medical sciences rather than the metapsychology of Freud's superego, ego and id. The Freudian libido theory dealt primarily with sex and pleasure precepts: the Columbia school attempted to encompass all emotions.

Two basic principles of Rado-Kardiner Adaptational Psychodynamics are especially pertinent to my group process. The first principle I accept outright. I have modified the second considerably:

*Premise One: All animal behavior is motivated by the pursuit of pleasure or avoidance of pain.* This premise is clearly true in physical terms. And it is true psychologically. We tend to go toward things that give us pleasure—sex, food, recognition, money, self-esteem, whatever. And we remove ourselves from things that give us pain. (What constitutes human pleasure and pain can be extremely complicated, of course, depending upon a person's individual programming and the values of the culture in which he lives.) The premise is well established and does not need a defense. I accept it.

*Premise Two: We react to pain or danger in one of two ways—flight or fight.* The anticipation of pain is experienced as danger. Once we perceive danger or pain, we adapt to the situation by responding with one of two major mechanisms of defense. These are:

1. *Flight*—the emotion of fear and the thought and behavioral intent of escaping from the source of danger; or,

2. *Fight*—the emotion of anger and the thought and behavioral intent of destroying or neutralizing the source of danger.

According to the Rado-Kardiner theory, flight or fight are the only basic major animal mechanisms of defensive response to pain or danger.

*I have observed a third mechanism, called "freeze": This is the repression of emotion—which I call "detachment"—and the thought and behavioral intent of isolating oneself from the source of danger.*

To my mind, there are thus three, not two, adaptive survival responses in the face of danger. The emergency emotions are fear, anger, and detachment (really, lack of feelings). Their behavioral counterparts are flight, fight, and freeze. A person can run away from the source of danger. He can stay and do battle. Or, like a turtle, he can detach himself, pull his head into his shell, and not move.

A healthy person is able to exercise any response or combination of responses, depending upon which makes sense in terms of the reality of the situation. For emotionally disturbed people, access to these mechanisms is often not based on objective reality. Such persons have been preconditioned emotionally to react the way they did in infancy and childhood. They do not know how to react emotionally as adults.

Flight, fight, and freeze; fear, anger, and detachment; are *natural* responses to danger situations. It is perfectly normal for a young child to throw a temper tantrum if his needs are not being met, or to hide behind his mother's skirts in a noisy room full of big people who are indifferent to him, or to run out of the room, or to refuse to come in. For many reasons in our culture, these emergency emotions and actions often are stifled in the child. Parents, feeling unentitled to their own emotions, become intolerant of these feelings in their children. They do not like the sense of responsibility that their child's loud sounds evoke, so they punish or ridicule the child who screams in anger, fear, or pain, or even for love. When parents are not able to empathize with their youngsters' strong feelings, they are not able to help the children. After all, it's easier socially when children are quiet. The world does not approve of angry brats or scaredy-cats, the attitude goes: "quiet kids are the best kids."

Two stories illustrate what has happened to many of my patients. These incidents were not traumatic, life-changing experiences. But they are typical. There must have been many similar events in the childhood of each patient, vignettes that revealed the household atmosphere and their conditioning.

One woman, Marie, used to yell at her brother and strike out at him when she was about five years old. Her mother solved that problem by making her sit in a chair with her hands tied. Marie was humiliated and furious. But she rarely expressed real anger after that—maybe once or twice, through adolescence, and on into adulthood. She had learned from her parents that anger meant humiliation, helplessness, enslavement, nonlove. Still, she was an anxious, fearful child, who suffered tremendously when she did not get A's in school (which was rare). She cried easily, and children her age usually would not play with her. As a teenager, she went to the movies alone. Often they would set her crying, and she would not be able to leave her seat until long after the movie was over. She was terrified the few times she went out on dates; she would remain silent and depressed throughout the evening. If it looked as if she wasn't going to get in right at her curfew, she would panic and insist hysterically that the boy take her home immediately.

Marie was terrified of anger in other people. It meant they were rejecting her, and she had no equal defense of anger available to her. She could not get angry at all, although she could do angry things, like deliberately dropping a dish while she was helping her mother. To become angry straight out was not only to risk rejection but also punishment. Not until she entered group therapy in her late twenties was she able to unclog the anger which had been stored inside her. She threw a temper tantrum, pounding the floor with her hands and feet, shaking her head and screaming. The rage poured out of her. And then the pain, the pain of a lifetime of having to deny her natural expression of a vital, survival-based human feeling. Now her anger emerges regularly. She is learning to exercise it in groups. She is struggling to understand it and to express it out in the world—or not express it—through her own volition.

Cal, a successful professional man in his early forties, still has a lot of difficulty showing fear and pain. He feels them often. But he stifles them, usually by striking out angrily. When he was six, he was forced by neighborhood bullies to bring them money every day on his way to school. He was so terrified of their threats that he began stealing change from his mother's purse. He was too frightened to tell her what was going on, to admit that he was afraid of the bigger boys. His mother had taught the little six-year-old Cal that he should "be a man" (his parents were divorced) and stand up and fight when faced with fear. When she discovered what was going on, she lectured the boy about manliness and sent him out to face the bullies without any money. Cal, of course, was beaten up, although thereafter the bullies left him alone.

Cal became an aggressive fighter as he grew up. It seemed as though he did not know the face of fear. He would pick fights with bigger boys and usually win. If he was hurt, he would never cry. If someone suggested he was a bully, that he was actually frightened, he would deny it fiercely and aggressively try to pick a fight.

Today, Cal has risen compulsively to the top of his field. But his personal relationships have been unsatisfactory. Through group exercises and confrontation, he is learning to show his fear and pain instead of defending it with aggressive anger. He is able now in groups to scream for help. He realizes that to show fear is not to admit helplessness. Rather, showing his fear is an admission of need which, as a human being, he is entitled to express and for which he is entitled to expect a response. Actually, to be able to scream for help when it is needed is one of the best cures for the feeling of helplessness. Cal is learning behaviorally, emotionally, and attitudinally that it is all right for him to be frightened. It is now possible for him to act effectively—even when he feels and expresses his fear—without feeling paralyzed, helpless, alone, and ashamed, ridiculed, or unmanly.

Whatever the particular childhood situation, the majority of children in our culture learn to disguise or avoid open expression of basic emergency emotions. I do not mean to suggest that conscious, voluntary control of these feelings is not a requirement of civilization. It obviously is. But too many children in our culture are forced to deny their survival-based emergency emotions before they learn to exercise them. Access to these survival feelings atrophies. The child loses his ability to summon up the feelings effectively when a realistic situation calls for such response. When grown-up, this individual will have limited emotional choices available to him in any situation.

A healthy family atmosphere provides understanding about all feelings—pain and pleasure, as well as love, fear, and anger. Parents should show the child that his feelings are natural, but that there are many times when some feelings must be held in check. Unfortunately, most adults today lack this kind of understanding and are unable to provide guidance for their children. The parents, no doubt, have been forced to smother strong feelings at an early age. Witnessing the feelings in their young-sters is unconsciously threatening and consciously demanding.

Unless parents, with responsible control and loving concern, allow a child to exercise his basic feelings, the child learns early that it is less painful and less wasteful of his energy to muffle strong feelings. He finds that his emotions provoke disapproval and ridicule and bring him only pain and other enervating moods which deaden everything around him.

People who suffer from the dynamic of *barely suppressed* anger and fear are caught up in the excruciating discomfort of unresolved anxiety, hostility, or both. These people fall within the neurotic profile in classic diagnostic terminology. The feel-ings just do not go away, yet their cause is uncertain and elusive. It's as though some incessant alarm system has been triggered in the near distance. They hear it in their peripheral awareness, but they do not know where it is or why it is ringing. And there is no way to stop the endless clamor.

A neurotic subconsciously attempts to reduce his immediate pain and tension through psychological devices such as phobias and obsessions, which I discussed earlier.

Whatever their form, the neurotic's psychological devices do not make the pain go away. Instead, they diminish his ability to function. They promote additional pain. They require more and more energy, more and more attention; they work less and less well in reducing tension. Even the most extreme behavior cannot quiet the neurotic's inner torment. Like a tyrant, a neurosis demands bigger and bigger payment to satisfy it. The exactions end only when the individual becomes and remains emotionally bankrupt.

A neurotic feels the pain of anxiety almost all the time. A character-disordered person, on the other hand, simply does not feel his belly emotions. He *represses* them completely. He isolates them, detaches himself from them altogether, like a child's Hal-loween puppet with head and chest, arms and legs, and no middle at all.

I do not mean that a character-disordered person experiences no pain, fear, or anger in specific crises. An alcoholic's neglected family can cause him severe discomfort and guilt after he has been on a weekend bender. (From his viewpoint, the discomfort would go away if his wife and children would "let me alone.") The desertion of a homosexual's lover will generally bring about strong depression. (Until a new lover materializes.) And a fat person's anxiety about not having a special friend can be extremely painful. (That is, until a date arrives on the scene.) Even though external pressures are at the heart of the discomfort, the emotional stress is very real. Depending upon the individual, the stress generates feelings of pain, fear or anger.

But each character-disordered person bypasses emotional stress just as fast as he can. The turtle seeks safety in his shell; the character-disordered personality looks for the shell that nature did not provide. He finds quick refuge in his particular symptom. Like Cal, he picks fistfights and claws his way to success. The alcoholic gets drunk. The homosexual cruises men's rooms. The fat man stuffs himself. The addict shoots up. The businessman works sixteen hours a day. The shy person withdraws into books. The nymphomaniac goes to bed with another stranger. All such shells reinforce the character-disordered person's repression of his fear and anger. He is attempting to make himself more secure, more comfortably detached. He often hurts other people with his irresponsibility, yet he is preoccupied with helping himself. He feels no real guilt or concern. Psychiatrists call his behavior "acting out." Through such behavioral devices outside his emotional self, the character-disordered person avoids experiencing even an anxious tremor from his innermost feelings, his pain in particular.

# "Freeze" and "Secondary Encapsulation"

The character-disordered person has learned the third response to danger, a self-survival response that involves neither flight nor fight. This is the mechanism of defense that I have called "freeze": *Instead of disguising or distorting his basic emergency emotions, the character-disordered personality represses these emotions altogether. He detaches his feelings from his conscious awareness, encapsulating them in a shell of unawareness, unconsciously creating an emotional isolation.*

Like the neurotic, the character-disordered personality has had no chance in childhood to learn how to express his survival-based anger or fear as natural emotions. This denial raises anxiety and hostility in a character-disordered person, to be sure. But he represses these cover-up feelings as well, and he detaches himself from them.

This survival mechanism employs neither flight nor fight, neither fear nor anger. Rather than utilizing a specific emotion, "freeze" is really a negation of feelings. I call this state of non-feeling "detachment." The disordered character's feelings are so repressed he can have little or no real emotional interaction with other human beings. His detachment is a true state of emotional isolation.

There are two ways a character-disordered personality can negate his emergency feelings. He can encapsulate them through "withdrawal" or through "control." When the emotional motif is substantially repressed anxiety, I call the person *withdrawn.* He may seem a mild human being, ineffective, passive, retiring, polite. If he has a severe withdrawn character disorder, he may even seem schizoid in human relations. When repressed hostility plays the major role, the person is *controlled*—tight-lipped, clenched-jawed, an obsessive character with an edge of aggression. Severely controlled character disorders suggest rigid Victorian patriarchs, demagogues, even paranoids.

Emotional encapsulation, whether withdrawn or controlled, is a self-imposed deadening of all feelings. Its function is to avoid severe anxiety, anger, and pain—the pain of awareness, the pain of deprivation, the pain of reality and struggle. In their state of isolation, character disorders are certain not to experience the emotional dangers of everyday functioning and maintaining significant relationships.

The certain sign of a character-disordered personality is that he is never victim to the severe pain that neurotics feel in the throes of their anxiety. The psychiatrist may sense, instead of conscious pain, a surface tension in a character-disordered person. But when he probes deeper, there will just be more tension, not painful anxiety. The patient may become aggressively angry, too, as a defense against changing his behavior. (This was typical of Cal.) But these feelings are not connected in any deep way with his basic emotions.

The adaptive mechanism of freeze is not always bad. It can serve a life-saving function at times. Human beings lost at sea have survived best when they withdrew their feelings and emotionally detached themselves from the pain and fear of a desperate reality. People who are completely unable to withdraw or control their feelings, who always react to danger with fear or rage, are on some occasions dangerously vulnerable to destruction. There may be no place to run, and fighting might get one killed.

But a continual retreat from feelings is self-destructive. Though the character-disordered person avoids feelings which might pulverize neurotics, at least the neurotic may be motivated to seek help that will ameliorate the pain. A character-disordered person is not so likely to ask for help; he simply does not suffer deep pain, no matter how corrosive and destructive his symptoms may be.

Too often, "freeze," the mechanism of detachment, becomes a pathological defense, and a flimsy one at that. The demands of the outside world are always there, threatening entry. When people have succeeded in removing themselves from painful reactions to stress, they must spend their energy reinforcing their protected positions. Their encapsulation requires constant bolstering in order to maintain a nonpainful state of functioning.

The defense of freeze, like fight and flight, developed for realistic reasons in the character-disordered person's early experience. But detachment becomes patterned and ingrained, an intrapsychic fortress of his own making. The person has taken flight without fear into a fortress where he feels secure. In truth, he is quite isolated, incapacitated, imprisoned there. His fortress has become his prison. The longer he stays in his own jail, the thicker the walls become. He is less and less able to cope with the problems of everyday living, yet more and more determined to stave off intrusion.

Once he has established himself in a detached world of minimal tension, the character-disordered person will fight anyone who attempts to destroy his prison-fortress walls. The thought of pain, fear, or anger becomes more unbearable in the imagination than the actual emotions would be in reality. The *adaptational* mechanism of freeze has become a *primary* mechanism, activating persistently whether danger is in fact at hand or not.

Standard psychoanalytic techniques which rely on lengthy, painful introspection and observations are useless in the face of such encapsulation. The patient, through he hears intellectually, does not understand emotionally. He cannot be reached. Though he knows the situation, his own vital reality is not at stake—or so it seems to him. He's like a man who says, "I know I should give up smoking, but. . . ." He will avoid the truth with or without deliberate lies. He may pay lip service to change, but he really devotes his psychic energy—consciously, unconsciously, or both—to strengthening his defensive detachment.

# CHAPTER 9

# The Limitations of Psychoanalysis and Individual Psychotherapy

FREUD WAS A GENIUS. Through his observations about human behavior, feelings, and attitudes, interwoven with his intuitions and insights, he contributed more to an understanding of human psychology than any man who has ever lived. His ideas transformed our conception of general psychology. The unconscious, infantile sexuality, free association, the significance of dreams, slips of the lip, transference, repression, regression, resistance—all represented brilliant discoveries about the human mind.

Yet psychoanalysis won very few supporters in Freud's own Victorian days. Its opponents were many and powerful— especially among established physicians. Psychoanalysis faced a long, protracted struggle for survival. Ironically, darker forces pointed to by psychoanalysis erupted into world catastrophe: Proud and antianalytic Europe, with its anti-sexual, authoritarian, patriarchal family, went down with World War I.

The victory of psychoanalysis then proved unexpectedly easy, though the triumph was in part obscured by severe splits among the psychoanalysts. From the present vantage point, however, it is clear that the victory of psychoanalysis brought more professionals into the new mode of treatment and inevitably brought about new advances in thought and practice. These led to legitimate, arguable differences of opinion among worthy adversaries. It doesn't really matter any more whether Freud threw out Adler and Jung—or whether they fled him.

Freud, in the Victorian era, had dared to see two great drives in man: sex and self-preservation (or ego). In that era of suppressed sexuality, Freud saw neurosis as the distortion of the sex drive. Freud's victory was a victory for sexual liberation. But as his success unfolded, it became necessary to correct Freud's exclusive interest in the sexual etiology of neuroses. This correction came first from Adler and Jung. Freud's initial reply was harsh and unjust. He accused them of watering down his doctrine and of currying favor with the Establishment (a point not without irony in those days of the Freudian aristocracy). But Freud also learned from *them*. They caused him to concentrate on the ego drive and a theory of total personality. It was then that he divided the personality into the ego, superego, and id.

The point is that Freudians and non-Freudians, whether they admit it or not, have long found common ground in ego psychology. This is more than a matter of theory. Operationally, there is a common technique and practice of psychoanalysis. The great advances in technique came in the 1920's with the work of Otto Rank, Sandor Ferenczi, and Wilhelm Reich.

Out of all this activity emerged a new approach. Its basic belief was that an individual does not suffer from a form of infantile amnesia, as Freud had emphasized. Rather, man's problems stem from the ways his past affect his current behavior. Thus came a significant shift from the individual's past to his present.

From this approach grew the focus of present-day analysis. Its core is the transference between the underling patient and the authority-doctor. Analysis today concentrates upon a *living* relationship, in the present, between doctor and patient. Today's analysts hold a wide range of theoretical viewpoints, yet the operational basis for every one remains that of establishing transference. Once transference begins, the analyst is able to see and understand firsthand the way in which the patient responds, in the present, to an emotionally significant person.

Transference reveals patterns that an analyst examines for clues to a patient's past relationships with important figures. In this way, he can help the patient work through the distorted feelings that emerge in the transference.

I include in this description the bulk of what is going on today in one-to-one therapy—that is, any treatment which involves an intensive, continuing relationship between a doctor and patient who meet on a regular basis with the intent of effecting personality change in depth. There is, of course, a great deal of one-to-one "supportive" therapy going on today. But that is usually for specific problem-solving—the breaking up of a marriage, for example, or the depression following the death of a loved one. Basic personality change is not the goal. I am also aware of experimental techniques, such as the use of electric shock by some behaviorists to reprogram the patient away from his destructive symptoms. And there are Reichian-related approaches, such as those of Alexander Lowen, where the therapists work with patients individually on body exercises designed to release feelings. Certainly I am intrigued by what Arthur Janov reports about his encouragement of screaming in private therapy. Clearly, we have both been dealing independently with some similar approaches to therapy. One important difference, however, is that Janov requires extensive private therapy before he puts patients into groups at all. I believe the function of groups is invaluable from the start.

Despite these therapeutic systems, the majority of one-to-one systems in practice today rely basically upon the analytic approach: one therapist and one patient are closeted together, session after session. Most of the input comes from the underling-patient, while the authority-doctor looks for clues to the patient's problems in relating to significant persons, using the vehicle of transference. Some analysts operate more in the here-and-now than others, contributing insights and directives. But the process basically remains that of analysis. It is a process which, in far too many cases, is destined for failure.

The key to the analytic process lies in Freudian discoveries: There are areas within the mind not readily accessible to the consciousness. (Psychiatrists call the recesses of the mind, with slight shift in meaning, the "unconscious," "subconscious," or "preconscious.") Repression prevents one portion of the mind from having direct access to another. Repressed feelings affect the patient's behavior and must be brought to the surface through the analytic process. Only then can the patient face the feelings and change his behavior.

Simply stated, the cornerstone of psychoanalytic theory and practice today is to explore repression and its damaging effects. When successful, the analytic process releases the patient from many unconscious repressions. But it also brings about the painful personal discovery of a whole new range of "conscious" conflicts.

Some of these freshly discovered conflicts require suppression, some do not. Part of the struggle, for example, has to do with letting feelings out through assertions and confrontations with friends, associates, co-workers, and loved ones. To take these chances is difficult. So is learning to control some impulses and let others flow. What is the "healthy" thing to do in a discomforting situation?

Managing such day-to-day struggles, of course, is what emotional maturity is all about. To learn to deal with problems of this nature with minimum pain and maximum effectiveness and pleasure is the goal of any kind of psychotherapy.

At this point important questions arise. How does psychoanalysis compare in effectiveness with other kinds of psychotherapy? With whom is it effective?

For a long time the victories of psychoanalysis stopped outside the doors of the psychiatric hospitals, which remained the stronghold of antianalytic psychiatry. The old psychiatry was little more than custodial care. Its defeat was long overdue. Even now that defeat is not complete. Some medical treatments for mental illness linger on regardless of their proven ineffectiveness. Lobotomies, shock-therapies, and other surgical procedures masquerading as mental therapies have often been in vogue and are still being used.

Nevertheless, during World War II, some young, psychoanalytically trained psychiatrists got a chance to demonstrate the superiority of their healing methods. They won brilliant victories over battle fatigue and rose to the challenge of the new mass need for therapy by creating the first methods of group therapy (associated with the authorship of S. R. Slavson, a nonphysician). Their successes meant that henceforth the majority of psychiatry professors in teaching hospitals were psychoanalytically oriented.

These victorious psychiatrists and analysts reached the height of their prestige in the 1950's. Many of them understood—as they understand today—that psychoanalysis is a long process suitable for only a small number of those seeking mental help. These hospital psychiatrists have in many cases encouraged the development of staffs of clinical psychologists and psychiatric social workers to provide individual and group therapies adapted from psychoanalytic concepts. Such staffs are often dedicated, but harassed and overworked. They are torn by contradictions between the modest amount of time they can give patients and the implicitly long time indicated by psychoanalytic concepts.

There is nothing really wrong with these professionals. They are, on the whole, conscientious and well trained. What is wrong is that the psychoanalytic process they are practicing does not serve their clientele.

Thanks chiefly to the psychiatric work done in veterans' hospitals during World War II and its aftermath, a new paradigm is in the making. I participated in that earlier psychiatric work, and it is one of the sources of the new models I am suggesting should take the place of psychoanalysis.

I am not an enemy of psychoanalysis. I was a practicing analyst for over ten years and I am a past president of the American Society of Psychoanalytic Physicians. I have undergone—and was helped by—seven and one-half years of my own psychoanalysis with Abram Kardiner, one of the deans of American psychoanalysis.

The substance of what I observe about psychoanalysis is not a polemic against the process. The facts and figures are not in dispute. They show *how few today are analyzable, and how expensive the process is.*

Among the most authoritative and current works on the subject is the textbook *The Technique and Practice of Psychoanalysis,* by the noted analyst, Dr. Ralph R. Greenson, clinical professor of psychiatry at the U.C.L.A. School of Medicine. Dr. Greenson usually requires patients to come five days a week for three to five years and indicates that successful psychoanalysis takes longer now than in the past. For many of his patients, he is the second or third analyst. He recommends a change of analysts when the long middle period of analysis comes to a stalemate, and after four years of treatment he reviews each of his cases to consider the advisability of changing analysts.

Dr. Greenson does not believe everyone is analyzable. "Only a relatively healthy neurotic can be psychoanalyzed, without major modifications or deviations," he says. Stressing the central role of neurotic suffering in successful analysis, he states: "Only a patient who is strongly motivated will be able to work wholeheartedly and with perseverance in the psychoanalytic situation. The neurotic symptoms or discordant traits of character must cause sufficient suffering to induce the patient to endure the rigors of psychoanalytic treatment."

Greenson makes no attempt to estimate what percentage of the emotionally disturbed is analyzable, but it would be fair to state that he limits the analyzable to the "relatively healthy neurotic," who suffers neurotic misery but whose ego functions remain essentially unimpaired. He thinks that varied forms of character disorders, such as impulsive neuroses, perversions, addictions, delinquencies, and borderline cases of schizophrenia are of "doubtful analyzability and would have to be determined by special features of the individual case." In my estimation, the neurotics termed analyzable by Dr. Greenson constitute at most 10 per cent of the population. Character disorders—including compulsive housewives and business executives, as well as homosexuals, delinquents, addicts, and so on—who are not analyzable constitute about 80 per cent of the population. The most important point (omitted by Freudians) is that in Freud's time these figures probably were reversed: neurotics were then predominant; now they constitute a dwindling part of the population.

For most people, the time and money required for analysis are prohibitive. Analysis requires three, four, five, six, and even seven years, or more, and three to five visits a week to the psychiatrist. Analytic treatment, at $25 to $50 an hour, adds up to at least $3,750 a year. And it can soar to $12,500. This mammoth cost eliminates all but the well-to-do. The poor, the lower middle class, and *most* of the middle class cannot afford it.

True, a few of these people can take advantage of low-cost psychoanalytic clinics. But these special clinics are rare, their waiting lists long. And clinics tend to select only patients with problems that are of interest to the staff at a given time.

The problem of cost is compounded by another reality. When one person in a family is emotionally disturbed, chances are that others in the household also need therapy. There is no question that therapy for everyone is the most certain way to help effect favorable changes in person-to-person relationships within a family. The expense makes analytic treatment for several family members almost impossible. At $3,750 per year per patient, even a man making $20,000 to $30,000 a year cannot afford the process for himself, his wife, and two teen-age children.

The analytic process demands that the analyst devote three to five hours to each patient every week. Suppose, for example, an analyst works forty hours a week. If he is seeing two of his patients five times a week, this consumes ten hours, or 25 per cent of his professional time. The remaining thirty hours permit treatment of, say, ten patients on a three-times-a-week basis. With this schedule, he is analyzing only twelve people at any one time in a three- to seven-year span. And he can only replace two to four patients a year.

There is no way to know the exact number of qualified analysts in America today. (By "qualified," I mean people who have undergone analysis themselves and received analytic training, but who are not necessarily M.D.'s, or graduated from or certified by a psychoanalytic institute.) The American Psychoanalytic Association and the American Academy of Psychoanalysis, two of the largest and most prominent organizations for M.D. psychoanalysts, number not many more than two thousand members between them. There may be some dual memberships, and no one really knows how many members are actually practicing analysis. The American Psychological Association has about thirty-four thousand members, but it estimates that only a few hundred practice analysis.

At the most, there are in the United States no more than three thousand qualified psychoanalysts. Assume, optimistically, that every one of them is capable and effective, that each is treating twelve to fifteen patients in analysis (eight is more likely). Assume, further, that successful analysis can be completed in three or four years. Then four patients are "cured" by each analyst each year. For three thousand qualified analysts, this means only 12,000 completed treatments annually: at most, 45,-000 patients are in analysis. (Actual estimates range from 20,000 to 24,000.)

The number of qualified analysts is not likely to increase rapidly. Training normally means a minimum of ten years spent in medical school, post-graduate studies, and residency—frequently undertaken fifteen years after graduation from college. In 1968, only 58 new analysts were certified by the American Psychoanalytic Association, the most elite organization of psychoanalysts (91 were graduated from their 21 affiliated institutes). In 1969, 38 were certified, 100 graduated. In 1970, the numbers were 31 and 76; and in 1971, 27 were certified (graduation figures weren't available).

Considering the millions of Americans who need psychological help, the number in analytic treatment is incredibly small. We desperately need a more efficient method of providing such aid.

Yet I believe the failure of psychoanalysis would be giant-sized even if the process were not prohibitively expensive and even if there were enough psychiatrists to go around. *The real problem lies in the technique itself.*

I say this as a psychiatrist who has used analysis for over a decade, and who has seen it help scores of my patients. I take this stand because of what I observe taking place in my group therapy practice. Most of my current patients make more real progress toward emotional health in *a few months* in group therapy than they would make in years of private analysis. I see this kind of progress constantly, and it is true for a variety of personality types, including those whom analysts have generally considered to be nontreatable.

Quite simply, the psychoanalytic technique is inefficient. I am not saying that it is not successful in some cases. I am saying that individual psychotherapy employs the longest, most expensive, most painful way to reach the causes of a patient's problems. And frequently it does not get to first base. In relation to my group process, it is as efficient as painting a house with a toothbrush. Individual psychotherapy is to me—at best—a fine, delicate finishing tool. Take a look at these problems:

1. *There are severe contradictions in psychoanalysis which limit the numbers of persons who can go through the process successfully.* Dr. Greenson has described these contradictions well: "The patient is asked: (a) to regress and to progress, (b) to be passive and to be active, (c) to give up control and to maintain control and (d) to renounce reality testing and to retain reality testing. In order to accomplish this the analytic patient must have resilient and flexible ego functions. . . . What is characteristic of the analyzable neurotic is that his defective ego functioning is limited to those areas more or less directly linked up to his symptoms and pathological traits of character. Despite his neurosis, the treatable patient does retain the capacity to function effectively in the relatively conflict-free spheres."

2. *I find that analysis drags out the most painful parts of this struggle.* Chief villain is the technique of closeting the patient in a one-to-one transference relationship. He must lie flat on his back, hour after hour, week after week, month after month, year after year, pouring out his feelings and thoughts in what is essentially a monologue, while a usually silent authority figure sits behind him. It is a lonely experience. It is a fearful and painful process.

The patient doesn't even have a chance to sense how the analyst is reacting or what he is thinking. The analyst supplies few signals, since he sits outside the patient's visual range. This arrangement is, of course, an integral part of analysis. Being cut off from most signals not only minimizes second-guessing, but also heightens anxiety. It is a method designed to bring up feelings. But it is an agonizing limbo—inhuman, really, in its denial of the most basic aspects of contact between people.

While psychoanalysis takes a torturous, drawn-out route toward emotional maturity, the group process does not. It cuts through rapidly to repressed feeling. Rather than going through years of painful emotional archaeology, a patient is ready in a relatively short time to learn how to deal with conflicts of repression and suppression.

3. *The patient must have the emotional maturity to work through the ambiguities of transference.* The key to effective analysis lies in the examination of the transference between patient and doctor. The whole process has to become an objective-subjective phenomenon. Both patient and doctor must see and feel what goes on, yet recognize that it stands for something else too.

That is quite a tall order. A patient's feelings about his doctor are one thing, his reality perceptions are something else. These distinctions must be sorted out for the patient to be able to work through his distorted feelings to reality knowledge.

The emotional attack that analysis launches on a patient's personality structure can be devastating. Of necessity, he must be emotionally close to adulthood to withstand the barrage. To ensure transference, analysis tends to regress the patient so that his neurotic feelings are magnified. This painfully emphasizes the underlying feelings that he fears and that cause him excruciating pain. Yet unless the patient actually develops a transference neurosis, analysis is not successful. Unless he recognizes and confronts the neurotic feelings he has for the doctor, the psychoanalytic process cannot reach completion.

This can be pretty tough going—and very painful for a patient. (It was for me.) If he is basically an adult, a patient can probably withstand this modification of his underlying fears. But the emotional make-up of many patients is not so maturely integrated.

4. *Transference often does not take place, so many people simply cannot have successful analyses.* This failure occurs even when an analyst *has* good intuition and is relatively free of personal distortions. What reasons do psychiatrists themselves give for this failure? As a profession, we don't have a satisfactory answer. We try to explain it by applying fuzzy labels to the unsuccessful analysand—too rigid, too character-disordered, too immature, pre-oedipal, not motivated enough, too many current reality problems, and so forth. As I have explained in a previous chapter, the over-all classification that psychiatry uses for these difficult-to-treat people is character-disordered. In over ten years of practice as an analyst, I had very little success analyzing severely character-disordered people. Most colleagues with whom

I have talked agree. With character-disordered persons, psychoanalysis in the full sense is invariably a complete failure, even though a patient can get temporary relief from discomfort.

5. *Many one-to-one therapy systems misunderstand the feeling of guilt.* Though guilt is not a primary, survival-based feeling, it is prevalent in our culture. I find that guilt results from a feeling of fear or anger about hurting someone you love. In our groups we get people to focus on the feeling behind the guilt. When he learns to express the real feeling, he is no longer victim to the guilt. The phantom of the significant loved person who first made him feel guilty no longer controls his present life. He is able to take direct responsibility for his actions and feelings.

Guilt can be experienced only when someone has been bonded in some degree to a loved object. If love has been minimal or absent, the guilt mechanism is deficient. I have seen this phenomenon often with criminals, drug addicts, and so-called "psychopaths." I asked one addict, on trial for severely harming an old woman he had mugged to get money for heroin, if he felt guilty about what he had done. He asked me in all sincerity, "You mean, does the judge have the goods on me?" That was the extent of his conception of guilt.

Freud observed that one could feel guilt only if he had reached the oedipal stage. If the person was pre-oedipal, he was not analyzable; that is, he was not treatable. This concept accounted for the basic attitude I learned in my training about the "untreatability" of many addicts and "psychopaths." They did not care about or trust any other person. They felt no regret about what they did to others, except the regret of being caught and facing punishment.

To my shock and amazement, at both Synanon and Daytop I saw supposedly irreversible "psychopaths" become racked with infantile guilt after they had involved themselves in the community. I was forced to restructure both the classical and adaptational views in which I had been trained. Although it is true that guilt is based on a love object, I saw that this feeling can be developed at any age. When that happens, the person can respond to psychotherapy.

At Synanon, for example, I saw a remarkable change in a once-hardened addict named Della. She hadn't even felt guilty about causing her husband to go to jail for ten or twenty years so that she could escape a drug rap. They had been crossing the Mexican border and faced a search by the police. Della managed to remove a supply of heroin from her vagina, where it was concealed, and slip it into her husband's pocket. The heroin was found, he was sentenced to jail, and she went free. Della was such a severe drug addict that she had been expelled from Lexington as "incorrigible." Once, after suffering an overdose, she woke up in a hospital just as she was being given an intravenous feeding. She pulled the transfusion needles out of her arms, slipped away from the hospital, "turned a trick" to get some money, and found her pusher. She was returned to the hospital in a coma.

After a few months at Synanon, Della began to have terrible, guilt-ridden dreams. Everything was covered with feces in her dreams. When she took a shower, shit would pour out of the faucet. When she flushed the toilet, shit would erupt from the bowl and innundate her. At the end of these repetitive nightmares, she would scream in terror. This was the beginning of her feelings of guilt, and as she became more bonded in love at Synanon, she was able to deal with her feelings and her behavior. Today, Della is married to a professional, has children, and is leading a happy life.

Certainly severely disordered people such as Della require treatment in a therapeutic community, where people are bonded in love and mutual concern. Apparently that atmosphere provides the interpersonal ties that the pre-oedipal personality requires before he can get in touch with his deep needs and begin to care about other people and how he relates to them. What is important is that many such people *are* treatable, given the right therapeutic system. When the guilt mechanism is faulty, one-to-one therapy usually fails. Not the least of the analytical failure has been the tendency to exclude "psychopaths" from therapy at the outset.

6. *The analyst's skill is immensely important to the success of the process.* So much intuition is required of the analyst that I fear the method will remain forever more art than science. After all, an active relationship between *two* people is involved. The relationship is very tricky. The analyst must know what he is

doing. And he must understand himself well enough not to let his own unresolved problems distort his perceptions of what is happening. Only then can the patient work through his own distortions to become a true peer of the doctor.

Let's face it: Many doctors are so threatened by peer relationships that they prefer to actively maintain and support a neurotic transference relationship between underling and authority. In effect, such a doctor will not allow a patient to grow up. That would endanger his own position as an authority. Certainly in my early days of practicing analysis, when a patient suddenly sat up and looked me directly in the eyes, I felt that he was being nasty and aggressive. The truth is, I was frightened. But I blamed the patients who made eye contact with me. I analyzed their *resistance,* rather than *my* fear. In truth, both were involved.

There is no getting around the fact that all therapists are "human," with their own special blind spots and distortions, as well as special perception and insights. The use of lay therapists in our groups acknowledges these mortal frailties. In fact, we try to make sure that patients are in a number of *different groups,* each group with a *different therapist.* That way, the patient is not confined to the inevitable personal myopia of a single authority.

7. *The analyst is susceptible to being duped.* Some clever patients can lie on the couch for months and years, completely turned off in their bellies, and play a kind of teasing mental chess game with the doctor. Many of my colleagues in analytic school were character-disordered personalities who were able to play this game. I was not. Neurotic when I started my own analysis, I almost failed in it. Not until several painful years later when I became numbed by the process did I learn to play the analytic game by the rules. The cost to me in historical and concurrent pain and anxiety was great.

There are too many people in a group system to let such a game succeed for long. You just can't fool everybody all of the time. Any kind of verbal chess game usually brings a quick confrontation, a kind of confrontation bound to stir up feelings of some sort in even the coolest gamesman. He'll be reached far more quickly than in a one-to-one therapy situation. By remaining aloof and authoritative, the analyst creates an emotional void that the patient must fill. He does this not knowing if the emotional "fill" is significant, valid, or true. My group process confronts people with *feelings*. Usually everyone can observe and measure the resonance of the anger, love, fear, pain and pleasure of another group member.

Most significant, we confront behavior straight on from the start. By struggling with symptoms right away, my patients are thrown immediately into the struggle of dealing with repressed feelings. We don't expect people to give up destructive symptoms permanently right at the beginning, of course. It is hard to drop lifelong patterns thrown up to defend deep hurts and fears. In this sense, psychoanalysts are correct in saying that permanent change takes time to bring about and to consolidate in the personality. A patient almost inevitably will revert to "acting out" symptoms periodically, usually when some stress situation comes up, either in group or out. But each time he stops his destructive behavior, each time he sincerely even *tries* to stop it, however successfully, his repressed feelings start to surface fast.

When this happens, my group patients are, at the very least, as confused as people in psychoanalysis. The chief difference is, my patients "get confused" and "unconfused" faster—years faster. The other group members have gone through the same kind of confusion. They understand how it feels. This lends a special kind of support to the patient as he experiences his confusion. It is a far cry from the "Great God's" grunt behind the analytic couch. With the group's support, the new member sees that he is not going to go crazy with anger, "fall apart" with pain, become helpless with fear, or perverted by love. He is not alone in his experience. He takes in knowledge and a mountain of awareness. Our group dynamic is not merely an exercise of introspection being verbalized to a tolerant but impartial listener—the analyst.

The new group member thus begins to develop a kind of trust which will lead him to open up more and more in the group. And, of course, he is encouraged in his struggle with his behavioral symptoms. That struggle becomes easier. More hidden feelings emerge.

Until this kind of emotional unfolding begins, no therapy can benefit a patient. In analysis, this may take years. In our groups, it often takes just weeks, sometimes even less.

I like the accelerated schedule for a number of reasons, most of which I have already discussed. But a reason I have not yet discussed is that the shorter time period permits more accurate testing than older, slower methods.

Biochemists, anthropologists, medical researchers, physicists, zoologists, biologists—all today are applying a scientific approach to their respective disciplines. And the approach is producing significant breakthroughs. Their discoveries can be replicated once they have been tested out. A practical application may not emerge for fifty to one hundred years. Or it may never develop. But the research results stand firm and can always be reproduced.

The scientific method rests on two bases: (1) careful and controlled observation and experimentation. (2) results (whether successful or unsuccessful) that can be replicated by others. When a researcher puts chemicals together to create a new formula, for example, he keeps precise records of the quantities of each chemical. Then he checks and rechecks results. Once the mixture, under test conditions, achieves the results he wants, he can write up the experiment in an article in a way that permits qualified biochemists in other parts of the world to reproduce the same results.

Of course, the behavioral sciences by their nature encounter a problem which other sciences do not. It is really impossible to set up controlled experiments which involve statistically significant numbers. This would require control of the lives of hundreds of families, and we all can guess how difficult this would be. It would violate what most of us value as the most precious right of being human: it would intrude upon our right *not* to be controlled.

Full-scale observations of significant human behavior interfere with privacy. Still, several Columbia anthropologists have formulated the beginnings of such studies. The idea is to have cameras set up in selected households in the Greater New York area, with observers at a headquarters control room who can view subject families in their "natural context." A push of the button, and there's a permanent film record of family members. (To avoid embarrassment, the cameras have not been placed in bedrooms.) The theory is that, after a few days, subjects would forget about the camera. In any case, they would understand that the filmed data is completely confidential, and they retain the right to request that the films be destroyed. Although the imperfections of this study are evident, these anthropologists do hope to gather an enormous amount of information about human behavior in our society.

In some areas of psychology, the scientific method has had a very practical application. Harvard's B. F. Skinner, for example, used experiments with pigeons to create a theory of teaching, called programmed learning. It has had wide acceptance and favorable results in many parts of the country today. First of all, Skinner applied Pavlovian conditioning to train pigeons to play ping pong. Observing their every movement, he rewarded them when they behaved the way he wanted and punished them when they did the opposite. Gradually, they learned the pattern of behavior he desired, leaving out all extraneous movements.

Such experiments led to a new method of instruction for human beings. The material to be learned is broken into minute steps, simultaneously teaching and testing the student in such a way that he is guided from one correct answer to the next. Pleased by his success with the answers (pleasure is his reward), the student apparently retains the information readily. In this way he builds knowledge upon knowledge until he has mastered the course.

The forward thrust of all sciences, including the behavioral, moves toward controlled and objective experimentation. This is the direction science is taking because the direction has proved productive. It consistently yields significant, desired results, results that come faster than with any other technique.

In the face of the scientific progress made in other disciplines, psychoanalysis remains an intuitive art. At best, a successful analysis is difficult to describe in such a way that it can be replicated and have broad application and success. After all, the one-to-one relationship between an analyst and patient is dynamic, highly personal, subjective, introspective. The sensitivity, experience, and intuition of a specific analyst cannot be transmitted, through words, to another analyst in another part of the world. Let's say a Wisconsin analyst achieves great success with a patient diagnosed as "character-disordered, with depression." How can the analyst possibly report this so that a colleague can be assured of successful treatment with a similarly diagnosed patient in Germany?

The truth is, psychiatry has done very little experimenting in laboratory-like situations. Such conditions would lead to solid, scientifically observed conclusions. But there have not been many attempts. As a matter of fact, those few experiments which do exist are not encouraging. In 1952, Dr. H. J. Eysenck, professor of psychiatry at the University of London, examined thousands of records of World War II British veterans who were hospitalized for mental illness. Eysenck arranged for some of these men to have psychoanalytic treatment. Some received other forms of therapy. Some none at all. Then he set up an "improvement rate" measurement scale. The results: 44 per cent improved under analysis, 64 per cent under other therapies, and 72 per cent improved with no therapy at all.

A few years ago, Dr. Werner Mendel, professor of psychiatry at the University of Southern California, set up another three-part experiment. One group of patients was treated by trained psychoanalysts and other top staff members at the hospital. The second group received treatment from a less specially trained crew of psychotherapists and clinical psychologists. The third group was ministered to only by psychiatric aides having no formal training in therapy. Those who received the nonprofessional attention fared best. Those treated by the most highly trained staff members showed the least improvement. Mendel was so surprised by these results that he conducted the experiment again with different patients and different psychiatrists. Nothing changed. The nonprofessional treatment was most successful, the professional ministrations least helpful to the patients.

I can think of hundreds of questions which would throw doubts on such experiments; certainly the studies are in no way conclusive. It is clear, however, that psychoanalysis is now in a kind of limbo. While other disciplines are staking their futures on a method whose progress is demonstrably more productive, psychoanalysis remains virtually atrophied.

It would be very difficult indeed to set up a statistically reliable test in which analysis was measured against other therapeutic techniques (including no therapy at all). The analytic process is so time-consuming and so expensive that a huge grant would be required to support such a test. It could take fifteen years or longer to establish results.

Admittedly, it is hard to apply the scientific method to any kind of psychotherapy, including my own. So many variables are involved. And, in the case of my process, the techniques are too new. Too much has been going on for me to find the time, or to set up the controlled conditions. Since our process does not take nearly as long as analysis, however, I can envision ways in which some aspects of scientific observation can be imposed upon my patients and my method. I look forward to the opportunity to do this soon, and hope to set up a computer program which will compile data about our patients and their progress.

Despite my criticisms of psychoanalysis, I do not deny its effectiveness in some cases. It is a delicate tool in the hands of a skilled professional. Analysis *can* work, provided the patient is mature enough to withstand the hardships of transference—and provided, also, that he has the money and the time to complete the process.

Ironically, groups have helped me "rediscover" analysis in an entirely new way. As I have reported in an earlier chapter, I began to run groups with patients whom I was treating in analysis. From their experience, and the experience of subsequent patients who came only for group, I concluded that our group techniques opened up patients' emotions much faster than analysis.

What happens then? Most of my patients develop quite satisfactorily within the group mode. No private therapy is needed. But other patients need and ask for private therapy, and I take them on once they have fully opened up emotionally in group.

The experience has been fascinating and truly exciting to a doctor trained in the tired old way of rambling analysis. The patient's emotionality, his rapid-fire insights, his special feelings and connections, make analysis an amazingly easier process. Thanks to his group experience, he is in touch with, and relating to, his emotions. Many once-repressed feelings are conscious.

Others keep popping up. None of them gives him shame or guilt. He has learned that if he experiences a maladaptive feeling—or attitude or action, for that matter—they are not his *fault;* they are his *problem.* Also, there is no underling-authority interference in such post-group analysis. The patient and I are peers at the human level. He respects my skill, but he is not in awe of it. He respects me the way one would appreciate a skilled craftsman, not the way religious people relate to a priest.

In analysis a patient who has been through my groups progresses toward an understanding of the nuances of his personality, at a pace that (to me at least) seems incredible. There is little time to chisel out such nuances in group. Many people do not really need to. Either they are capable of making more intricate perceptions on their own, or they can live healthily without them. But for some patients, the subtleties of analytic insight mark an important final step of therapy.

For me, sharing a patient's insights at this post-group stage is a real pleasure. The analytic hour has become beautiful, full of feeling and stimulating perceptions. That is a far cry from what I found in my early years as a psychoanalyst.

I suspect the same observation can be made about any form of therapy in which a doctor or psychologist and a patient closet themselves together in a room to work out emotional problems on a one-to-one basis. For truly therapeutic results, the patient should start by having full access to his deeply felt emotions. Our process gets him to that point rapidly.

CHAPTER 10 | *Triangular Man: Behavior, Feelings, Attitudes*

As the effectiveness of my method became increasingly evident clinically, I began to explore the theoretical basis for its success. The evidence that was accumulating was substantial. It indicated that many people were making progress toward emotional health in significantly less time than they had in private analysis with me, in therapy with other professionals, in institutional programs, in hospitals, or in therapeutic communities. Also, there was success in treating personality types whom psychiatrists had historically pronounced "incurable." My training in Freudian theory and in adaptational psychodynamics could not help me account for the extraordinary results I saw.

Why was this particular approach to group therapy producing good results, in such rapid time? To my knowledge, the same results were not occurring in verbal, intellectualizing groups that failed to focus on behavior.

My search led to the formulation of a schematic Triangular Man. I saw one part of the triangle as man's *behavior,* the second part as his *emotions,* and the third as his *attitudes.* Taking a broad view of psychotherapy, I saw that my profession had focused primarily on only two parts of the triangle: emotions and attitudes. Psychoanalysis, for example, began with a rambling attitudinal exploration which led eventually—if transference took place—to a deep comprehension of the patient's feelings. Adaptational psychiatry concentrated on how emotional reactions were shaped in childhood and affected the adult life. Carl Rogers and his followers also concentrated on feelings. And while it is true that existential psychiatrists had put some stress on behavior, it was only in terms of how behavior grew out of attitudes. Change the attitude, the reasoning went, and the behavior will change, too. With its interest in developing the total awareness of an individual, Frederick Perls's gestalt therapy *did* countenance the importance of behavior. Still, existential psychiatrists were not concerned with feelings in the sense that my groups were. To me, their approaches seemed moralistic and philosophic—full of verbalization that stressed the *shoulds* and *musts* at the expense of deeply felt emotions.

The more I thought about the idea, the stronger became my conviction: No psychotherapeutic method had tried to deal effectively with all three sides of Triangular Man, beginning with an emphasis on behavior. Yet such an approach seemed to be the central reason why the group technique growing out of Synanon encountering was proving unusually successful.

From the beginning, Synanon confronted a symptom by saying "stop it." If alcohol is your problem, give it up. Do you use dope? Stop. Right now—cold turkey. Furthermore, *start* acting like a responsible human being. Do your job in the community. No verbal games, no rationalizations.

True, there was moralizing. There were shoulds and musts to be heard. But, behind the moralizing, there was the behavior-focused wisdom of the streets. The wisdom said one thing very loudly and very clearly: Give up your symptom, right now, at the start. Behave like a responsible adult. If you don't know how, *act as if* you do. When that makes you anxious or angry, save the feelings for group. Then let it all out, and take a look at it.

# Behavior

My groups were at first not as vigorous in attacking destructive behavior as the Synanon groups. I began to think, with increasing seriousness, about the need to stress behavior with my middle-class patients. I had one patient, for example, who was a kind of Don Juan. Through the two years he had been in treatment with me, Charlie had had extramarital affairs with seven women. Each relationship had been started with Charlie's complaints about how misunderstood he was at home. Then, after several months, when the newly won mistress began to make demands upon Charlie's time and emotions, he found another female to whom he could unburden his problems. For a brief period of time, he would function with two mistresses, as well as a wife. Finally, the previous mistress would be abandoned altogether, and the new mistress would replace her.

One of Charlie's problems was that his wife understood him too well. A character-disordered personality, he was quite insulated from most of his deepest-level feelings. And he lived on a tightly balanced teeter-totter between fear and anger, without being able to get to either side. To camouflage his fear and anger, Charlie had developed a tough-guy manner that was, in truth, rather charming. (He reminded me a bit of Humphrey Bogart.) He concealed his fear and anger, also his pain and loving feelings. His job was boring and unfulfilling, although the pay was good. It gave Charlie no sense of fulfillment or achievement. Charlie had absolutely no male friends—only co-workers and neighbors. He had no hobbies—no interest in sports or stamp collecting or skiing, for example. He was, he believed, an inferior athlete. In fact, Charlie felt very insecure about his masculinity. Hence, his dependence upon women. When Charlie made love to a woman and brought her to a climax, he felt entitled to accept her love. He continually sought new women to whom he could make love. With each new woman, he could be "open" for a while about the emotional impoverishment of his life, stressing the needs he concealed from the rest of the world. However, when the woman began to fill Charlie's needs, he became terrified. Charlie's ability to accept love was very limited. His solution was to find a new female relationship to allay his insecurities.

What if Charlie were asked to give up extramarital affairs? Maybe he would be forced to face up to the fear, anger, pain, and need for love which were causing him to "act out." Perhaps, with the symptomatic behavior eliminated, Charlie would find the emotional pressure building up inside himself in a new way.

Another patient, Clara, drank too much (although she was by

no means an alcoholic). An attractive and winsome woman of twenty-eight, she was the daughter of a minister. Somehow her father had conditioned her to have an altruistically unreal conception of what life should be like. Clara was intelligent, talented, articulate. She worked as a copywriter in an advertising agency and dressed well, though not with much flair. Clara was responsible on her job, with her parents and relatives, with her friends, to the institutions to whom she felt she owed loyalties. When Clara's boss asked her to take on an extra copy assignment over a weekend, she always said yes, even though other writers could have done it. When an account supervisor wanted copy revised for an unreasonable client at five P.M., Clara always agreed without protest to do it. When her married ex-roommate from college wanted a babysitter, Clara always agreed to be one. If a friend from out of town called and wanted a place to stay, Clara found space on her divan. She lent money to friends, served conscientiously on her college's fund-raising drives, and invariably found time to listen to the problems of others.

Clara's problem was not so much that she drank, but rather that she used alcohol as an excuse for "acting out." All the time she was sober, she lived out the goody-goody role her father expected. She avoided angry or painful confrontations, avoided displaying selfish feelings or motives, and avoided the strong emotions which are the basis of genuine intimacy. She also avoided sex, saying good night to her dates with a brief, nonintimate kiss at the doorway of her apartment.

When she had had too much to drink, however, Clara was very different. She had slept with her ex-roommate's husband, as well as her best friend's fiancé. During any given year, she had intercourse with at least a dozen strangers. The drinking usually began on a Friday night, as Clara visited several of New York's East Side boy-meets-girl bars. At one of the bars, she would pick up a man—any man who was persistent, extraverted, and attentive. (Clara's preference, in her own words, was for "outgoing emotional Mediterranean types.") Then she would bring the man to her apartment for a forty-eight-hour sexual orgy. During the weekend, she would do everything possible to ensure the man's pleasure. She would perform fellatio, permit anal entry, experiment with contorted sexual positions. (One position Clara described I still think is a physiological impossibility!) But she was so intent on bringing pleasure to the man that Clara never had an orgasm herself.

The pressure of trying to sustain such an unreal Monday-through-Friday existence was too demanding for Clara. She felt her need for love and her sexual deprivation too strongly. Liquor was the mechanism that permitted her to do things she would not otherwise have done. On Monday morning, she could always blame liquor, and thus avoid responsibility for her conduct.

Clara never felt good about herself on Monday morning. If she did *not* start drinking seriously over a weekend, she would devote her time to reading, listening to good music, going to an occasional movie or opera, or seeing some friends (without true intimacy). The tension would mount, and by the start of a new work week she would feel unbearably anxious. On the other hand, if she *did* begin to drink, it would lead to a sexual encounter that left her feeling humiliated and guilty.

Clara's pattern was never to let two weekends go by without starting on a bender. What would happen if she stopped drinking altogether, the way real alcoholics are asked to stop? What would she do with the emotional pressure which built up? Would she, as a result, be able to express the anger and pain she had not been able to show in private therapy?

I talked to a group leader about these two patients, and also about several other group members. Emphasizing my interest in the Synanon idea of giving up destructive symptoms immediately, I requested that both Clara and Charlie be asked to stop acting out their respective symptoms.

The results were astonishing. Clara (who was programmed to want to please others) agreed at once to stop drinking altogether. In the weeks that followed, she had one relapse (when a former lover arrived unexpectedly from out of town), but then kept to her no-alcohol regimen. After about six weeks of abstinence, she screamed out intense feelings of pain and anger about her relationship with her father. She also experienced deep-down pain about the hostility she had always shown her mother—hostility that had prevented a warm, loving relationship from developing. Expression of the feeling led to valuable new insights for Clara. She saw her father as a manipulator with a bellyful of problems (including severe sexual ones) about which he had never been honest. And while she also saw her mother as a manipulator (with a backbone of steel, despite her image as a fragile china doll), Clara began to develop a warm, respecting love for her mother.

Charlie was different from Clara. Resisting the group leader's edict, he maintained that he loved the woman he was seeing and that she loved him. He insisted that his wife didn't understand him, that his sexual desire was too strong to be satisfied by intercourse only with his wife, and that he was an exceptional man who needed to maintain intimate relationships with two women. Charlie felt so strongly about the group leader's demand that he came to see me privately, asking that I transfer him to another group. I refused, telling Charlie that his starting point in becoming healthy had to be to give up his series of mistresses. Charlie left my office angrily, and for the next two weeks was absent from his group.

Then, one evening, he came into my office, sheepishly. The relationship with his current mistress had started to break up, he said, and he was considering beginning a new relationship with "a broad who works in my office." But before he "asked the new broad out," he said he would like to hear once more why it was important to stop having love affairs.

Perceiving that Charlie's question was a test of my personal involvement with him, I explained the reason as clearly as I knew how. I told him about the fear and anger I sensed in him, and how much I felt he needed to show these feelings to others. I reminded him how few friendships with men he had, and how much he needed to have such friendships. I told him I cared about him and wanted him to be happier. When I was finished talking, I spontaneously grabbed Charlie's shoulder with my hand.

There was moisture in Charlie's eyes as he agreed to return to the group and commit himself to "not having an outside broad for six weeks." Within two weeks, Charlie was screaming in fear in groups. It was the start of a new relationship with his wife (who subsequently began to come to groups with her husband).

# Feelings

Clearly, getting people to struggle with their symptoms right at the start speeded up the therapeutic process considerably. The technique of encountering, as it broke all the social rules, did a lot to uncork feelings that people had learned to hide throughout their lives. But many group members were adept at counterattack or at suppressing their reactions to encounter. We couldn't get to their deeper feelings just through encounter techniques. Depriving people of their symptomatic outlets gave us a new tool for tapping hidden feelings. The pressure built up internally, rather than from outside confrontation. As long as people did not neutralize the internal pressure by "acting out," the feelings were sure to emerge before long.

About this time, I began to see the importance of working on *feelings for themselves,* rather than just as an interactive expression of the individual through encountering. We didn't abandon encounter techniques, however. We still encouraged someone to get angry directly at whoever sparked his anger. Feeling the right to do that was an important part of growth. For someone not used to getting angry, it helped break a "nice guy" image and often led to deeper feelings. For someone who was used to getting angry, his attack on a group member gave us a chance to see how honest the feeling really was. Did he feel securely entitled to get angry, as an adult, taking full responsibility for the feeling? Or did he try to bully people with his anger? Did he strike out with a rapier-like insult, then retreat before he could be confronted himself? Who made him angry? What clues to his childhood could we see in his attacks?

All of these possibilities made encountering valuable to our groups. Still, I saw that encountering sometimes became a way to release energy without tapping deeper into feelings. By the same token, as love became important in our groups, many people would be satisfied with a brief cry and the warmth of a hug or two. As someone started to show pain, someone else would hold him while he cried—often with great release of feeling. But then it would be over. The tension of the mounting pain had been appeased, and deeper feelings weren't touched. I saw more and more that feelings had to be expressed *full measure* in order to be therapeutic.

Our focus began to shift from encountering to exercising specific feelings as they arose. At the beginning of one of our early marathons, for example, Sally spoke up after an angry exchange between two other women. She had been frightened by the exchange, she said, and she realized it was because anger had been forbidden in her family. I told her I could understand her fear and suggested that if she felt scared again, she should try to let out the tears which she had been controlling. She should also try during the marathon to get angry whenever anybody made her feel that way.

For several weeks prior to the marathon, Sally had been struggling with her symptom. She was a shy girl who spent her nonworking hours alone with a book, while all her contemporaries were out at parties and on dates. We had asked her to make herself go out, struggle to meet and be with people. She got several dates through a computer dating system. Some hadn't been bad. She also went to parties with her fellow-workers and joined a ski club. She still wasn't having much fun, though, and you could feel the anxiety mounting in her. I felt Sally was ready for an emotional breakthrough, so I watched her carefully as the marathon progressed.

Intense feelings built up throughout the room during the next few hours. By dawn, Sally had burst into tears of pain which had been bottled up for years. It was a good experience for her. After the marathon, her face was open and her feelings about herself good. She maintained the euphoria for quite some time. It was reinforced by the fact that dates were coming to her more easily (after all, men are attracted to the vitality of good feelings in a woman). There really wasn't much need to struggle with her symptom. But in groups, Sally's emotional progress came to a standstill. She still got frightened when there was a particularly angry encounter. It would even stir some tears in her. But pain had become an easy feeling for Sally. She still couldn't get involved in any angry group interaction, and if she felt fear, it turned to tears, which ceased after she had cried a little and taken comfort from someone who hugged her.

One day, as she started to cry, I cut in before someone could hold her. "What's making you cry, Sally?" She looked at me, a bit startled. "The way they were yelling at each other. You *know* that always makes me afraid." There was a hint of anger in her voice.

"Then why don't you show each of us that you're afraid? Don't hide in one person's arms. Tell Doug, there, and then Jane. Just look at each one and tell them, 'I'm afraid.'"

Sally looked more terrified than I had ever seen her, but she went ahead. "I'm afraid," she whispered, looking fleetingly at Doug. "I'm afraid," to Jane. "I'm afraid." "I'm afraid." "I'm afraid." Halfway around the room, the feeling began to connect. She said the words louder and louder. Their force scared her even more, but she kept on around the room, one by one. Tears were streaming down her face. Still, she stayed with the fear, rather than sliding into hysterical pain. "I'M AFRAID. I'M AFRAID, Jim. I'm AFRAID, Dan. I'm AFRAID." When she had gotten almost around the room, she started screaming the words. And then the real pain came up, in racking, tortured sobs. Almost everyone was crying by this time. They all could identify with the depth and honesty of her feeling. When people hugged her, it was with a strong feeling of bondedness. She had had an experience they could all understand, with empathy.

After that episode, Sally began to deal with all her feelings in group. She learned how to get angry. She learned how to express her feelings with a sense of entitlement. She began to sense her strength as an adult, feeling human being who was not helpless. And she began to apply these insights to her everyday life. Before long, she was involved in a good relationship with a man. They were married about a year later.

# Attitudes

Sally's "as-if" behavioral changes at the beginning of group helped lead her to important emotional insights which she explored and exercised in group. She was able to apply those lessons to her life outside group. However, I saw many other group members reach a deep stage of emotional awareness such as

Sally's, and then falter, reverting to old patterns of behavior and falling victim again to historic, distorted feelings which had supposedly been dealt with in group already. It became clear to me that the third part of Triangular Man—attitudes—had to be confronted, too. Struggling with behavior, delving into misprogrammed feelings, and learning to express real, healthy feelings, were not enough. It was too easy for people to reach a certain plateau of emotional awareness, return to group week after week to express feelings, but make no progress at all in their daily lives. They were indulging in little more than emotional masturbation. We had to explore further to learn that maladaptive attitudes were keeping them from real growth.

Bernard is a good example. He was a high-school teacher, Jewish, married with two children. Bernard came to groups quite suicidal. He had been unable to get an erection for months, and he was convinced that he was a homosexual. He had had one homosexual experience in his teens, but hadn't thought about it until his sexual performance went sour in his marriage. He was in an hysterical, desperate state when he came to groups. We were able to help him get to his feelings quite readily. He quickly learned to express his pain and fear. He gained immediate sustenance from the group's concern and understanding. After a few weeks, he even exploded in anger at a man in the group who had been riding him hard about being "henpecked."

Bernard really let loose that day with a barrage of historical anger stored away against his father and brother, who had taunted and belittled him all his life. He was so pleased with the sense of his anger that he would exercise it in every group that he could. At home, he began to get an erection occasionally, although his sex life still wasn't good. We knew he had trouble asserting his needs to his wife, and we encouraged him to use his new-found feelings, when warranted, at home. If his wife made him angry, show the anger. If he felt the need for love, show the need.

Bernard reported each week how he had stood up to his wife, showing his anger when she made him mad or tried to control him. Then he would jump up to do an anger exercise in the group. The feeling was certainly connected. Bernard was as angry as could be. He felt entitled to that anger. But something was missing. Finally, one week, I asked him to tell the group what had gone on in his life since the last meeting.

"It was a pretty good week," he said. "I had some trouble with sex, but I really stood up to Joanie about the weekend."

"What happened?"

"She wanted to go for a drive in the Catskills, and I wanted to take the kids to the beach. I really yelled at her about that."

"Where did you go?"

A pause. "To the Catskills. . . . But she sure knew I wasn't happy about it." The group burst out in laughter.

I raised my hand to quiet them. "Does that kind of thing happen often, Bernard?"

"What do you mean? Yeah. I've been getting angry at her a lot."

"I mean, does she always do what she wants instead of what you want? Even though you get angry at her?"

Bernard swallowed and looked nervously around the room. "Yeah. I guess she does. I never thought of it that way."

What had happened, of course, was that Bernard's attitude about anger hadn't changed at all. He had thought that getting in touch with anger and learning to express it to his wife was enough. He did not see that the purpose of assertive anger was to maximize the chances of getting what he wanted. The assertion of the feeling did not mean much if he could never change the reality of his situation. Clearly, his wife still had her way all the time.

Bernard was bearing another attitudinal burden which became evident once he brought his wife into groups, as we demanded. To his mind, their problems were all his. He couldn't get an erection, so their sex life was shot. He had acted out homosexually years ago, so his wife was stuck with someone who wasn't a real man. From his description, Joanie was a loving women, a bit controlling (but "all women are"), a good mother and efficient wife who was stuck with a failure for a husband. No wonder she ran everything: he was just an incompetent who couldn't get a hard-on. He was pleased that he could get angry now about how she took charge of everything, but the reality was she really was "better at running things anyway."

Once Joanie came into groups we saw right away how these

attitudes were distorted. She was a pinched, sullen person who obviously had terrible feelings about herself as a woman. She would strike out at Bernard with shrill accusations, then lean back and watch him dangle on the hook, trying to please her yet defend himself at the same time. No wonder he couldn't get an erection! Joanie was the epitome of the castrating bitch. (In all fairness to her, Bernard's helplessness and lack of assertiveness were difficult to cope with.)

It took several weeks in groups together and separately before they began to break the symbiosis which had devastated their marriage. Once Bernard saw that healthy anger was a way of speaking up for himself and getting things his way at least some of the time, he began to assert his desires more healthily in their marriage. Joanie was very frightened by the change in him. When she saw her old tricks of denigrating and controlling him didn't work, she withdrew and sulked for a while. Then she began to work on her fear in group. And she made healthy demands on her husband. She really wanted him to stand up and take charge; she could not respect him when he didn't. They're still in groups, but their relationship has grown tremendously. Rather than get into hours-long harangues, or martyred capitulation, each is able to get angry healthily. Each can show his need. Sex is infinitely better. They're having more fun with each other and with their children.

Bernard had had the misprogrammed attitude that anger does not do any good. Even when he learned to express his anger, his attitude prevented him from accomplishing anything with it. He had to deal with all three sides of Triangular Man in order to grow: He had to *behave* like an assertive man (even though he often did not feel like it). He had to experience his fear and need for love and learn to express his healthy *feelings*. He had to combat maladaptive *attitudes* which kept him from functioning like an emotionally healthy, adult man. (Such attitudes are numerous, and often hard to pin down.)

# The Dynamic of Triangular Man

The interplay of behavior, feelings and attitudes must occur with any member of my groups who wants to find an emotionally healthy life. There was Louie, for instance, a beautifully sensitive, tender man who was an exclusive, compulsive homosexual when he came to groups. We required Louie to stop cruising men's rooms and start dating girls. He did, and soon he was lying on the mat in group, screaming out his need for love. Eventually, he began living with a girl. They were later married.

Although Louie has worked through most of his problems, he still has one significant maladaptive attitude which he must cope with all the time. Louie was programmed to believe that pleasure invariably brings pain. Every time he spent an especially good evening with his girl or with friends, every time sex was good, or he got praise at work, he felt tremendous anxiety. His struggle each time was to realize that the unpleasant feelings resulted from a maladaptive attitude. He had to discount them and concentrate on other, good feelings.

For Clara, once her abstinence from liquor led to her deeper feelings, things progressed well. Her historic feelings had erupted, and through new group exercises she was learning to assert her sense of being an attractive, adult woman. She only had an occasional drink for sociable purposes. That was all right on dates, but when she went to parties, she felt very uncomfortable. One weekend, she leapt back into her old symptom. She went to a party on a Friday night, felt totally inadequate in comparison to all the chic women there, had a miserable time, got drunk on Saturday, and ended up in bed with a young man she picked up in a bar. When he did not call her Monday, as he had promised, she went to his apartment building. She saw him putting another girl into a cab, but waited a few minutes and rang his bell. He invited her in. They had some drinks and went to bed. She did everything in bed he wanted, but got no physical pleasure herself.

Again, he didn't call her. By group on Friday, Clara was miserable. She got very angry in a group exercise, but it didn't seem convincing. There were mixed signals. When she told us how inferior she had felt at the party before she had acted out, we got her to express her fear of being a woman, and then assert that she was a beautiful woman. Still something was wrong. She didn't have that clean, joyful feeling of self which I had seen her have after such group exercises before.

We talked some more, and she began to describe how elegant all the women at the party had been. She said she had walked in rehearsing the feeling of, "I'm a woman and I'm beautiful," but when she looked around, she "knew" she didn't have a chance. As we probed further, it became evident that Clara held the firm attitude, subconsciously, that all women were prettier than she. (This was certainly not the reality!) In other words, she was beaten before she started. That attitude kept her from looking as attractive as she could. Instead of emitting the signals of a relaxed woman who feels confident of her femininity, she seemed tight and unresponsive in social situations with men when there were other women around.

For Clara, it was essential to keep this defeatist attitude in mind as she practiced her feelings in group of, "I'm a woman. I'm entitled to love. I am lovable." Until the maladaptive attitude and attendant feelings are replaced with healthy ones, she will have to struggle to hang on to her good feelings about herself. But the task becomes easier with practice.

James was a rigid, emotionally closed character-disordered personality whom one group member accused, rather creatively, of "taking baths with your vest on." James came to groups just because he was unhappy, without knowing why. His mother had been confined to a mental institution when he was a boy. James didn't remember any feelings one way or the other about her. His father raised him and indoctrinated him thoroughly with the idea that all women were inferior. Groups helped James behaviorally by insisting that he loosen up, make himself enjoy parties, try new activities such as photography (so he could join a club). Still, he could not get involved in any kind of a committed relationship with a woman. His sex life was fine; his love life was awful. He would live with a girl for a while, then boot her out because she didn't do something or other right—keep house, cook, converse, or whatever. Groups opened him up to all of his feelings quite a bit. Still he had trouble with women. Not until he came face to face with his attitude that women were inferior could he begin to relax his demands on his relationships and enjoy himself. Hidden behind his maladaptive attitude about women was a tremendous need for the love of a woman, of course. James also feared that if he accepted an "inferior" woman, he would be considered inferior by his father, the only person he respected. It looks now as though James has found somebody who is filling his needs. Most important, he is allowing her to fill them. Each time he finds himself becoming critical of her, he tries to examine his reaction before expressing it. More often than not, it is distorted, related to his father's bitter attitude. James concentrates instead on showing her his need.

Sol and Miriam are a couple in their early fifties. He's successful in business. She's an accomplished painter. They have one daughter, grown, who lives away from home. Both Sol and Miriam are well-educated, highly verbal people. Sol had been in psychoanalysis for years, but they came to groups when they began to see that their marriage was faltering. Sol was a rambler, talking on and on with no affect, just data and attitudes. Miriam, though somewhat in touch with her feelings, usually withdrew when he became critical of her. They had very little sex life and had never really enjoyed sex with each other, or with anyone else prior to their marriage twenty-one years ago. Yet they were extremely close and dependent upon each other. Their marriage was an exquisite "don't make waves" contract: "I won't ruffle your feelings if you won't ruffle mine."

Sol's symptom really was his anxious, incessant chatter. Miriam's was her way of isolating herself behind a sweet, but ingratiating, smile. She would listen to everything he had to say, agree with him, praise him, and then paint feverishly for hours while he was at work. Both really were in truth very bored with their lives.

We handled Sol's symptom by cutting him off each time he began to ramble. Before long, he was getting very angry at the group, and then he worked around to a lot of "Fuck you, Mommy" feelings which were at the heart of his problems. Miriam worked on anger and need. Our behavioral assignment for both was to have sex at least twice a week, and to force out feelings as they arose, rather than act by their old contract of not making waves with each other.

I'll never forget their sparkle and joy one day when they came into group to announce that they had had a fantastic time in bed together. The sex had been great for both. Afterwards, they lay in each others arms, weeping openly. In that group, their joy was like that of two happy children romping together. Sol sparkled with wit. Miriam danced about, giggling, and even clicked her heels in the air in total defiance of her normal façade of a proper, demure woman. It was a great pleasure for everyone.

The next week, I walked into the group to see Miriam sitting alone in a corner, Sol across the room from her, his hands on his knees, glowering. All the good feelings were gone. A couple of nights before, they had been preparing for bed with the intent of making love, and Sol had walked over to the window, in the nude. The shade was wide open. Miriam was sure he was showing himself off to the neighbors. She got very angry, and her sexual feelings disappeared. The truth was, as we explored the story, that both of them had to grapple with some maladaptive attitudes about sex. Miriam's reaction to Sol came out of an old belief that sex was dirty. His "exhibitionism," as she called it, evoked that assumption. Sol, in turn, was behaving a bit like a naughty boy who was showing off his penis. It was a defiant act in the face of uneasy feelings he had about sex—feelings which arose from his misprogrammed attitude that pleasure in sex was not allowed.

Although Sol and Miriam were eventually able to work out their problems, I want to be careful not to imply that the Casriel Institute has been therapeutic for everyone who has attended a few group sessions, or even many. To be truly effective, the process requires a continuity of treatment over a period of time that varies with each individual. Many troubled individuals who are deeply entrenched behind a set of symptoms and defenses are immediately threatened by the process—and they leave groups. Others are excited by the emotionality of groups, or intellectually intrigued, and they stay until their symptoms become an absolutely central issue. Then they leave. In neither of these cases does the process prove genuinely therapeutic.

For example, Nora, a female homosexual, left group when her symptom became the issue. A highly intelligent woman who worked from time to time as a professional entertainer, Nora entered groups because she was lonely (her lover had run away with an already established female singer). Nora was commercially unsuccessful in an intensely competitive field, and she was emotionally isolated from practically everyone. She had learned to exist behind a façade of prideful self-sufficiency. Although she was good company socially, her signals and behavior really told the world, "Don't get near me. Don't help me. I can take care of myself."

In a marathon, Nora experienced an emotional breakthrough which helped her shed some of her defenses and begin to reveal her vulnerable needs. Then, in postmarathon sessions, the group asked Nora to begin dating and to have sexual intercourse with a male. (She had stopped being an active lesbian when she entered group.)

Nora did start dating, but found herself becoming extremely anxious when she was alone with the man. She did not even want to neck with him, she told the group. The group persevered. "Act as if," they told Nora, advising her at least to start to neck. The reason Nora's group was putting such pressure on her about her symptom of homosexuality was that they were reacting to her feelings about being a lesbian. Clearly, she did not feel good about it. (I have known homosexuals who have reached an emotionally adult accommodation with their symptom. If their desire is not to change, and they feel content with their lives and are functioning well in the world, there is certainly no need to pressure them to change. However, in Nora's case—as in that of most homosexuals who come to me—the basic discontent with their lives and unhappiness lying behind their symptom is evident.) Nora was the female equivalent of a "closet queen." Publically, she acted out the role of a seductress when men were around. She didn't want her associates to suspect she was a lesbian. Yet she didn't want to face the painful conflict between her public and private life.

After several weeks of group pressure, Nora did not show up for a number of consecutive sessions. Then a tersely-worded note arrived at my office saying that she was "giving up group." Later, through acquaintances of Nora who were in my practice, we learned that she had returned to active lesbianism. We weren't surprised. It seemed fairly certain that Nora would return to her familiar role as a proud, distant beauty—without friends—who depended completely (and smotheringly) on one female to be her cherished lover, companion, and intimate. It was a life that would inevitably cause Nora to become emotionally closed once again.

I ran into Nora by accident a few weeks later, and we talked for a few minutes. I told her that I thought we had failed her, and I hoped she would come back to groups. She said no. To her mind the process was unfairly demanding, and it required a kind of performance which she found unreal and unhelpful. "Everybody asks you to show *your* feelings so they can get rid of *their* anxiety," she said. "And there's too much anger. Those people don't really know how *I* feel. They're too busy trying to get me to do what *they* want."

Performance had been a special problem of Nora's, and I can understand her reaction. She had had particularly demanding parents, and it seemed that her whole life had been one of performance for others. She had no real sense of who she was, without performing. (Typically of many actors and other entertainers in my groups, Nora had chosen a career which reinforced her lack of identity. She felt most real when she was on stage, yet the approval of the audience was never enough, because she had no other identity.) But Nora had hit upon a continual problem of the group therapy process. There are rules to follow and skills to develop about showing feelings. Group pressure to "follow the rules" can be great—and sometimes insensitive to an individual's emotions at a given point in time. Usually the leader or an experienced group member can put a stop to a "group dump," when everyone is attacking a single individual more to relieve his own anxiety or frustration than to help the person. I remember one woman, an alcoholic, who had gone off the wagon briefly and was defending herself sullenly against the group. Everyone was yelling at her, and she was withdrawing more and more. Suddenly the man next to her took her hand and said to the group, "Cut it out. I think she's a good person." She burst into tears at the unexpected kindness and concern, and it was the beginning for her of emotional openness. That one gesture got her to drop her defenses and trust another person long enough for the process to begin to reach her.

For Nora, we were not able to sufficiently establish that trust in others for her to begin to trust her own feelings and worth.

The same was true of Paula, who was perhaps more typical of my group members because she had no obvious antisocial symptom. Paula entered my process because a friend, already in groups, urged her to get involved. A personnel worker of about thirty, she was intelligent, hard-working, and attractive. As a teenager, she had gone through an irresponsible phase—pot parties, bad grades in college, numerous affairs, a couple of abortions, and later a drop-out from college and the middle-class world of her mother. But, in her twenties, with the aid of some directive therapy, Paula had become a solid citizen who returned to college, got a degree, came to New York as a "bachelor girl," and took a job with a job placement agency.

The chief trouble with Paula was that she didn't know how to relate to other people. She was a bit like a wounded bird, fragile, with no trust in herself and, consequently, in others. Curiously, she always seemed able to meet and get involved with new people, particularly men. But in a short time each relationship, whether a love affair or a friendship, deteriorated into quarrels and disagreements—then into a split-up. Paula handled the termination stages of each relationship with strong attitudes, built on a foundation of "shoulds" and "oughts," which covered up her painful, deep needs: "Men shouldn't talk about other girls when they're with you on a date." Translated: "I need a man to love me." "Friends aren't supposed to be critical of you." Translated: "Please love me just because I'm me."

Even at her job, a similar pattern prevailed. Paula developed a quick relationship with a female associate. Then, in a matter of weeks, the relationship proved to be too demanding and difficult, and the women began to pull away from each other. A period of silences followed when the women met in the halls of their office.

Why did such a pattern exist? It grew out of the fact that Paula was a character-disordered personality with giant emotional needs. She was somewhere between the child and adolescent stage of emotional development. She could be emotionally seductive about her needs, then would get hurt and angry when they weren't met. Yet she was unwilling to put her needs aside long enough to sustain a relationship when problems developed. She would extricate herself from a relationship when even a modest problem occurred. And, with absolute certainty, problems had to arise out of the needs Paula kept hidden, because she did not express them straightforwardly.

Paula needed love, but hid her need. She needed praise and never asked for it. She held back the pain she needed to show to others, and she concealed her fear and anger behind a smokescreen of appropriate conduct. Worse, Paula consistently accommodated her friends or lover. In doing so, she had an expectation that, through some secret contract, she in return would be accommodated. It seldom worked out that way. As a result, Paula would get angry about the things she had done for her friend, or lover, or associate.

The result was that Paula's life assumed a destructive circular pattern. She went from one lover to another. She would leave a job because "the boss didn't like her," then take another job equally undemanding of her intelligence and talents. She moved from one apartment to another, always having to find new roommates, and not being able to afford a place by herself because whatever job she had did not pay enough. But then it was "too difficult and took too much time" to try to better her career by going to graduate school or entering a training program which promised advancement. She said she wanted to get married, but she would not truly look at what went wrong with her relationships with men, or how her hidden needs were driving males away.

Paula eventually left groups. She had learned a little about how to get angry and assert her need for love within groups, but she couldn't apply these lessons to her life outside of group. She never learned to trust the group enough to reveal her deep pain and terror. I think that a few weeks in a twenty-four-hour-a-day community such as AREBA could have helped. She really needed that continual exposure to other people in order to learn to trust others and to trust her own lovability. She needed to feel secure in a loving, family situation—the kind she had never had in childhood. That sense of security could eventually have led her to take the chance of dealing with her feelings, behavior, and attitudes.

Paula acted out one pattern, among others, which I find

typical of many of my patients. When she would begin to get involved with a man and have some pleasure with him, there would be fights soon after, and she would finally break off the relationship. I see this inability to handle pleasure all the time in my groups. Sol and Miriam had special troubles with sex right after they had had a particularly close experience in bed. Louie still has to work through his maladaptive attitude that pleasure brings pain. In our culture, people feel they must pay a tremendous price for pleasure. As any member in my groups works through the interplaying facets of Triangular Man, he comes into conflict with this basic problem sooner or later. Some people find that they have been programmed to believe that the price of pleasure (having their basic needs met) and love (the anticipation of pleasure) is worth the pain. These people (like Clara), whom I call Acceptor Types, will gladly pay the price, no matter what the pain. Others in my groups (like Charlie) find that they have been programmed to believe that the price of pleasure and love is too great. It involves too much pain. They would rather depend upon themselves to fill their own needs. These are Rejector Types.

Acceptors and Rejectors, whom I discuss in detail in the next chapter, are the two basic personality types in my groups. Within the dynamic of Triangular Man, each type learns to strive toward the common goal of gaining new, healthy ways to handle pain and pleasure.

# CHAPTER 11 | *Acceptors and Rejectors*

THE CONCEPT OF TRIANGULAR MAN serves primarily to explain how our group dynamic operates. We deal simultaneously with behavior, feelings and attitudes. To focus upon the development of the human personality itself, rather than the dynamic of groups, I have devised a second three-part scheme of man. Roughly parallel to the three elements of Triangular Man, this new diagram presents the human being in three levels:

1. On the surface is the *symptomatic level*. This involves how the individual behaves. What are his acting-out symptoms? For the character-disordered personality, what is the nature of his secondary encapsulation? For the neurotic, what psychological devices make up his anxiety reactions? What healthy modes of behavior does the person exhibit?

2. Below the symptomatic level is the *dynamic level*. This has to do with how the person reacts emotionally to himself and the world. What feelings are distorted, what feelings healthy? What mode of emotional defense does he use? A neurotic's "flight" or "fight" reactions to danger have been painfully distorted. He suppresses most of his survival feelings, yet they appear in twisted, anxious ways. A character-disordered person-

ality represses most of his feelings, using the mechanism of "freeze" to cut himself off effectively from any conscious contact with his real feelings.

3. At the base of the personality is the *identity level*. Here, we see what the individual's deepest attitudes are about himself and the world. How does he see himself? What does he expect from others?

There is constant interplay between these three levels of the human personality. Each affects the other. A significant change in one can cause a change in either or both of the others.

Most basic to the total personality is the identity level. It becomes clearly defined early in life and dictates in large part how the dynamic and symptomatic levels function. It profoundly affects the nature of significant relationships with other people. And, like attitudes, the identity level is the hardest to get at and change. Yet until that level is confronted and altered in an emotionally disturbed individual, the road to emotional health has not been traveled to its end. All our rules and exercises are aimed, ultimately, at the identity level. When the dynamic is successful, we can perceive a significant change in identity. That's why I call my group therapy dynamic the "New Identity Process."

I see three basic personality profiles at the identity level. One is that of the emotionally healthy individual, which I described in Chapter 4. The people who seek help in my groups fall basically within one of the other two character types: Acceptors or Rejectors. (No one fits exactly into just one profile. What follows are theoretical descriptions of what I find to be over-all tendencies within individual personalities.)

Each identity type evolves in terms of the first principle of Rado-Kardiner Adaptational Psychodynamics (see Chapter 8): All animal behavior is motivated by the pursuit of pleasure or avoidance of pain.

# Identity Development of the Child

From infancy on, the motivation toward pleasure and away from pain is basic to a human being's development. It begins with the nature of parent-child relationships. The baby's needs are fairly simple: food, warmth, bodily contact, sleep, emotional response, and so forth. Having one's needs satisfied is pleasurable to a baby or an adult. Not having them satisfied causes pain. The physically helpless infant must depend totally upon his parents to meet his needs. He is at the mercy of their willingness, capacity, and ability to relieve his tensions, absolve his pain, bring him pleasure.

An infant becomes conditioned, or programmed, by the significant person or persons in his life. It learns to respond in patterned ways. The programming begins before it can talk (think) or physically care for himself (act). Its basic mode of response is emotional. A human being's early conditioning is primarily emotional.

In most cases, in our culture, an infant's earliest sustained relationship is with its mother or mother surrogate. (Other people, such as fathers, siblings, uncles, aunts, maids, nurses, may or may not be significant. To make things simpler in the descriptions which follow, I will use "mother" or "parents" to indicate the significant person or persons.)

Everything that happens contributes to the conditioning of an infant: things that give pleasure, as well as things which cause pain. Inevitably, the child learns there is a great deal of frustration (that is, pain) in having its needs met. Sometimes the pain is minor, and sometimes it is great. After all, parents are human, too. They have their own needs, and the needs are often distorted. Even in the healthiest of households, there are inevitable delays or mistakes in meeting an infant's demands. As a child grows, he or she must learn that some needs cannot be filled immediately, if ever. The lessons are realistic, but they can also be very painful.

Any number of factors, often unavoidable, can contribute to a child's pain. An emotionally mature mother will still have difficulty filling her child's needs if she is physically sick, pressured by poverty, isolated from peers, or without an adequate and responsible mate. An emotionally healthy father will have severe problems fulfilling his children's needs if he is worried about holding on to his job, paying off an accumulation of large debts, doing his military service overseas, and so on.

Trying to meet a child's emotional and physical needs is demanding.

Aside from practical roadblocks, it's not always easy to separate your sense of your child's needs from your own. About four years ago, I came into my apartment one evening and reached out to hug my then-two-year-old son, Seth. I tried to pick him up and cuddle him. But, at that moment, Seth was playing with his toys. He turned his back on me, rejecting my stretched-out arms. I felt hurt by his rejection.

A couple of hours later, I was relaxing on the couch after dinner. Seth made a running jump into my arms, knocking my book to the floor. I was annoyed because of the interruption, and I still felt hurt about Seth's earlier rejection of my love. My first reaction was to lower him to the floor and go on reading. But after a few seconds of internal struggle, I realized that Seth's needs worked on a different timetable from mine. I hugged Seth, kissed him, and roughhoused with him. Quite simply, I saw that Seth was not *me*. When I had the need to love him, *he* did not have the need or desire to be loved by me. Seth was the child, and I was the adult. It was easier for me to understand and adapt to his needs than for Seth to adapt to mine.

Without being tyrannized, parents should try to meet their children's emotional needs—provided, that is, that it is pragmatically feasible to do so. Avoiding tyranny isn't easy. The key is to distinguish between your own needs and those of your child. Children have needs which are quantitatively and temporally different from those of a grown-up. It is not enough to cater to a young person's biological and physical requirements such as food, water, rest, warmth, a change of diapers. A parent must also meet an infant's biological-based psychological needs. If physical needs are not met, a child can die or grow up physically stunted. If psychological needs are not met, a child may become psychologically stunted. In our culture, middle- and upper-class parents are consistently the worst offenders. They tend to cater to their children's physical needs, but fail to understand and meet emotional needs. Many of us who have been brought up in middle-class homes suffer, I fear, from emotional malnutrition. To make matters worse, our culture has reinforced the malnutrition.

Much of the human growth process has to do with retraining one's understanding of the differences between Self and the rest of the world. What is Me? What are They? How much of what I perceive and feel comes from Me? How much is actually going on out There, in the objective world?

Most psychotherapy is concerned with such distinctions. My group educational process involves this struggle: Reveal and deal with your own feelings, reactions, and attitudes so that you can learn which are distorted legacies from your past and not realistic responses to what is happening in the present. By understanding your own feelings, behavior and attitudes, you are better able to discern what is going on in other people! Which dangers are real and which are imagined. What pleasures are possible. When pain can, to your best advantage, be avoided. When you can make such distinctions, you are much freer to make a choice. You are no longer a slave to the childhood misprogramming you carry in your belly.

Much of a small child's growth entails the process of separating his sense of himself from his sense of the world. At first, he experiences his parents as part of himself. Little by little, through experience, he comes to realize a separation exists. He gradually changes his idea of his parent from that of his private genie to his private slave, then to his private servant, and finally to a private mother who will meet his needs, but who more and more demands that he in return fulfill some of *her* needs.

*What goes on during this period between a child and the significant adults around him matters for the rest of his life.*

If adults are emotionally healthy, children will be conditioned to respond healthily to others. But if adults are emotionally disturbed, then their pathological feelings, attitudes, and behavior will be transmitted to their offspring just as surely as their language. Distorted emotions, incompetence, ignorance, unyielding attitudes, poverty—all play critical parts in the programming of a child.

Suppose, for example, a mother feels resentful of the time she must devote to the feeding of her baby, changing diapers, washing clothes and dishes, and doing other ignominious household tasks. The couple is new in the community, and the husband goes away on business trips two or three days a week. The wife has nobody else to talk to. She is too scared to try and meet people on her own. When her husband is away, the woman sits alone, with only a television set as a companion. Under these circumstances, it would take a remarkable mother not to be continuously angry at the baby, who restricts her activities without providing enough compensatory rewards. The woman cannot help but transmit these frightened, depressed, angry signals to her baby. Every time she feeds him or changes his diapers, he senses her anger, fear, or depression. Chances are, this baby is learning that pleasure entails pain.

As a child matures, he learns to anticipate pain. He becomes aware of *danger*. With the help of his eyes, ears, nose, touch, and memory, he recalls his earlier experience and realizes that certain situations cause pain. While he is learning each day to do more for himself, he has no primary control over his environment. Realistically, he is quite helpless.

How does the infant react? Remember, he is in a dependent state. He cannot physically flee or fight. Physically and cognitively helpless, the child can only react emotionally to defend himself against pain and remain open to pleasure.

Unfortunately, what will bring pleasure or pain is not always so clear-cut in the complicated world of human interaction. What does a child do when pain comes hand in hand with pleasure, when the pleasure of human warmth, caring, understanding, and love are accompanied by a high price tag? How does he react if, say, his mother feeds him whenever he is hungry, but while feeding him holds him angrily or coldly? Or what if his father tosses him up in the air, but through roughness stemming from unconscious anger or tension he hurts the baby slightly each time?

The pleasure-pain constellation of a child's early life profoundly affects his lifetime capacity to feel love. Love is built on the anticipation of pleasure from a person, the awareness that someone else is giving you something, supplying your needs, and asking for nothing in return. When someone continually gives you pleasure, or resolves tensions and removes pain, the responsive feeling is pleasure. And the anticipation of that person who has been the constant source of pleasure evolves into the feeling of love. When you anticipate that pleasure from someone, you love him. The pleasure or pain can be physically or psychologically determined.

Pleasure is a biologically based survival feeling. Just as danger is the anticipation of pain, so love is the anticipation of pleasure. The infant comes to know, when he is lying in a wet crib and he cries in displeasure, that something large hovers over him and dries him. She not only removes the displeasure, she adds the pleasure of her touch and loving concern. He starts to learn to love the thing. It resolves his pressures, his tensions, his uncomfortable feelings. It feeds him, nurses him, warms him. He learns the being is his mother. Then, he begins to be prepared to extend his newfound feeling of pleasurable anticipation—his love—to his father, to his brothers and sisters, to relatives and friends in the community, if they act in kind. And, finally, to the world at large.

A person who loves the world usually gets a lot of love from the world. Conversely, a person who expects to be hated usually gets hate in return. People get what they expect, because their attitudes, behavior, and feelings combine together to induce anticipated results. So a child who is loved by his family, who is protected and given to by his family, learns to love them. He anticipates love from, and gives love to, the world. Throughout life his relationships with others tend to be good ones. But when the love from significant people is not right in early childhood, when physical or emotional needs are denied in unhealthy ways, a growing young person develops trouble with love.

*An infant's core identity takes shape around his biologically-based need for pleasure/love, on the one hand, and the "price"—pain/danger—he has to pay for it.* The basis of his identity is formed by how he responds in thought, feelings, and actions to the love/pleasure, danger/pain he perceives from the significant people in his life.

The pattern is established by the specific mix of pleasure and pain at the beginning of a child's life. There are many contributing factors: His genetic make-up. What he gets physically and emotionally from significant people. What he senses in their signals. The manner and time in which his needs are met or not met. The nature of the household's stresses and strains. The vitality of a home. All these, plus countless other factors, affect the role of the anticipation of pleasure and pain in his life.

If the mix works right, the child grows into an emotionally healthy adult. If not, he becomes maladaptive and develops what I call an *Acceptor Identity* or a *Rejector Identity*. Relationships with significant people in early life condition the *maladapted* human being to become basically one type or the other. Almost certainly, unless a person gets into effective therapy, there will be a continuation of this misprogramming in every significant relationship he has for the rest of his life.

It is seldom that anyone fits precisely into one identity type or the other. With each individual, the orchestration of characteristics is different. And characteristics of one type invariably show up in the other. But these basic profiles are useful.

If the pain outweighs the pleasure a child experiences while obtaining his biologically-based needs in the most significant human relationships, sooner or later he emotionally *rejects* the relationship as a source of obtaining his need. He takes on a *Rejector* Identity. Frequently this rejection is apparent. Sometimes it is hard to tell exactly what happened. Perhaps he had to cry too loud or too long all the time in order to get fed. Or his mother was consistently irritable, and the child experienced her irritation only when he had to be in contact with her—at dressing or bathing time, for example.

In my process, it is not important to know all the causes or nuances of the major factors. What is important is the child's reaction. Sometimes the love and care received were not worth the pain. As soon as the child is old enough to manage some things for himself, he says to himself unconsciously, "I'll do it myself, as soon as I can. I don't need her—or anybody—to help." In very early life, this child learns to feel that a human relationship is more painful than pleasureable. As soon as he can, he'll do it for himself. He'll give himself the pleasure. Although it might not be as pleasureable this way, at least there will be no pain, he reasons unconsciously. And so he continues to cut himself off from the anticipation of pleasure—love—from significant human ties the rest of his life. Symbolically, he sucks his own thumb for the rest of his life.

For other infants, no matter how painful a relationship, *the pleasure exceeds the pain.* Or, perhaps, the child feels so helpless that he learns to tolerate the pain in order to fulfill some survival needs. He feels helpless in the dependency of his needs. Whatever the reasons, this child *accepts* the human relationship despite the pain. He develops an *Acceptor* Identity. A human relationship seems the best way, or the only way, to have his needs fulfilled: not only does it seem to be the way to obtain pleasure, it seems to be the only way to survive.

This early childhood decision to emotionally reject or accept significant relationships occurs unconsciously—that is, without a continuing, conscious awareness of the decision. Even if the decision initially is made consciously (I personally, and some of my patients, have been able to recall just that point in our lives), the decision quickly sinks into an area of which one is not aware or conscious. Buried though it is in the unconscious, the decision has ramifications which affect the person's life in many, many ways.

# The Rejector Personality

Charlie, whom I described in the previous chapter, was a Rejector. He avoided significant relationships in order to escape pain. In so doing, he also avoided love. The Rejector locks out the potential source of emotional pain; but he also locks out any anticipation of having his needs for being loved met by other people. He feels this need cannot possibly be filled, so he represses the need. He denies, at a conscious, preconscious, or subconscious level, that he wants emotional love at all. He is a free, self-sufficient being. He does not "need other people." He can "do for himself." The realism of such a person's gut feeling of self-sufficiency depends upon the individual, of course. Hostile juvenile delinquents may be Rejectors; so may productive, responsible businessmen. What is most significant is that the identity feeling of the Rejector has to do with the unconscious fear of pain, which causes him to avoid significant human relationships. Deep inside, the Rejector *thinks* and *feels* he does not need anybody to help him survive. Whether he can function productively in a job or profession or not is another question altogether.

By removing himself from the pain-love complex, the Rejector lives emotionally alone. He tends to be stoic. No matter what hurts—or how much it hurts—he can grit his teeth and get by on his own. He will not share his pain with others. Doing so would make him too vulnerable. He represses or suppresses the pain.

Having denied dependency upon others, the Rejector exists in a constant state of tension, which he has learned to live with. He senses danger: he anticipates pain and fears it. He must maneuver all the time to avoid the dangerous situation. Yet he cannot count on anyone to help. He must always "do for himself."

The Rejector's emotional isolation in the significant aspects of his life makes him use his head. He is what I call a "Thinker." Though feelings are a basic source of communication, the last time the Rejector attempted to share his feelings, he felt too much pain. Since that time in his infancy or early childhood, he has not expected loving concern and help from others. His feelings tend to be "atrophied" from disuse, so his thinking fills the void. It would be difficult for him really to scream for help—even if he were drowning. He is reluctant to scream, or to lose control of any feeling, even with the danger of being killed. Thus the Rejector learns to rely only on his own thinking ability, since emotions have little or no value to him. He attempts to be inflexibly self-reliant and independent.

This type of person is usually highly verbal, since words do not require emotional hook-ups. In groups, the Rejector often will use words in order to avoid getting in touch with his gut-level feelings, especially his pain. He will ramble on about the facts of his existence, chop down other people with verbal ripostes, and sometimes put forth brilliant explanations of what is going on in the room. He may even have wit and humor and start the group laughing. He can *give* pleasure and love, if he wishes. But he will not dare to cry in pain or scream out his need for love.

That need for human pleasure/love is a survival-based trait common to hominids for a minimum of 1,750,000 years. The Rejector lacks secure human pleasure; he will not have his need for love filled by another human being. Yet when love is denied, something must take its place, so he attempts to compensate for this lack through *object* pleasure. He seeks pleasure in things he can do for himself or control for himself. He may find satisfaction in a career. He may strive for good marks in school or for lots of money in business. He may turn into the leader of a gang. He may become expert at woodwork or at sewing or sexual conquests like Charlie. Or he may just collect glass bottles. He may even enjoy, to some degree, giving love to others. Whatever the choice, the Rejector finds satisfaction in the *things* he is accomplishing, creating, or accumulating.

Rejectors keep themselves out of significant emotional relationships, no matter what the price in loneliness or isolation. That's not to say that they do not associate with people in what seems to be close binds; there is just nothing of what we call "gut level" emotional attachment. Rejectors can and do have affairs and get married. But they are not really involved emotionally.

Sooner or later, Rejectors start to feel trapped. They feel they give a lot and do not get enough love or pleasure in return. The reason Rejectors do not get enough, of course, is they do not let enough come in. It is a vicious circle. A Rejector becomes irritable and annoyed with a relationship and isolates himself even more from his partner.

## The Acceptor Personality

Clara, described in the preceding chapter, was an Acceptor. Remember how eager she was to please everyone and do what they wanted, no matter what her needs. She needed, accepted, and would maintain significant human relationships no matter what the price. An Acceptor feels that he would die if he were not in a relationship with someone. Acceptors are often martyrs. Some will stand for being beaten up, cheated on, lied to, humiliated, enslaved to their partner's beck and call. They'll do anything to keep the loved person in their lives. They feel they cannot survive without some object they need to love.

Acceptors pay many prices. The biggest price is loss of their identity. They lack a sense of their own worth and strength and self-respect. Their only real identity lies in the pain of their relationships. They show pain easily; rarely can they live with the kind of pain-avoiding tension familiar to Rejectors.

Acceptors are "Feelers," not "Thinkers." They do not make efficient use of their intelligence to perceive, understand, and anticipate problems. They make excuses or obscure facts. Otherwise, they might really see what they are putting up with to gain love. They might come face to face with the fear of not having a strong identity. They might see what they would have to give up, and the loneliness they would have to face, if they rejected a relationship.

As with Rejectors, the Acceptor's identity feelings do not necessarily have anything to do with in-the-world competence. An Acceptor may function extremely intelligently and effectively in the business world or school, but he will still refuse to look clearly at the realities of his personal relationships. The point is, Acceptors sacrifice their self-respect by depending so heavily on a relationship with the pleasured person. Their identity depends upon the love relationship.

# Rejectors vs. Acceptors

Unlike an Acceptor, a Rejector has a clear self-identity, thanks to his feeling that he was the only one who would love him (self) without inflicting pain. He gives himself pleasure from his own performance, his productivity, work, the objects he has accumulated. He cannot conceive that one can join into a love relationship and still not lose his identity, productivity, possessions, or freedom. Rejectors frequently look down on Acceptors for settling for so little in their lives.

Acceptors, in turn, cannot understand Rejectors: How can a human being live alone? What meaning does life have if it is not to share love with a significant person? How futile seems the Rejector's search for self-love. What a valueless, unfulfilling experience. Acceptors feel sorry for Rejectors.

The operative feeling of an Acceptor is pain. The experience of pain, as a price for getting love, is familiar to him. He can live with it. As a matter of fact, many Acceptors do not trust or believe love unless it is accompanied by a greater or lesser degree of pain. They have become pain-dependent personalities to whom love has significance only when it is painful.

What an Acceptor cannot live with is the fear of being alone. That is the danger he fears dreadfully. Being alone would confirm his innermost terrifying secret: "I am not really lovable, so I will pay any price to get love, because I can't survive alone."

The operative feeling of a Rejector is tension. He thrives on it. And survives on it. What he cannot tolerate is the pain he believes love brings. His greatest fear is to be trapped in a love relation that will be painful; that possibility is danger to him. In his most secret self, he believes he is entitled to love, but that the price is too high. He fears love will smother him and be accompanied by a terrible cost. He fears betrayal.

In summary, the Acceptors (martyrs, feelers) make their identity dependent upon a relationship with a significant other person. Their pleasures come primarily from being with that other human being. Their pain derives from the many prices they pay to maintain the relationship. But being alone would be worse. They fear that most, for then they not only would have no identity, which they gave up for the price of a loved object, but they would have no loved object. They would have nothing. It would prove they were not lovable, because no one loved them. Not being lovable, and existing without an identity, feel worse than death. Indeed, for some Acceptors death is preferable to nothingness. (Some in despair choose death. The papers always carry stories of a spurned love ending in suicide or homicide-suicide.) So the Acceptors accept the lesser pain of a degrading relationship in order to get love. Pain is the operating emotional motif of the Acceptor Personality.

The Rejectors (stoics, thinkers) have conditioned themselves to expect more pain than pleasure from human relationships. They feel more secure in their aloneness. They have a strong identity which stems from their own constant doing for themselves. They become self-reliant. To have that identity taken away in an entrapping love relationship seems like suffocation or jail. They will not allow themselves to feel severe pain consciously, but the threat is always there. Rejectors live in a constant state of tension, sensing the danger of pain in a love relationship, mustering their forces to ward off even the possibility of such pain. This tension is the motif of the Rejector Personality.

Needless to say, most marriages, affairs, and even close friendships take place between Acceptors and Rejectors. They hardly fit together like the smooth curves of Yin and Yang, but each identity type does have characteristics which the other lacks and seeks—however abrasively they intermesh. Rejectors tend to be less emotional; they are warmed by the vitality of an Acceptor's feelings. Acceptors tend to be less verbal or clear-thinking; they are fascinated by the precision with which Rejectors view the world. The Rejector, though he fears being smothered, enjoys the strength he draws from the Acceptor's dependency upon him. The Acceptor, though secretly angry at his dependency upon the Rejector, is comfortable in giving his mate the power to take charge of his life.

Acceptors and Rejectors may sound like what Freud called "masochists" and "sadists." I do not find this to be true. According to Freud, masochism occurred as a kind of self-punishment resulting from feeling guilty about sex. Sadism was a projection of this feeling to the other person. I find Acceptors and Rejectors have to do, instead, with Rado's understanding of the pain and pleasure syndrome, rather than guilt over sex. The Acceptor is what Rado calls "pain-dependent." He'll put up with almost anything in order to gain his identity from the loved one. The Rejector, on the other hand, acts out an angry defense against the anticipated pain (danger) from a love relationship. Before he can enter into a relationship he must "neutralize" the love object. Often this can involve "sadistic" behavior. By treating the Acceptor with anger and hostility, the Rejector eventually reduces the Acceptor to a state of helplessness, where he is vulnerable and humiliated. At this point, the Rejector feels no threat and he can love the Acceptor. To the Acceptor, the whole process is exactly what he expects from a relationship.

It is important for every individual to understand his basic identity type. Once he does, he'll begin to see why he has chosen the people he has for close relationships, and why there may have been severe problems with these relationships. He will also know what to focus on in groups in order to change the maladaptive attitudes, feelings, and behavior which stem from his basic identity.

# Neurotics or Character Disorders

Acceptors and Rejectors can be either neurotic or character-disordered, depending upon the basic defensive dynamic they learn in their early development. A common neurotic symptom of Acceptors is the depressive reaction over the death or rejection of someone important to them. (Sophie in Chapter 8, who was depressed about her sister's death, was an Acceptor.) A typical neurotic Rejector is a current patient named Steve, who has his own retail business and used to suffer extreme anxiety all the time about its success or failure. Just as he had learned from his uncle, an angry, "self-made" man who had raised him, Steve refused any help from his wife or friends. He had to do it all himself, even though his anxiety reaction was causing such severe pain that he was on the verge of a breakdown when he came into groups.

Sandy, a middle-aged teacher who never married, was a character-disordered Acceptor in our groups. She had grown up in a well-to-do family, with parents who loved her openly. But she had an older brother who was their obvious favorite. Sandy learned very early in life to stay in the background, go about her business quietly, not show her feelings, and to be grateful for whatever attention her family showed her. She became a schoolteacher and had a brief affair with a rather glamorous Frenchman when she was twenty-nine. When he rejected her, Sandy followed him to France. She discovered he had a wife, but she stayed on as his mistress for a while. Finally, he broke off the relationship completely. Sandy came back to the States and went about her business quietly once again.

Mary Ellen is a character-disordered Rejector who recently joined groups. A stunning fashion designer, but rather brittle and aloof in manner, she has been divorced twice, and runs her business with efficient expertise. She has lots of boyfriends, but as soon as anyone gets close, she ends the relationship and takes on an extra-ambitious work project.

Mary Ellen hasn't been in groups very long. She faces some difficult tasks with our process. She must stop acting out her symptom by using her business as a safety-valve for her feelings. She must also treat her current affair (with a man who is both eligible and responsible) with a sense of commitment. Typically, after they have had a close, pleasureable weekend together, she has found excuses not to see him the next week. She has cut off his phone calls rather abruptly, pleading that she's too busy to talk or too tired to see him. She must begin instead to accept the dates and tell her boyfriend about the anxiety she feels, rather than turn off her feelings and work late hours in her showroom. In groups, she must work at expressing her fear of close relationships and her need for love. As a Rejector, screaming out that need, and accepting the love of group members, as well as her boyfriend's, is crucial.

Sandy, the schoolteacher, began to make progress in groups after a few weeks when she learned to get angry and accept others' anger. Unfortunately, she accepted a job in another part of the country after she had been in groups for three months. Her idolized (and hated) brother had been putting extreme pressure on her to leave therapy, and I think she may have moved away just to avoid the conflict. Hopefully, she'll come back.

Sophie's dramatic breakthrough in her first group really provided the therapy she needed. Because of her age, plus the circumstances of her life, we didn't push in groups for full character change. She really was able to pick up things with her job and her children and grandchildren soon after the group experience lifted her depression over her sister's death.

Steve, however, has been in groups for over a year. He is managing his business quite well now. When he feels especially anxious, he has learned to ask his wife to hold him lovingly. He has also learned in group exercises to express the full depth of his need for love. He is at the point now where he is gaining rapid insight into his maladaptive attitudes and how they affect both his work and his family life. Just the other day, he reported proudly that he had promoted a man who had worked for him for years to second-in-command. This man had presented Steve with a creative plan for expanding the business, and Steve's first reaction had been to dismiss the idea out-of-hand. But he felt the familiar old anxiety rising in his belly. He realized he was operating out of his misprogrammed attitude that no one else was capable of doing things for him. In other words, he had to remain in complete control. With considerable struggle, he told the man he would look over the plan. When he saw that it was indeed a good one, he adopted it and put the man in charge of that operation. Overall, Steve today is a much more relaxed, loving person than he was a year ago, and he is getting a great deal of pleasure out of his life.

For each of these people, the task in group has varied somewhat, according to their particular problems and character. The process has been more successful for some than others. But the basic road map to emotional health is the same for everyone, whether Acceptor or Rejector, neurotic or character-disordered: each person must deal with the Symptomatic, Dynamic, and Identity Levels of his personality in order to effect true growth in his behavior, feelings, and attitudes.

# CHAPTER 12

# *The Process: Taboos, Structure, Leaders, Marathons*

New Identity Groups deal simultaneously with the symptomatic, dynamic, and identity levels of the human personality:

1. We confront the *symptomatic level* by outlawing it. We do not waste time discussing destructive behavioral patterns. We just tell the person to stop the behavior. We tell alcoholics to stop drinking. We tell homosexual males to give up men and start dating women. We tell students who are flunking to start studying a lot more. We do not allow group members to dwell on their symptoms by talking at length about them in groups.

2. At the *dynamic level,* we encourage people to reveal their feelings, and we provide exercises to help them get deeper into their feelings and strengthen their healthy feelings. The name of the game is emotions. In fact, group members get their biggest rewards only by showing honest feelings.

3. At the *identity level,* we help people discover who they are. If they are Acceptors, our main thrust is to give them anger exercises to help them assert the force of their own personalities. If they are Rejectors, we try to teach them to feel their pain and learn how to take in other people's love, so that they do not feel so much alone. For both, we examine the attitudes which may be diverting them from leading a healthier life.

In a very practical sense, my New Identity Groups are an emotionally-charged, but disciplined, dynamic of introspection (like the analytic process), inspection (encountering), projection and transference, with some essential structure, a few basic rules, and a number of valuable exercises.

The structure is based on experience. The objective of the structure is to modulate and control the group dynamic for optimum therapeutic results. We are not just trying to have angry encounters or pleasurable feelings per se. We are trying to help group members grow in emotional health. The rules are part of the structure.

# The Basic Rules

### 1. *No alcohol before or during groups.*

All group members are asked to avoid drinking even one cocktail before group meetings. If an individual has a "drinking problem," he will of course be asked to give up alcohol completely. Even if he has no problem with alcohol, he is asked to give up drinking on nights (or afternoons) when he comes to group. The reason: Alcohol is a depressant. It tends to reduce anxieties and tensions. It can cause users to sustain a false bravado. Quite simply, alcohol defeats the prime objective of group therapy: getting people into better contact with their gut-level emotions.

### 2. *No drugs before or during groups.*

This taboo exists for the same reason as the anti-alcohol prohibition. Drugs can give users false highs and lows and defeat the purpose of the group-therapy process. This prohibition includes drugs which are "acceptable" in society—tranquillizers and diet pills, for instance.

### 3. *No cigarettes during group sessions.*

Cigarettes release tensions and anxieties. When faced with a difficult-to-show feeling, most smokers will light up to ease the tension. I believe it is better therapeutically to let the anxiety build up. It may help bring an individual to a more intense feeling.

### 4. *Group members must focus on showing feelings, not on relating facts or discussing history.*

Emotions, not history, are the medium we deal with. Reality problems are crucially important, but groups are not designed to provide social-service counsel. Whether or not to marry a specific girl, whether or not to take a new job, what to do about a pregnant sister, how to ask the boss for a raise, how to confront a business partner—these are reality situations which group leaders and group members simply are not best qualified to advise upon in the group process. All the facts are not known, and in all probability the group member has emotionally colored the facts he does present. We have learned, however, that the nature of reality problems is usually affected by the person's inability to feel entitled fully to his feelings, and his inability to utilize his full feelings. When those feelings are freed, often new avenues of awareness open up pointing to new choices about how best to deal with a current problem. After the feelings have been exposed and expressed, then there is time to discuss what the emotional experience means and how it may relate to his behavior and attitudes.

### 5. *Group members must be honest.*

Groups are not meant to be parties or social gatherings. Therapeutically, one of the ideas is to show disturbed persons how others are really reacting to them. True, this can be discomforting, hurtful, sometimes destructive. But where else can a person get such honesty? Where else can someone develop trust that people will believe what is being said about them? It is because so much of our social world is dishonest that we need the honest and sometimes painful directness of group therapy.

### 6. *No physical violence.*

This rule is necessary because group members are being both emotional and honest. People may be shouted at, ridiculed, insulted, in some cases accused of acts for which they feel unfairly challenged. Few civilized amenities are obeyed. Anger can become intense. Sometimes, punching and kicking seem only a few seconds away. The no-violence rule is not only for safety, but also for better therapy. It forces people to deal with their feelings, rather than let the feelings escape through released physical energy. We thus prevent might from making right.

These are the only rules imposed on group members. There are no rules which control what goes on among adults when they are *outside* of New Identity groups—although we do pressure people to drop their symptoms. A Don Juan can sit in groups, hear what unhappy women have to say, and then, with that inside information, pursue as many as he can seduce. There is one hitch: The women will talk in groups and finally confront him. The Don Juan will have to face the anger of the group. Somebody can come into group therapy with a massive load of anger, built up in his daily life outside group, and focus his anger on everyone in group. It won't be long, however, before group members catch up with him. He will find someone angrier at him than he knew possible, and the anger will hurt him and make him look at his own distorted anger. We want to promote freedom of action in our New Identity groups, but we want people to learn to take responsibility for their actions.

# Structure and Dynamic

My first group consisted of eight patients, two peer leaders with experience in encounter groups, and myself. These were basically encounter groups. We started with a "go-around," with each person reporting briefly on what had been happening to him and what he was feeling. Before long, someone would challenge someone else, and the encounter dynamic took over. From these groups, we learned about the therapeutic value of love, as well as anger. And we began to understand the role of the other three basic feelings, pain, fear, and pleasure.

Gradually, the size of groups expanded to about twelve to fifteen people, plus a leader. We found that effective interaction could still take place with that number. Within the two to three hours that a regular group ran, a significant number of people were able to work and most others were emotionally involved with those working. It was still the basic encounter approach, but we were also learning at that time the value of expressing feelings through exercises. If someone burst into tears in the face of an angry encounter, we wouldn't just discuss why or goad him to get angry back. Often, we asked him instead to show each of us what he was feeling. If it was fear, he would say the words "I'm afraid" to each person and concentrate on feeling the feeling "full measure," to its depths. If he was in pain, or felt isolated, we asked him to show his feeling with words such as "I hurt" or "I need." As these exercises led to deeper feelings, often other group members would identify with these feelings and start to express their own. From these beginnings grew the many different exercises described later, in Chapter 14. From these beginnings also grew our understanding of the therapeutic value of *screaming* out one's feelings.

Some of my groups today are even larger than those earlier groups. In marathons, I'll have up to twenty-five people in the group. With the scream techniques we have developed, we have found that having many people in a group does not necessarily hamper the process. Our techniques make it possible for several people to be working at once, with a few other members helping each person get out his feelings. The emotionality in such an atmosphere can actually speed up the process by leading more people to their feelings faster. Then we'll take periodic breaks to discuss what has been happening. Each person who has worked tries to see his experience in the light of certain behavior and attitudes. Other members contribute their insights as well.

At this stage, such a group is involved more in a teaching/learning discussion than an encounter. This is important in dealing with attitudes, which sometimes require great subtlety of insight to ferret out and confront. Often during attitudinal exploration we'll ask someone to do another exercise in order to grapple with a distorted feeling his attitude entails and to exercise healthy feelings in its stead. A man who has been a perfectionist his whole life might have this experience: First, during his workout on the mat, extreme anger and pain concerning his father, who was remote and demanding, without showing love. Then an intellectual understanding about how that feeling has made the patient see himself as incapable of doing anything right and unentitled to do anything wrong. Also, how the attitude/feeling has made him extremely critical of other people. Finally, an assertion of the feeling, "I can make mistakes. I can make mistakes and still be loved. Fuck you, Daddy, I'm lovable . . . for Me!" Such an experience works best in an atmosphere of love and concern. Encountering at this stage sometimes can be detrimental.

The encounter technique still has value in my groups, however. It can help open people up to their feelings (although our exercises often do as well). It provides important insight to the individual about how he actually presents himself to the world. It also is an effective tool for holding people to account about their behavior and getting them to be responsible to themselves and the group. For example, there was a pretty young brunette from a middle-class family who had come to me addicted to heroin. Katie was an A student at New York University, yet she had recently nearly died from hepatitis. Her childhood had been a sad one of rejection by both parents, beatings by a sadistic maid, excruciating embarrassment over an uncontrollable desire to walk around holding her genitalia. (Her mother had dragged her angrily to the doctor about this habit when Katie was about five. He made the little girl lie spread-eagled and naked on a table and told her that if she ever touched herself there again, she wouldn't be able to have babies.)

Katie grew up an isolated child, compulsive about good performance in school, estranged from her family. She had an early marriage which ended in divorce. By that time, she was hooked on heroin.

Like most addicts, Katie was an emotional infant. A month of groups taught her a bit how to express her anger. She also found refuge in the loving atmosphere of groups. Yet she still had a lot to learn. As she reports it:

"One day during my first month in groups, I was sitting in class at N.Y.U. feeling terribly anxious. I didn't know why I felt so unbearably anxious, but I did know that I wanted to get high very badly. Suddenly, in the middle of the class, I jumped up and walked out. I got into a cab and gave the office address. I couldn't wait to get there. I kept wanting to get out of the cab and run all the way up. When I finally got there I burst into the middle of a group. The tears started rolling down my cheeks. The group leader asked me what was going on. I started talking through my tears, saying how much I had wanted to get high and how I couldn't bear how I was feeling, so I had run out of my class and come up to group.

"When I finished my explanation, I really started weeping and sobbing. I was feeling pretty righteous about coming up there, so it came as quite a shock when I looked around the group and saw nothing but contempt and disgust on the faces around me. One guy angrily said, 'Where's your determination?' I just didn't understand. Whenever I had felt like I did then, I felt as though people had to be very careful and gentle with me. I had always believed if anyone even looked at me cross-eyed when I felt bad, I would just fall apart into a million pieces. I really would have liked to wear a sign saying FRAGILE, but I counted on my haunted eyes to give the message. What was wrong with these people? Why couldn't they see how dangerous this was? A cross word, a mean look, could kill me when I felt this way (which was most of the time). Why didn't they understand? And especially now, since I felt so righteous about having come to group instead of getting high.

"This attack was incomprehensible. The more they got angry, the weepier I got. Finally I decided they must all be insensitive and sick. When the group ended, I stayed for the next group. I told this new group of people my story. I felt so sorry for myself about the unfair treatment I had received, I began to whimper even harder. And again I got the same reaction. Disgust, contempt, and even boredom. No one wanted to be bothered. My worst nightmare was coming true. I was being attacked when I felt most helpless. And the group leader, who had always been so nice, was the meanest of them all.

"I sat through the whole two-hour group weeping quietly, feeling sorrier than ever for myself. Everyone ignored me. No one cared. And then that group was over. I had been there three hours and another group was coming in. I stayed and told the third group my sad story, and my God if the same thing didn't happen! The leader was even worse than ever—downright cruel.

"Suddenly I was on my feet screaming every filthy word I could think of at the damn bastards. I was in a rage. I screamed and screamed, and when I was finally through and looked around I saw smiling faces looking back at me. The group leader asked me how I felt. And I realized I felt strong and good about myself. I no longer felt weak and helpless. My worst fears had come true. I had been attacked—and I hadn't died. I had fought back, and I felt damn good. I felt like a woman.

I had really learned a lesson I've never forgotten. I'm not a cripple. I'm not damaged. And I can do anything I really want to do. That's a good thing to know."

It took Katie several weeks of groups before she began to feel the deep identity anger which could help her assert her needs as an adult, rather than an emotional child. Most patients when they first enter my practice attend at least three groups a week, then taper off to two times a week once they have gotten in touch with their basic feelings and are functioning better in their day-to-day lives. Whenever possible, I try to assign people to a more intensive number of groups to begin with—three times a day for a week or two. Usually, the process reaches them that much faster, and the depth of emotional experience gained in a concentrated immersion in groups for several days seems to have a more lasting effect than for some people who begin with only a few groups a week. Janov's initially intensive work with new patients would point to the same conclusion. In contrast to Janov, however, we start with the group process, not individual therapy.

# Projection and Transference

The interaction of encountering also gives us clues to people's problems. Group is not the real world, of course. It is a special, vouchsafed situation. But people inevitably reveal in group how they behave, feel, and think in the world outside of group. Group interaction and verbal feedback force a person to begin seeing himself as others see him.

Both projection and transference play an important role in groups. *Projection* is the psychological device of unconsciously spotting (and often attacking) traits in other people which we have in ourselves, without taking the personal responsibility for the feeling. I have seen many an emotional child scream at others in the groups for being "so helpless," when in reality the confronter feels and behaves helplessly in his own life. Verbal controllers will deride other verbal controllers, hysterics will point out hysteria in others instantly. Part of the value of having several people in a therapy session, rather than just patient and doctor, is the rapid stripping away of façades. Projection is a valuable part of this dynamic. It allows the group to see things about both the person being confronted and the person confronting.

The group member who is projecting may also learn how such projections affect his life outside the group. The incessant talker can see how his dislike of a fellow worker who talks a lot is really a defense of his own garrulousness, and he may then be able to get along better with that person. A mother who screams at her children for not admitting having done something wrong can see better that she has a terrible time herself acknowledging her own mistakes. Such an insight might come after she faces the intensity with which she has been challenging another group member about "always being so perfect."

Projection also can lead to a negative element in groups. That's the setting up of what we call "contracts." People with specific symptoms will often try to protect others with similar symptoms. They'll avoid confronting each other and come to the defense of each other when the group is bearing down. We try to expose such contracts rapidly, so that each person involved can see that what he is actually protecting is his own symptom.

In day-to-day existence, we all develop contracts with a wide range of people—bosses, secretaries, uncles and aunts, nieces and nephews, neighbors, golfing and tennis partners, and so on. A contract involves the tacit agreement *not* to criticize another person about specific areas, in return for the other person's not criticizing you in other areas. For example, a boss might never complain to his secretary about her consistent tardiness and prolonged lunches with personal friends. In turn, she might never complain about extracurricular and overtime projects he asks her to do. That's essentially a practical contract, concerning behavior. A contract can also extend into more subtle areas that are purely psychological. A dating couple might develop a relationship in which she plays the part of the little girl while he assumes the role of a competent and authoritative parent. This "contract" fulfills their respective emotional needs. The only problem is that in a real situation it might be destructive to both of them and not lead to a healthy, growing relationship. If they get married and have children, they could have real problems. The woman's "little girl" approach to life might make her an irresponsible mother and household manager. The husband's "superman" role is an impossible one to sustain, yet he would be unable to relax his image and share his fears and needs. There is bound to be dissatisfaction and conflict sooner or later.

In group therapy, such contracts usually develop as a tacit agreement not to criticize defenses which are similar to one's own. Not only is this not therapeutic for the people involved, but such contracts can be detrimental to the whole group dynamic. Imagine a group made up primarily of younger people, most of whom are resentful of authority. If a parent were to come into the group to confront his youngster, the chances are that he would face considerable hostility from all group members who have tacitly agreed to blast authority and not face their own irresponsibility. Or imagine a group where most members have learned to defer to authority, and the leader is someone who enjoys power. The contracts between authority and underlings could keep the dynamic fairly subdued and not produce real growth possibilities for the group member—or the leader!

With *transference*, someone unconsciously assigns to a group member the role of a significant person in his life. Typically, a strong man becomes someone's domineering father or competitive brother. A mature woman becomes one's mother—warm and loving, or overbearing, depending upon the past of the group member who makes the transference from his unconscious. A sexy woman who acts like a little girl may make a man extremely angry because she reminds him of an older sister who teased him provocatively when he was young.

Such transferences occur all the time in group. They also occur in real life. A young man who has difficulty standing up to his boss may be conferring on him the special "magic" he imputed to his father. The wife who pouts or becomes hysterical when her husband asks her to clean the house could really be acting out the way she did as a child when her mother kept after her to be neat.

Understanding transferences as they occur is important in our groups. We sometimes use the transference as a therapeutic device. The milquetoast who is afraid of his father and has transferred these feelings to an imposing male in the group will be encouraged to get angry at that man, for instance. But basically we try to expose the transference quickly, so that it can be understood, then grappled with behaviorally.

Unlike psychoanalysis and some other one-to-one therapy systems, our process does not nurture transference or probe it indefinitely. Take the shy girl whose mother was beautiful and who feels unpretty and unsexual in the presence of, say, a model in group. She does not just go on and on in our groups about how inferior she feels. We may ask her to express the pain of inadequacy or the fear of moving her body in a way that feels sexual. But the goal which we aim for as soon as possible is to have her express her own adult femininity—despite the presence of the model in the room. We'll have her assert "I am a woman and I'm lovable" to everyone in the room. Doing the exercise as well as taking in the group's affirmation and approval eventually will help teach her what it feels like to be a secure, sexual, adult woman. We focus on her healthy feelings for herself, not on the unhealthy feelings which permeate the transference.

# Multiple Groups

The inevitable occurrence of projection and transference has led me to set up groups so that most patients (especially new ones) go to different groups, rather than the same one each time, and are exposed to more than one group leader. That way we avoid some of the problems of contracts arising from projection and from people clearly becoming too comfortable with one another. We also minimize the dangers of transference—especially to group leaders, who inevitably are assigned special "magic" by group members by virtue of their roles as leaders.

I have residual blind spots, prejudices, and distortions, and so do my group leaders. By going into groups with different leaders, patients are exposed to different ways of operating, different distortions, differing intuitive capabilities about defenses. It is possible for an individual to fool one group leader (a constant danger in one-to-one psychotherapy), but it is almost impossible to deceive two or three *in groups* for very long.

In one group, for instance, Roland claimed to be impotent. He was not able to get an erection with the girl he was taking out, who was also a group member. The group—and the girl—gave him a lot of sympathy about his problem. He talked about times in the past when he *had* been able to engage in normal sex, and everyone felt sorry for him. He "worked" on his pain and his anger. Then, in another group, someone sensed some "mixed signals" as Roland talked. When confronted, Roland revealed that he had been having intercourse regularly with a cute young girl who appealed to him. The first group, which had given him sympathy, was furious, and so was the woman he had been dating, who promptly broke up with him. Unfortunately, Roland left groups after that confrontation. However, the point is that one group, meeting weekly, could have been taken in for many more months. But two groups, with two different leaders, could not be deceived as easily. There were different questions, different reactions, different kinds of probing.

When new people are introduced into a group, at least some will see through a manipulator's defenses and attack them. The continual change in attendance is discomforting to many, but therapeutic for virtually everybody. It is a cardinal principle of my group system. We try to put a few new people, now and then, into each group.

# Peer Group Leaders

Most of my group leaders (whom I also call "catalysts") have not been professionally trained in psychology or psychiatry. The lack of formal training can be an advantage. It permits my group leaders to become actively involved in group dynamics without fear of breaking a professional image. Catalysts must be able to scream in anger at a group member, lovingly touch and embrace other people, show fear, cry in pain, and even display distorted or inappropriate feelings they may feel. After all, group leaders are people—peers—not the God-like authority figures most psychiatrists and psychologists feel they have to be in front of a patient.

Significantly, the psychologists and psychiatrists whom I would choose to lead New Identity groups must undo the professional's ingrained emotional isolation to become an effective catalyst. Few professionals are open emotionally; their classical training reinforces their emotional closedness. But if they do not make themselves emotionally vulnerable, group members will not trust them.

As a professional, I do not do a number of things as well as some of my group leaders. One excellent catalyst, for example, was extremely effective at getting angry at group members. His ability to challenge certain group members with anger opened them up to their feelings much faster than I could have done. My professional training and image also interfere sometimes with my ability to touch and embrace the way I should and would like to. Some of my catalysts have been better at that, too.

All my group leaders were once group members in my practice. There, through their perception and empathy, they proved unusually helpful to others. They made things happen, demonstrated unusual insight, showed an ability to be honest with their feelings. Selecting a few, I offered them a special training program: a lecture course on the theory of my groups, a series of peer groups, a peer marathon. Following this, there were groups with catalysts and other prospective catalysts. Then, the person got a few opportunities to work as a "co-catalyst" with me or with another group leader. Finally, if all went well, he was ready to lead his first group, solo!

Being human, my group leaders make mistakes, just as I and other psychiatrists do. Nevertheless, they have three important attributes: the ability to show honest feelings fully; the ability to empathize truly with the emotions of others; and the capacity to be perceptive without too much personal distortion. All things considered, my group leaders are very good indeed at what they do.

I ask each group catalyst to write a monthly report on the progress of all members of his groups and I hold regular internal meetings with group leaders to keep track of each individual patient's progress in the group system. We discuss problem patients, treatment techniques, when a change of group leader might be helpful to a patient, and so forth. Sometimes, it seems apparent that a spouse should be in groups. In such a case, following our discussion, the group leader will confront the individual in group about why the husband or wife is not in therapy. (Frequently, an entire group will demand that someone ask a mate to "come to group." Remember: The path toward greater emotional health *starts* with actions.)

In addition, catalysts and I meet regularly in training groups. These sessions have many purposes. One is to maintain an emotionally advanced group which my group leaders and I can rely upon to work out our problems connected with leading groups. Second, I want to stay in continuing contact with the emotional development of my catalysts. Third, all of us build up feelings of anger, fear, pain, and love toward each other, and these feelings need expression and release.

# Special Groups

Our basic groups of about twelve to fifteen members include people of varying ages, from teenage to sixties or seventies. Most are in their twenties, thirties and forties. I try to compose groups in terms of the members' sophistication about group therapy—newcomers (with a few more experienced); middle; and advanced. Other than that distinction, groups are fairly eclectic.

During the past few years, I have experimented with new approaches and techniques. We are, for example, running special groups for younger teenagers (aged thirteen to fifteen), and the groups seem to be effective. However, we often put older teenagers (aged sixteen and over) into adult groups. We have learned in groups that teenagers often are limited in what they can teach one another. They can learn some things better from adults. Also, in passing from childhood to adulthood, teenagers are going through an identity crisis. Who are they? What resources do they have? What is expected of them as an adult? What does it feel like to be an adult? They have more chance of finding the answers by relating to adults in groups. By mixing up groups, we also destroy the pecking order that tends to develop in any fixed group. Such hierarchies are especially prevalent in teenage groups, where peer opinion is so vital.

The teenagers who join adult groups are a refreshing and therapeutic influence. Their honesty and insight embarrass many grown-ups and prod others into working. And the teenagers benefit from learning firsthand that adults do not have all the answers but that they do have *some*. The mixed groups help the youngsters a great deal more, in my judgment, than the pure teenage groups had done. For younger children, we have some groups divided by age—six to eight, eight to ten, ten to twelve. We modify the process because of their age, but they do learn to get to their honest feelings, accept what feels like a forbidden feeling as just another feeling, take in love in better ways.

Occasionally, as the need arises, there are groups that focus on specific symptoms—homosexuality, for example. Currently, I am running a group for fat people. The results have been excellent, with significant weight loss on the part of a number of patients. One key to this kind of group is that transference is readily established through symptom identification. The group gets down to serious work very rapidly.

We also run special married couples groups. At least one member of each couple is required to go to other groups, too, and we try to see that both members go to other groups in which their spouse is not a member. In the married couples groups, people gain some insights into their marriages by getting involved in the dynamics of other marriages. Sometimes, too, the safe atmosphere of the group allows people to confront each other in ways they would not have dared at home.

There are some special problems with these groups. First, there is a danger that they can become a kind of social club. Couples will get together for parties and dinner regularly with each other, develop strong friendships, and too often set up contracts which are not therapeutic. Second, the infamous battle of the sexes becomes evident. Men tend to side with men, women with women, in defensive patterns which have more to do with gender than with individual health. The therapists and group members must be especially alert to these problems in order to make the groups effective. When I see these tendencies develop, I reconstitute the group.

As another experiment, on some occasions we have used videotape in groups, so that group members can benefit from instant playbacks. Although people are initially self-conscious about the camera, they forget it is there once the dynamic takes over. I have used the equipment occasionally, but don't use it for treatment purposes at this time. I believe that the insights people

gain from seeing themselves immediately on tape can have therapeutic value; but the time spent with a group leader in reviewing
a videotape can better be spent in learning and doing more in
additional groups. Nevertheless, videotape is an excellent means
for training group leaders, demonstrating my process, and
teaching in a way which saves time for me and other teachers.

# Marathons

After a person has been in groups for a few weeks, we usually
suggest a marathon. Sometimes a marathon is advisable after
only a week or two of group therapy; sometimes, it is not
recommended for six weeks. There is no definite schedule. It
depends upon the individual.

Marathons originally lasted thirty hours, generally from a
Friday evening until a Sunday morning, with an interlude of
four or five hours on Saturday afternoon for sleep. The objective
of a marathon was to break down emotional and attitudinal
defenses in order to help a person get at long-buried, deeper
emotions.

From the beginning, marathons were extraordinarily effective.
They established a new sense of bonded love among participants.
Through insights gained in marathons, I also was able to develop
much of the early theory and techniques utilized in my groups. It
was as though I had a new instrument, a microscope of human
needs and feelings in which I was able to see things I had never
witnessed before.

It is difficult to find words to adequately describe those first
marathons. Some were better than others. Most had this in
common: the essential feeling, at the end, was one of openness,
kinship, love. There was a new awareness of others, a new
identity of Self. People felt bonded, the way members of a
healthy family feel toward each other. Marathon participants
would hug each other lovingly. Their faces were full of life,
despite the tiredness. They were "high" on the sense of life and
kinship which they all felt.

Marathons could be very dramatic, too. Often people would
have significant breakthroughs to feelings and specific memories
which they had completely blocked out up to that time. One

woman, in her early forties, had had an extraordinarily unhappy life. Her alcoholic mother had "raised her by the book," and a cruel book it was—beatings with a shrub branch twice a day, banishment to a locked closet when she wet her bed. Sue's relationship with her father was a seductive one. He would hold her in his lap, stroking her legs and thighs. When she was a teenager, he rubbed her legs every night to relieve the cramps she got from hormones taken to stem an effusive menstrual cycle (often six weeks of bleeding without stopping). The massages soon led to her genitals and breasts, and although Sue knew that her father's ministrations were sexual, she found them too enjoyable to stop. She had a vague memory of her mother always waiting impatiently in the next room while her father was stroking her.

When Sue grew up, she married a man who forced her into sexual situations with him and other women simultaneously. They had two children. Sue began to drink heavily, and finally she divorced him. Sue married another man in 1965, then came to see me a couple of years later, as her current marriage began to flounder, too.

Through groups, Sue was able to express some of the feelings she had had about her mother, whom she remembered as always taunting her and laughing at her. But she had trouble getting at feelings about her father. By that time, she had become involved in an extramarital liaison with a sensitive, loving man who was struggling with severe sexual problems, including a long history of homosexuality. Sue went into her third marathon, knowing she ought to break up this relationship, but she was reluctant to do so. Robert was a kind of knight-in-shining-armor to her, despite their sexual problems. Sue described the marathon this way:

"I was very scared. Somehow I knew beforehand that it would mean the break-up between me and Robert. It was not only that I knew the coleaders were against our *liaison*—I could fight that for my love if I had to. It was more a fear of what was to come out in the marathon, of my own feelings. In any event, Robert and I went into the marathon. I was interacting with others, but not being 'on' with my own feelings until about 6 A.M.

"Then I went to the bathroom. I was wearing a pink sweater

and slacks. I sat on the toilet and looked down at myself, nude from the waist down. I was very tired. All my defenses were broken down, gone. Suddenly, I remembered sitting on a toilet, wearing a pink pajama top, and Daddy standing over the sink, running water over his bloody penis. Mama was leaning against the door jamb, laughing hysterically or drunkenly.

"Somehow I managed to leave the bathroom in Dan's office and get back to the marathon room. Inside I was screaming. Outside I was trembling. I interrupted whatever was going on and spilled out the story of the night my Daddy came home drunk and raped me. I had had no memory of the incident until that marathon. Every minute detail came back, crystal clear. The nights I had gone to bed wearing only my P.J. top, hoping he would come in to 'rub my legs' again. Then finally he came. But this time it wasn't the caressing, fondling 'love' of before. He pulled the covers down and got on top of me. He pried my legs apart and all I felt was the searing burning excruciating pain in my vagina. He put his hand over my mouth when I started to scream, and then he put a pillow over my face and pushed his fist into it so that I gagged. I began to vomit. I fainted. The next thing I knew was I was being dragged to the bathroom and was dumped on the toilet seat. I saw him washing the blood, and I thought he was seriously hurt. I was angry with Mama for laughing at him when he was hurt. I tried to get up but I was bleeding. I asked Mama to get me a Kotex—I said, 'I think my period has started.' She got me a belt and a napkin. I put them on. She was in my room pulling the sheets off the bed. They were bloody. I didn't understand. I thought my period had started and I had messed up the sheets. My vagina was on fire. I lay down on the bare mattress and cried myself to sleep. About a month later, Daddy took me to a doctor, an aged and reputable man in medical circles. We went on a Sunday. This doctor did all kinds of tests on me, and the following week I went into the city's best hospital for a D&C.

"During that marathon I experienced all the horror of the rape, its aftermath, and the abortion. I screamed—I could feel Daddy's hand on my mouth, the pillow smothering me. I could smell his drunken breath and feel his scratchy beard. I could feel his penis ripping me apart. I relived the entire episode in that marathon room. All the while, people were with me. There was Dorothy and Penny and Robert and the coleaders. Robert kept telling me to get it all out. All the horror, all the shit. It was as if I was vomiting out my soul. I had started sitting in a chair. I ended up on the floor wretching and screaming.

"Finally, it was done. I felt ugly, filthy, despicable, loathsome. I could not look at anyone in the room. From far away came the voices of the group leaders. They were telling me 'You were only thirteen, Sue . . . just a child. There was nothing wrong with your wanting his love in the only way you knew how to get it—seductively.' They kept saying that over and over. They kept telling me to look at the people in the room. Finally I did look. I saw compassion and love. They kept on and on and on. I just wanted to crawl into a hole and die. But they kept on, telling me to get up and into my chair. Finally I said, 'I never told anyone that before, not even myself.' Then one of the leaders kept talking to me in his basso voice—gently, tenderly. He kept saying that it was a criminal thing that they had done to me and that I must admit that and then fight it. I said, 'I know, but I am so tired.' I truly felt exhausted. Some of the guilt and humiliation had left but I felt wrung out. He kept insisting, 'Sue, you must do it *now*. *Now* while the whole thing is fresh in your memory.' I protested weakly. Then the other leader came in and said, 'Sue, would you fuck your son?' I flew up at that. '*No! Never!*' 'But don't you feel sexually attracted to him?' 'Yes, of course.' Then: 'Why can't you get angry at your Daddy for doing that to you?'

"They pushed and prodded me until finally I stood up and got ANGRY with every portion of my body and emotions. It was GLORIOUS total ANGER.

"It was very clear to me then that all my pathological behavior was an outgrowth of the 'contract' between me and Daddy.

"After the marathon, I wanted *sex*. I felt my whole body tingling with desire and anticipation. Robert was not there for me. He understood my rejuvenation, but he simply could not cope with my open desire for a man's love. We broke up. It was terrible. I wanted to hang on to the shining white knight, but I wanted more. I wanted the knight to desire me as a woman. This one could not. And so he left. I sat in his lap and cried like a six-year-old who just found out about Santa Claus. He held me and understood, but he could not be someone other than himself.

"Then I began to date other men. Among them, Steven (her estranged husband) who had been through three marathons, many groups, and was quite different. He was open, warm, loving—he even cried *in public* on our first date.

"After several months we were reconciled. Now I am able to show Steven all my feelings and the kids are also in groups. We're beginning to become a family."

Not all breakthroughs are so dramatic. (Thankfully, most people's histories are not so tragic, although the frequency of incest in our culture, as I have seen with my patients, might surprise many people.) For Sue, it took three marathons interspersed with many groups to exorcise that dreadful secret which had affected her life so deeply. And it took many groups after that, plus hard work with her husband and children, for her to strengthen her healthy feelings and begin to live a life of some pleasure and happiness.

I don't know whether Sue would have gotten to that frightening memory faster through our newer scream techniques. I have discovered, however, that these techniques generally make a lengthy marathon unnecessary. Before we had developed those techniques, the prime value of the thirty-hour marathons was that there was so much time. A great deal of emotion churned up. Extended fatigue broke down defenses. The intoxicating spirit of love and bondedness encouraged people to reach for new insights.

With scream techniques, we don't need all that time. Now a marathon can have as many as twenty-five people in it. Although it doesn't last much more than sixteen hours, everybody will work. The main reason is that we have switched the responsibility for action from the group to the individual. In longer marathons, we would sometimes spend two hours on one person with hardened defenses, prodding him, cajoling him, urging him to work. Today, I tell people in marathons (and in all groups) that it is *their* responsibility to work for themselves. That's why so often there will be several people on the mats at once. That way, everyone has a chance to get to his deepest feelings, and most do. When a group member takes the personal responsibility of pushing himself over the threshhold into new feelings, the experience has more value to him. Too often, in earlier marathons, people would later deny their experience, saying the group had "pushed them into it," or they were "just tired."

Running marathons this way has lost some of the giddy joy we felt after thirty-hour sessions. Many people had never experienced that kind of bondedness before, and a taste of it certainly gave them something to reach for again. Actually, our current marathons haven't really lost that feeling of bondedness. Instead, they have cut into the intoxication which, I found, was often misleading. People would come into group after a marathon hopelessly depressed, because all the good feelings had disappeared. They felt robbed and distrustful of the whole process. The truth is, no one can maintain such joy continually. No one should expect such a "high" out in the real world all the time. These people had expected the good feelings to remain magically. The reality is that life is full of ups and downs. What one needs is a mature sense of self as a person capable of maximum choice about feelings, attitudes, and behavior within the realistic framework of the day-to-day world. To gain that sense of self requires the kind of hard work which our current techniques demand.

We do bolster the marathon experience by what we call "post-marathon groups." People entering a marathon make a commitment to meet one night a week for twelve weeks following the marathon. In those twelve post-marathon meetings, the people who have come to know each other so well usually become even closer. The bonding is strengthened. Also, insights gained through the scream experiences are examined and reinforced. Some people fail to meet their commitment to come to post-marathon groups. Almost always, these are people who, through criticism and the anger of others, have had a "bad marathon." There are some marathoners who cannot come on a particular night because of prior commitments. After a few weeks, we replace these people with others of comparable emotional maturity. The dual purpose is to keep up the intensity of the group and to disrupt special "contracts" which may have developed.

# Being Responsible to One's Feelings

We have learned in the format of more recent marathons that an experience is best embraced and learned from if the individual takes responsibility for working on his own feelings from the start. Such responsibility takes several basic forms in the over-all group dynamic.

First, one assumes responsibility for his feelings by working to show whatever he is feeling with honesty and intensity no matter how "bad" the feeling may seem. That way, he can begin to understand the hidden feelings which have been affecting his life. If he can fully accept that he has those feelings, he can learn to recognize how they affect his behavior. When a phobic neurotic who cannot ride subways experiences and accepts the anger he has felt toward his father, he may see how that anger has been translated into his particular phobia. The insight will help him overcome his fear each time he nears a subway.

Second, by accepting responsibility for his deep feelings, a person also gains the strength of his own identity. He is a human being entitled to his feelings, no matter what they are. Someone cannot control what he feels, nor should he be punished for what he feels. What counts is how he deals with these feelings—what actions he takes as a responsible adult living in a world which must have some rules, with other people who have needs, too.

Third, an individual must be responsible to his feelings about others in the group. He must not sit on the sidelines to avoid letting people know what he feels or sees about them. He must become part of the dynamic through the interaction of confrontation and the loving concern of helping others get to their feelings. When a newcomer has trouble expressing his own feelings, we tell him to get involved with other people. In the process, inevitably his own feelings will emerge.

A fourth responsibility a group member must assume is that he must work hard with his feelings. There are many occasions of dramatic breakthroughs in our groups, when someone has an epiphany of understanding as a result of an exercise of a feeling or feelings. However, he must continue to work with his feelings. Often he will have to do the same exercise again and again over many weeks or months before he is freed from a distorted feeling. He must also practice his new-found, healthy feelings. For instance, he must assert his anger or need for love many times before he has easy access to them. With that reinforced access, he will gain the free choice of when and where to express the feeling with adult insight and responsibility, rather than distorted attitudes.

It's not easy for a new group member to understand what these responsibilities are. (Many old hands at group forget them when the going gets rough.) But as someone is exposed to the process and learns to see himself and others in new ways, the responsibility becomes clearer and easier to maintain. One important aid is the growing realization about how the *signals* of what one is feeling can be in contradiction with what one *says* or *thinks* he is feeling. Getting signals in alignment with symbols (words) is a critical component of our group dynamic.

# CHAPTER 13

# Signals: The Foundation of the Group Therapy Process

WHETHER WE ARE CONSCIOUS OF IT OR NOT, all of us are conditioned to be sensitive to the human reactions of the people around us. We know, for example, what an angry expression looks like. We perceive the face of fear. We learn to see when another's concern is real and when it is phony. We recognize what pain looks like. Some expressions go beyond the bounds of our particular culture; we might recognize them in almost all human beings. But some human reactions would not be identified except within our own familiar world.

Through observation, we begin to know when signals confirm the truth of what somebody is saying and when signals fail to agree with words. If a coquettish girl, teased by her dates, says, "Stop it, you're making me angry," and *grins* as she says it, the boy is unlikely to stop. ("Stop it—I love it," is a bemused commentary on the female role in dating.) Imagine the same girl annoyed because the boy has walked another girl home from school. How would identical words sound? Chances are, the boy would stop teasing immediately. Her tone and manner would tell him something was really wrong.

And we understand human sounds which express strong emotions. When somebody in one of my groups starts to scream out intense anger, the meaning is unmistakable. A scream of pain is very different, and communicates a totally different emotion to group members.

My guess is that 60 to 70 per cent of face-to-face communication between people takes place—not through words—but through gestures, intonations, mannerisms, and other "signals" which indicate what we are feeling. (Dr. Ray Birdwhistle, expert on what he calls human "kinesics," cites comparable figures in his works.) An anxious cough, a nervous twitching of the knee, snapping of fingers, an emphasis on certain words, drooping eyelids, pulled-together eyebrows, quickened breath, a yawn, a swallow—all are signals communicating attitudes and inner feelings. Such signals can be camouflaged so as to be hard to see. But even a skilled actor has difficulty disguising *all* his true feelings.

In civilized society, adults are forced to concentrate increasingly on words. Parents, older brothers and sisters, teachers, bosses— all criticize us when we fail to comprehend ideas and remember facts. A child is told to go to Mother's sewing machine and bring back a sewing needle and the *black* spool and thread. If the child forgets the needle or brings back the *gray* thread, he is in trouble. A teacher tells the class to write a two hundred-word essay. If your essay is only a hundred words long, you are in for a low mark and, possibly, a bawling out, as well. As time goes on, many of us act as though most human contact takes place through symboling, the uniquely human ability to make one thing arbitrarily stand for another—i.e., words stand for things. But even as we understand the content of words, we are also tuning in on the accompanying signals—what Julius Fast has called "body language." As products of a complex society, we tend to relegate many signals to our unconscious levels of awareness. We work hard to comply with civilization's rules, even though a part of us is continually alert to the significance of human signals. We sense socially inappropriate signals in others, then try to ignore the signals. We see and hear signals which show hostility, but try to pretend the signals don't exist.

In truth, civilized man is involved in an elaborate social game. The prime rule is to ignore awkward, inappropriate, or hurtful signals. Enmeshed in such a game, civilized adults become increasingly less sensitive to signals. Many people act as though communication with other adults is effected only through words.

This is not the case. Despite the social rules we attempt to obey, all of us rely enormously upon signals to understand what is going on. Despite society's attempts to muffle feelings which create awkward or discomforting situations, each of us is aware of the significance of signals. We know that nobody can control his feelings with the facility with which he can manipulate words. As we talk, most of us signal our feelings. (Often, we signal emotions we are not consciously aware that we have.) This fact is the working foundation of my group process. Among others, Frederick S. Perls seemed to agree about the importance of signals in his groups. During a series of lectures delivered at Esalen from 1966 to 1968 Perls gave group members this advice: "So don't listen to the words, just listen to what the voice tells you, what the image tells you. If you have ears, then you know all about the other person. You don't have to listen to *what* the other person says: listen to the sound: listen to the sounds. *Per sona*—'through sound.' The sounds tell you everything. Everything a person wants to express is all there—not in words."

Emotional signals may be fuzzy or clear. Signals of important feelings frequently sputter faintly behind a barrage of words or a series of practiced gestures. Defenses developed over a thirty-five-year lifetime are, after all, designed to cover up deep-level emotions. Even so, when signals fail to align with words, we trust signals—*most* of the time, at any rate. And why not? Throughout most of hominid's time on earth, survival has depended upon quick and accurate reaction to the signals of others. An armed man from a nearby tribe might articulate peaceful words while his objective was to steal food or women from your camp. A stranger you encountered on the road might ask for a drink of water while positioning himself to steal the fish you were carrying. If your welfare depended upon discerning the difference, you would watch every gesture and movement with extreme care. You would study the man's eyes, listen to his tone of voice. In a literal sense, noncivilized man's survival depended upon accurate comprehension of signals. Signals are what communicate most strongly and most immediately to us. When signals failed to jibe with another person's symbols, noncivilized man's adrenal system told him: "Something is wrong."

The effectiveness of my groups depends upon the same kind of perception. It is not something group members discuss. Rather, it is something which even new members rapidly take for granted. After participating in only a couple of sessions, new patients will tell another group member things like: "You're really angry. Why don't you admit it?" The basis of the challenge: Angry signals emanate from the person, despite an attempt to talk in a modulated, reasonable manner. Continually, you will hear people make statements like these: "If you're angry, *get angry!*" "Are you afraid?" "What he said hurt you, didn't it?" "You're feeling a lot of pain." Each means, "You're signaling a particular feeling, no matter what you are saying. Why don't you relate to the *feeling?*"

Vocal signals play a pivotal part in our groups. Many signals are onomatopoetic, a human attempt to imitate the sound of a feeling, at a preverbal stage. We all recognize the meaning of sobs, of gasps, of screams and growls, sometimes in subtle variations. (We even comprehend the meaning of the sounds in animals. I shall never forget the death wail of a dog who had been hit by a car!) Such sounds pour forth freely in exercises going on in my practice today. We did not start out that way; these preverbal screams emerged as our groups developed. At first, we did not ask people to "make the noises" of their feelings; we told them instead to say in words what the feelings were. But noises burst out anyway, and group members identified the noises immediately.

Many of our exercises evolved like this: First, we tried a description of a feeling in simple words, such as, "I am angry at my mother because she always laughed at me." Later, a simpler verbalization: "I am angry." Then, nonverbal feelings, screams of rage or fear which echo sounds of the earliest days of man and the infant years of our lives. Depending upon the group and the individual, each of these approaches has great value in our exercises today.

All our exercises have to do with the five basic emotions—love, anger, fear, pain, and pleasure. Specific exercises deal with specific emotions, but often one feeling will reveal another, and then another. Thus what starts out to be an anger exercise may go through layers of fear and pain, become anger once again, and end up as a joyful, loving feeling.

When the emotions resonate truly, the person's signals and words are in harmony. He is an emotionally open person, at least during that exercise, and he is learning to have access to such resonance at his choice for the rest of his life.

In my group, we try to keep verbalization to a minimum. Most groups begin with a "go-around"—which is a verbal report on what has happened since the last group meeting, and on how each individual is feeling at the moment. But even during the go-around, a group leader will not let anyone report endlessly about facts. Pointed questions from the group leader or from other group members will cause the person to reveal emotional reactions. "How did you *feel* about that?" "How do you feel about the people in this room?" "Who do you dislike most in this room?" "How many times have you been told you're a creep?" "You're boring me." "Is there anyone in the room you trust?" "When he told you you're boring, didn't that make you angry?"

Groups at the Casriel Institute are more interested in immediate dynamics than in someone's history. Here is an example that is typical of at least one hundred new patients a year. A woman comes to me because she feels a great deal of emotional discomfort. Her marriage is bad; the fights she and her husband have been having for years are exhausting and painful and never seem to resolve anything. She feels rejected by her children. Life is "boring" and "without meaning." Now something has happened which, to her, indicates the end of everything is at hand. Perhaps she has discovered her husband is having an affair. A child might be seriously ill. Perhaps her husband is going to be fired, and she anticipates severe money problems. In other cases, a sister or parent may be dying, or she may be so much overweight that none of her summer clothes fit anymore.

Invariably, when the woman first comes to groups, she will attempt to tell about her history, concentrating on historic emotions rather than on here-and-now emotions. Groups can help this woman learn to express her fear and pain. Behind the fear and pain, there will be intense anger, which groups can help her learn to express, and also warm loving feelings, which she can be reprogrammed to show.

New Identity therapy can help this woman abandon controls which isolate her from her family and others. Group therapy can help her change the way she behaves toward others. The process will not work if she is allowed to discuss historic anger and pain, for by blaming her parents she remains an emotional child. In my groups, such an individual will generally be confronted in the first few sessions. She will not be allowed to ramble or just *tell* what her parents did to her. Nor will she be permitted to be charming or pleasant. At the very least, the individual will be forced to talk about her feelings. Then if the words and signals fail to align, she will be confronted about it. Being honest about your feelings, and letting your signals align with your emotions, is difficult. It bewilders a lot of people when they first come into group. Some have defended themselves all their lives with words. They feel relatively comfortable as long as they are allowed to verbalize while hiding the feelings behind the words. Other people can show feelings to some extent, but the expression is exaggerated and defensive. These individuals are bewildered when the group confronts them about the signals they have been hiding and accuses them of being emotionally dishonest.

The fact is, most of us have been conditioned *not* to talk about deeply-felt emotions. We have learned to relate to the words and surface signals. Our strongest and most vulnerable emotions seem to get us in trouble. So we try to control our most important feelings while learning society's game of camouflage.

Part of the learning process is to understand the difference between what people say and what they do. "Be honest," a father tells us as he cheats on his expense account. "Nice girls don't get angry," chides a mother full of controlled rage. "Be polite," says a teacher who constantly interrupts. "Consider others." "Turn the other cheek," "Love your little brother" (when he has just smashed your toys). "A job worth doing is worth doing well."

But a child *sees!* Not yet dependent upon words, he observes and understands adults' signals. Aware of discrepancy between words and signals, he relies mostly on signals. Since the adult world operates importantly in terms of symbols, the child learns to maintain a "double standard." This way, one half of the discrepancy no longer rides in his conscious awareness, and the confusion is a bit dissipated. By the same process, one day at a time, he learns to repress a lot of his own spontaneous signals.

The result? A world where "counter-signaling" constantly goes on. People *say* one thing in words—show it in a mannered way—and we know instantaneously (though not always consciously) that something else is meant. Counter-signaling pervades our lives in thousands of ways. Consider a few, and you will see how disturbing it can be to keep your words and signals in alignment. We complain about hypocrisy at a cocktail party, for instance, yet greet someone we intensely dislike with a cordial smile. Or we denounce a "yes man," yet agree too readily with our own boss. We often insist upon counter-signaling for reasons other than social appropriateness: We hasten to reassure a man who faces his wife's almost certain death from cancer. We tell him, "There's a good chance the operation will be successful"; yet we know his wife is mortally ill. Our signals tell him we know; we just do not want to be reminded of the feeling.

Counter-signaling is also evident on a national scale. It is the target of much of youth's outcry against the establishment. Young people see that moralizing about democracy and equality, urban renewal and black integration, cannot disguise the injustice, corruption, bigotry, and pollution which exist in our society.

Yet counter-signaling is not totally bad. This makes its prevalence even more confusing and poses a special problem for new group members who are trying to learn the discipline of emotional directness. Counter-signaling often enriches conversation, makes plays on words effective, emphasizes perceptions and insights in a subtly human way. Humor is full of counter-signals: Describing a two-hundred-pound woman as a "real beaut" obviously does not mean she would win a beauty contest. Sarcasm involves a kind of counter-signaling: people state one thing while, by vocal inflection and perhaps a raised eyebrow, they signal the opposite. Even literature often deals with something akin to counter-signaling. Much of Western thought has irony as its foundation. One thing seems to be happening, with predictable results; yet something hidden is actually going on, with results taking an unforeseen turn. Think of Socrates' use of irony;

Kafka's nightmare world; the fall of tragic heroes who were supposedly invincible.

On a practical level, everyone in this culture practices counter-signaling some of the time. A realistic sense of survival leads us to say and do appropriate things while we hide what we truly think and feel. And civilized control obviously has its merits. No one can walk down the street striking people just because he is angry. Or tell off his boss because he is annoyed by something the boss said. Judgment and control in such situations are not difficult for most people. What is difficult is to have true choice in our day-to-day lives about when to show feelings, when to match signals to words, or when to withhold overt expression of the feelings.

In my groups, we try to help people develop the ability to choose. Through a group dynamic of therapeutic exercises, we practice the discipline of matching what one says with what one feels. I do not mean that we teach people to develop mannered signals or appropriate words to show what they are feeling. They must learn, instead, to express their true feelings. Then the words and signals emerge naturally, directly, and clearly aligned with the feeling. Our discipline also conditions group members to select for significant relationships people who can be equally honest emotionally.

It is not an easy process. Learning emotional honesty often requires doing things which are socially distasteful, such as telling someone in the group that you disliked him on sight, even though you had no justifiable reason for doing so. It means giving up self-images. It can mean dropping a practiced charm or pleasant façade. It can mean admitting that you get angry when you do nice things for other people. Being emotionally honest can mean showing fear openly, even though you were conditioned to believe it is unmanly to be afraid. It may mean *not* acting like a gentleman or a lady.

New Identity therapy requires painful self-examination, discomforting frankness, chance-taking, and continuing practice of the discipline of being honest. Our exercises are designed to open people up to their feelings. Our exercises also provide a way for people to *practice* expressing their feelings, so that the emotions become increasingly easier to experience and show.

At the start, most people are understandably afraid to become involved in such a discipline. Most will avoid being emotionally honest, at least about some things; and, of course, many newcomers genuinely don't know how to be emotionally honest. Consequently, the human ability to tune in on signals plays an immensely vital role in our group dynamic. For one thing, by watching to see how someone's signals match—or do not match—his words, we know whether people are acting behaviorally as they should outside of group. Signals make it difficult for a group member to lie for very long. No matter how guarded, no matter how clever, he cannot long hide his signals from a number of alert and concerned people. One person, or two, or three may be so programmed that they do not catch his particular countersignals. But when ten or twelve others are in the room, several are bound to pick up signals which do not match the words.

Sometimes the discrepancy is obvious. A nervous look, for example, when an alcoholic claims he has not had a drink. A milquetoast whimper of "I'm angry" which will not convince anyone. A rigid embrace coupled with the words, "I love you." None of these signals necessarily indicates a lie. They may be feelings other than the fear of being caught in a lie or of taking full responsibility for what one feels. But it is up to the group and the individual to catch and explore such signals and find out what the signals are about.

Sometimes the gap between words and signals is remarkably subtle. I have seen people roaring and stomping about the room angrily, or sobbing loudly, without convincing group members of their sincerity. Something *felt* wrong, although those same signals may have seemed perfectly valid when another group member got angry or showed pain. For the first person, the anger or pain was not hooked up; for the second, it was. The group can usually tell the difference. Sometimes a group's sense of the truth is uncanny. Once in a while there is a "group dump," with everyone taking off on someone for distorted reasons. But I generally trust the occasions when most people in the group challenge what a member says. When I personally believe someone and am feeling for him, and if others express doubts, I am professionally respectful. They have been right too often—right because they have learned to hook up to their belly feelings and

be open to the subtlest variations of human signs. Also, I know
that my own childhood programming still makes me insensitive
to or distorts certain signals.

For instance, I once saw a charming man, Ted, whose symptom had been homosexuality, successfully lie to his group for two
sessions. Having abandoned his symptom, he had been directed
by the group to start dating females. For several weeks he had
failed to comply with the group's directive, providing excuses
about "how difficult it was to meet a woman." Finally, Ted
entered the group and said: "Well, it happened." "What happened?" three or four people in the group asked at once. "She
moved in. Now I can't get her to move out." "Who is she?" "Tell
us about her?" "Where did you meet her?"

Ted proceeded to recount an anecdote with the skill of a
professional humorist. (He had been an actor for his first years
after college. And he used humor and wit as well-honed tools of
defense.) He had met a fat woman at a party. ("Two hundred
and forty pounds of elephant—and she's mine, all mine.") He
had brought her home. She had been the sexual aggressor. They
had had intercourse, and she (as well as Ted) had had an orgasm.
Now she loved him and had moved into Ted's bachelor pad,
with "two suitcases of Lane Bryant clothes and her overweight
hair dryer."

As Ted told the story, one man was rolling on the floor,
holding his belly with hysterical shrieks of laughter. Everybody
was roaring uncontrollably. Some people were crying as they
laughed.

Ted continued the story the following week, recounting details
of their sex life and emphasizing his embarrassment at how the
woman looked. The group was fooled again.

The third week, as he started to talk, one man quietly said,
"Cut the crap, Ted. There's no woman in your apartment." Ted
admitted the hoax, tears of pain clouding his eyes. He had
invented the fat woman, he said, to avoid another confrontation
with the group.

Several group members shouted at Ted about his manipulation, but most just told him they were hurt. Once again, they
said, "Start dating a girl." In a week or so after the discovery of
his hoax, Ted did begin dating a girl, then had an affair with

her. It lasted for a few weeks, but when it broke up, Ted left group. He complained that the group pressure to comply with its rules and demands was "dehumanizing." I understand that he is living a homosexual life, but that he isn't much happier than he was when I first saw him. Clearly, however, we failed to reach Ted successfully in our groups.

The group's grasp of signals is not just a check on lying. Often group insights help suggest ways these people can connect up more deeply to their feelings. When other group members sense a misconnection between signals and words, they may make suggestions on how to jump the gap: Try a different emphasis on words. Don't clench your belly that way. Or try different words: maybe the feeling is not anger at all; maybe it is pain or fear. Time and again in our groups I have seen that a conscious effort to change a signal—even as deliberate a signal as putting one's hands on one's hips to show determination while trying to get angry—can lead a person directly to a feeling. Signals and feelings are intimately tied to each other! Sometimes group members come up with highly creative suggestions about how to reveal the connection.

In a crucial sense, signals are the foundation upon which the effectiveness of my group process is built. Without signals, group members would not have a reliable way to "read" the words of others.

My process is a humanizing one—it reconditions over-civilized people to be *less dependent* upon word content, and *more aware* of the emotions and attitudes lying behind the words. All of our group exercises point toward that goal.

CHAPTER 14 | *The Process:*
*Exercises*

ALL OUR GROUP EXERCISES deal with the five basic feelings: fear, anger, pain, love, and pleasure.

When I refer to exercises, I do not mean physical rituals in the manner of calisthenics. Some exercises do require specific physical postures—leaning back in the chair, clinging to another group member, lying on the mat, pounding a pillow, perhaps shaking a fist. But these postures and gestures are to facilitate or accentuate the emotional experience. The essence of the exercise is primarily vocal expression through words or screams. We have discovered that there are patterns of emotional experiences which can be reproduced through the repetition of words and sounds. In that sense only are we performing exercises.

To make these exercises easily understandable in the discussion which follows, I have categorized them according to the basic feelings. This does not mean that an anger exercise will always be an anger exercise, or an expression of fear remain an expression of fear. For one thing, a person often does not know exactly what he is feeling to begin with. He may think he is angry, then find that his assertion, "I'm angry," rapidly turns into pain or fear. That pain or fear could be his programmed reaction to expressing anger. Or it could be what he was really feeling all along. It

253

may require some exploring and hard work by the individual—and group members, as they read his signals—to discover what he is really feeling. If there is ambiguity, we'll often ask him to drop the words and just scream out the feeling. Frequently, the nature of the scream will tell him and the group a lot more than the words.

Secondly, one feeling often turns into another as the individual delves more deeply into his belly. Time and again, we have seen that gut-level feelings reveal themselves in "layers." A person expressing intense fear for the first time since infancy may find a "layer" of deep anger under the fear, then additional fear under the anger, followed by a "layer" of terrible pain, some even more intense anger under the pain, and, finally, a joyful, loving feeling. All these feelings can be triggered by a single exercise. It happens quite spontaneously. Sometimes there will be words, which change as the individual intuitively realizes he is in a different emotional place from where he started. "I'm scared" can become "I'm angry" and then, "I hurt." Usually, as the experience intensifies, the words change to sounds—the shriek of fear, a raging growl of anger, the wail or whimper of pain.

I have often held people as they were screaming on the mats and have heard and felt in them an almost total regression through one feeling to another—back to the helpless, piping cries of infancy. It is a wordless, feeling reliving of their emotional history. Though it is a painful experience, it leaves the individual light-hearted and open. I remember holding one young man recently who had had this experience and was lying quietly right after his last screams had died down. All of a sudden, a chuckle rumbled out of his belly. He began giggling and laughing like a child. The laughter was so infectious that I started to laugh too, and the two of us lay there in hysterics for several minutes. "*That's* the secret," he kept on saying, then doubling over in more laughter. "That's *it!*" What he had discovered was a whole vision of himself as an open, happy child, free and full of spontaneous joy. He really knew in that moment what it felt like to be himself. That sense of his identity was the "secret" he had been keeping from the world most of his life, behind the encrusted bastions of a character-disordered Rejector.

Not all exercises will lead to such an experience every time, but each of them has that possibility. Because the deepest experiences in our groups usually occur with the sounds, not the words, of feeling, we try to get people to those sounds as soon as possible. Most of the exercises described here do involve some words to begin with. This can be some simple phrase naming the feeling, such as "I hurt," or it can connect the feeling to a significant thought: "I'm angry at *you*, Mommy," or, "I need you to love me, Daddy." Keeping the phrase simple minimizes the interference of verbiage. It also allows the person to repeat the phrase readily. We have found that such repetition helps him connect to the feeling more rapidly. If the exercise is carried through so the feeling is experienced full measure, however, the words usually will turn to sounds. With experienced group members, and often with newcomers, we are able to bypass the words and start with screaming right off.

All of our exercises are aimed, one way or another, at discovering a new sense of self—a New Identity, free to choose and feel and enjoy life's pleasures with emotional openness and adult responsibility. The path for each individual may be different, according to his personal history, but the goal is the same.

Some of the exercises which follow are used frequently in our groups, others less so. Occasionally we will try new devices— variations on regular exercises, or perhaps a surprising new approach which seems appropriate to the problem of the person working at the time. Recently, for example, I suggested that a middle-aged accountant who relied on a rather passive, "nice guy" image, go around the room giving a "Bronx cheer" to each group member. As silly—and as simple—as it seemed, he had difficulty making the noise. He could not look people in the eye and show the "to-hell-with-you" feeling which the "Bronx cheer" suggests. Finally he learned how and soon became a master at the gesture, much to his delight and that of the group. It was only one of many ways he learned to relax his image and realize that he was entitled to assert his identity rather than cater to the demands of others at all times.

That man needed considerable prompting from the group to get into the "Bronx cheer" exercise. We try not to pressure group members into doing specific exercises until they are ready to do them. It is important that they trust the group process and the group members in order to maximize the chances of having a significant experience. However, there will be urgent prodding if someone balks for clearly defensive reasons. It is the subtle task of the group leader and other group members to see that someone is moved to do an exercise rather than pushed farther into his defenses. If the individual balks, it is often out of fear. Group support—and perhaps a fear exercise—will frequently get him through the barrier.

# Fear Exercises

Fear is the feeling that throttles most people when they first come to group. Quite simply, they are afraid to show any feelings, including their fear. I have rarely talked to anyone who was not scared the first time he sat in on a group. For most newcomers, it is an extremely frightening situation. Although we do not do as much encountering as we once did, occasionally people may say cruel things, interrupt impolitely, ask hard-to-answer questions. Within any framework of what is considered acceptable emotional behavior in Western society, groups are "out of control" and therefore frighteningly different. Worse, to a newcomer unprepared for what goes on, groups seem to reward "out-of-control" behavior. (I am often struck by the familiarity of words and sounds that I hear from the lost souls who occasionally wander New York's streets in severe mental distress. One wonders what would have happened if they had had a "safe place," such as our groups, in which to express their outcries. Much that I hear is no different from what we hear in groups all the time.)

During the go-around, most newcomers are able to admit their "anxiety" or "nervousness" to the group. Group members remember their own uneasiness in their first group and fully understand. Usually, very little is asked of a newcomer. No pressure is put on him to do an exercise. As the group comes to a close, the leader may ask: "How do you feel about your first group?"

The group's reaction will depend upon how honest the newcomer is, how involved he has been with others, and the feelings he has shown.

Consider the responses of two different girls to the question about their first group. Both girls have been feeling quite intensely. The signals they release show it. Everyone in the group knows it.

The first girl, Marge, says something like this:

"I was scared to death the entire time. Anger terrifies me. I wanted to run out the door and disappear every time I heard somebody shouting. I was kind of shocked at the swearing, but then I got used to it. . . . I felt close to you, Nancy. I understood your feelings. But I was just too scared to help you. I wanted to sit here like a little mouse so that nobody would notice me."

The group inevitably will react to Marge in an understanding way. She is showing her fear, and they can *see* it. They identify with the fear and understand her. Chances are, the next session, they will help her "work" on her fear.

Sandra has sat silently and tightly throughout the group. In a singsong tone, her answer is:

"The group was different from what I had expected. I couldn't see the point of those exercises on the floor. I didn't understand all the shouting. There are some really angry people in here. I don't think people should get so angry. I really felt out of it all."

The group probably won't react as kindly to Sandra as it did to Marge. Sandra is trying (unsuccessfully) to camouflage her fear behind verbalized attitudes. Her signals show fear, while the content of her words tries to conceal and control the fear. The misalignment of words and signals is confusing and disturbing—really untrustworthy—to group members, and to everyone in or out of group who tries to relate to Sandra.

Our most basic fear exercise in group is to ask a person to state his fear openly. He is told to make eye contact with each member of the group and say, "I'm afraid." As he "makes the rounds" of the group and says these words, the chances are good that he will connect emotionally with the fear in his gut and *show more fear*. Eye contact is the key factor in the exercise. It permits emotional contact between two people, which causes the exercise to work. The person begins to face the fact that he is afraid; and he begins to see that it is all right to feel afraid. Others will understand and accept his feelings.

People often are not so much afraid of fear as they are afraid of the baby-like feeling of helplessness accompanying it. This

misconditioned feeling of helplessness—not the fear itself—
immobilizes many people. After all, a baby *is* helpless when it is
afraid. It is almost totally dependent for survival upon the
actions of others. But an adult is in a different position. He has
many resources and strengths, whether or not others give him
assistance. Remember that fear is a basic survival feeling. Physiologically, it mobilizes one to act—to flee—not to remain in a
helpless, immobilized state. We try always in our groups to show
people that it is all right to feel fear—indeed, that fear is a means
to help protect oneself from danger. This is an especially important lesson for Rejectors.

Frequently the phrase "I'm afraid" is combined in our group
exercises with words relating to specific actions or other feelings.
Someone might be asked to say the words, "I'm afraid to get
angry, but I feel angry." Or: "I'm afraid to hunt for a new job,
but I'm going to start looking anyway." The actual phraseology
chosen is a function of what group members and the individuals
feel are "the right words."

Generally, group members respond by nodding or saying, "It's
okay to be afraid," or, "I'm afraid a lot, too." Such support is
important. An individual accustomed to muffling his fear must
be re-educated to understand that others can understand and
share it when fear is shown. This concept is hardest for men in
our society. Males often are conditioned to believe it is unmanly
to reveal fear, and this attitude must be combatted. Fear is just a
feeling. Everyone experiences it at various times. True bravery
means acting in the face of fear, not denying its existence.

Sometimes we confront the "unmanly" attitude by asking the
man to say, "I'm a man, and I'm afraid." Such words can start as
an "as-if" exercise, then become a fully-connected feeling which
brings tears to the eyes of even a powerfully-built he-man. When
a man first realizes in our groups that it is not shameful to show
his fear, it is a very painful experience. He has been conditioned
to believe that to be manly is to be approved of and to be loved;
his initial admissions of "unmanly" fear feel as though he will be
rejected and unloved. The experience also is painful because he
senses all at once the amount of energy he has wasted by using
it to hide a feeling which he was entitled as a human being
to express.

The words "help me" bring up a great deal of fear in people who feel intense loneliness. Showing the need for help is very vulnerable; the request *might* be rejected. This vulnerability raises giant fear. Again, eye contact is vital so that the person can learn it is all right to show his vulnerability. Often anger comes up to protect the fear or the underlying pain. That feeling can be so overwhelming that the person is not really in touch with his fear. He must struggle to put aside—"push through," as we say in groups—the anger so that he can get in touch with his fear.

Each of us maintains an image of some sort, designed to prevent the world and ourselves from seeing who we really are, what we really feel, where we are really vulnerable. The "nice guy" at the office is probably tremendously angry inside, but hides his anger even from himself; he was programmed to believe that anger is wrong and that he will not be loved if he expresses anger. The aggressive male who spits on homosexuality may well fear those traits within himself. The "do-gooder" is really full of selfish needs which she dare not face.

These examples are oversimplified, perhaps. The subtleties of self-images can be as varied as a particular human being's life experience warrants. But the fact remains that self-images are usually defenses, often destructive and personally defeating walls which require enormous energy to maintain. The problem is to help a person break the image and show him a new path to honest and spontaneous self-expression. That way, he can know who he truly is and learn how many choices actually are open to him.

Our group dynamic challenges self-images all the time. One way is through verbal "feedback," when people tell a group member how he strikes them and what they see him doing—whatever he *says* he is doing. Another thrust against self-image comes through group members' emotional reactions. If everyone continually gets angry at someone, or scoffs at his helplessness and refuses to treat him like a child, that person eventually must face the fact that the image he is presenting just is not real. There is a group adage which says, "If everyone tells you you're an elephant, you'd better start hunting for peanuts." Even someone very well-defended, if he stays in groups long enough, cannot help but recognize that people are reacting to him in certain ways because who he really is evokes such responses. He sees finally that their honest reactions to him are valid—not his self-image. And that image begins to crumble so that his real feelings and needs emerge.

It can be tremendously fear-provoking to accept the truth of group feedback and reactions. Someone must trust the atmosphere and enough of the group members to some extent before he can "let in" what they are showing him. As soon as he begins to face how unreal his image has been, he is left without a major defense—however self-destructive or wasteful—which has protected him most of his life.

The group dynamic is designed to promote trust in two ways: First, group support through shared feelings and the sense that other people have "been there" too helps a person trust the dynamic. Second, group challenge breeds trust by showing the individual that other people believe he has the strength and ability to change—and that they really want him to for his own good. In other words, they *care* about him. Sensing this concern helps many people work through a lot of fear.

As a kind of exercise, we often ask a new group member with an "image problem" to tell the group the worst thing he ever did. The reaction is fascinating. Inevitably, there is silence as the person censors his first thoughts. Then he will tell a not-very-interesting story which makes him seem brave and heroic, or even (safely) a little foolish. As he recites the story, his signals hint that it is really something else which ranks as his topmost secret sin. Careful prodding and challenge from the group brings the new member eventually to reveal something that does break his image.

Immediately, the dreaded secret seems not so frightening at all. Other people in the group have had similar experiences, or worse, and most at least know and understand the fear and other feelings which his admission entails. The secret may be something truly shocking by society's standards, like incest or a serious crime. It may be something which seems mild or old-hat to other people—a fantasy of murdering a parent or sibling, perhaps. Whatever it is, revealing it to a group of people often bridges the gap between signals and words so the monstrous secret never seems so threatening again. This is not just the release of "confession." It is a true revelation to most people that their "secret" involves just another feeling. Once the secret is out, the person has a chance in group to exercise his feelings about it safely. It is a tremendously freeing experience. And it is a sign to us that this member has begun to trust the group.

In some fear exercises, the person slouches down in his seat, puts his head back, closes his eyes (to reduce the initial fear), and screams out his fear, starting with whatever words seem right. No matter what words he begins with, he generally ends up making an animal sound—a scream of terror. The scream is repeated over and over again until he has gone through the feeling and does not feel as frightened.

We also get group members to express fear on the mats. Usually other group members gather around the person working. He starts to scream—just the sound, or, "I'm scared!" He may begin to thrash and twist about, striking his fists and feet against the mat, shrieking out his fear: "I'm scared," or "Don't hit me." The words often relate to specific childhood experiences—a pattern of beatings administered by a father, for instance; or the death of a grandparent; or just the terror of being alone in bed with the lights out. Usually any words quickly turn into animal-like screams.

During each of these exercises, the person often "gets off" the feeling at some point—usually as it connects to a deeper, more fearful level of awareness. When that happens, the group encourages him to open his eyes and take in the emotional feedback showing in the faces of other people. This brings him back into contact with other people and reassures him of their concern and involvement with him. He is encouraged to plunge deeper into the exercise and get all the way through the feeling. When he pushes through to its depths, his fearful screams often turn into other feelings—anger, pain, and, finally, joy.

## Anger Exercises

Our first groups concentrated on angry confrontation, such as I had experienced at Synanon. We soon learned that angry interaction generates other feelings. Some people become frightened and cannot defend themselves against attack. Some cry instantly in hurt or fear. Some withdraw into hostile silence. Some don't come back. (Anyone who leaves my practice today is followed up with letters and a phone call inviting him to come in for a conference—free of charge—to see if or how we have failed and how we might help him.)

In our beginning groups we discussed all reactions as part of the dynamic. But it became apparent that these interactions often were not getting people to the depth of their anger. So we tried something new. We tried to get people to express the feeling *for themselves,* rather than just direct it *against* people in the group. We asked them to assert the feeling that they were angry because they were *entitled* to be angry as human beings who have been hurt unfairly, not because they had to defend themselves behind anger. (This emphasis on *feeling the feeling for oneself* is the basis of most of our exercises today.)

As we developed anger exercises that concentrated upon feeling the emotion for oneself, it became evident that the feeling had specific, different levels of intensity. We see now that there are four very clear-cut stages of anger. Each must be explored and exercised, but only the fourth is truly therapeutic. We recognize the levels basically through the individual's signals as he does the exercise. Each level of anger actually comes from a different part of the body:

1. The first level is from the head, an "intellectual" anger, quietly thought and expressed. It may include hostile putdowns or signals of disdain. It may be a verbal declaration like "You made me angry," without much affect to back it up.

2. The second level of anger emerges as a loud scream. You can hear it stick in the person's throat. Invariably, it is mixed with anxiety. I call this level "riddance" anger, because it always comes out with something like "Get away from me" or "I've got to get away from it" or "They have got to get away from me." It's a defensive, panicky feeling.

3. The third level of anger delves deeper. A murderous rage, it comes out of the chest. It is the type of anger that wants to kill: "Let me at him! I *hate* him!" People have to feel this third level before they can proceed to the fourth. They must feel secure enough in their rage to have taken the chance of showing that

they sometimes feel like killing. Once they have survived that exposure, they become free to show their real anger, the fourth, deepest level.

4. The fourth level of anger rumbles loosely and rhythmically from the depths of the belly. I call this "identity anger." People feel all connected up and relaxed, strong and alive. There is self-assurance, not bravado. It is the kind of anger which says, "I'm angry because I've been hurt. What happened to me wasn't fair, and I'm angry. Nobody is going to do that to me again. I won't *let* anybody do that to me again. No more! No more!" It is the assertion of an individual who is fully connected to his feelings and aware of what he is entitled to feel as a human being. There is no tentativeness, no threat, no frightened pain or anxiety.

This fourth level of anger is felt throughout the entire body. You feel aware of a total you, a total identity. You become aware that you are entitled to be loved without pain. You are entitled to be loved without paying a huge price. The feeling comes out as the realization, "I am really lovable. I am lovable because I am me. I am lovable from the moment I was born, and if somebody doesn't love me now, I can find someone who will." This is an especially important feeling for Acceptors.

Going to the depths of anger does not just clean out pent-up feelings. It has a decidedly positive effect. When someone really hits the fourth stage of anger, the assertive "don't you dare do that to me" sensation shows clearly in all his signals. The voice resonates. The body relaxes. The rhythm of the words flows. He begins to *enjoy* the feeling. He feels strong and entitled. Entitled not to be hurt. Entitled to be loved. When he first gets to this level, he may feel severe pain at the lost years when he did not allow himself this assertion. But then, invariably, a good feeling takes over. He will break into a grin, switch his stomping into a prance, his yells into the happy laughter of self-discovery. He feels open and free. His body tingles all over—even his genitals— for this assertion of self is a strong, pleasurable, sensual (if not sexual) feeling. The person at this level of anger is anything but helpless. His is a truly joyous feeling. It's contagious, too: most of the group responds to the joy and shares it in hugs and laughter.

All anger exercises point toward this fourth level of anger. Most of them begin by asserting the words, "I'm angry!" over and over again. Usually the person stands up, with feet planted firmly, head thrown back, fists clenched at his sides. He will start by trying consciously to "connect up" to the feeling, repeating the words again and again until they begin to resonate. He may strive to connect to the feeling at first by concentrating on a specific reason he is angry. But eventually the feeling takes over. He becomes a mass of angry energy, throwing out the words again and again—"I'm *angry,* I'm *angry!*" They vibrate even deeper in his belly. You can hear the difference as someone begins to connect. It is no longer a choked-up, red-faced scream from the throat or an hysterical, frustrated roar. Instead, the words and finally the sound of the feeling roll forth from the belly, easily and forcefully, in deep, assured tones.

Specific reasons for being angry often flow through the person's head in fleeting images while he is performing the exercise, but there is not time for them to become thoughts. The force of the feeling is too great to pause for symboled sorting. If someone does pause, he inevitably "gets off" the feeling. Later, when the full feeling is up and out, he may describe to the group the images which flashed by while he was getting angry; in so doing, he often will make attitudinal connections that have therapeutic value.

These connections would have little worth if the person had not experienced the intensity of the feeling first, or simultaneously. We saw the truth of this in our early groups as the anger exercise developed. Too often, people can "understand" what their feelings are about, but the understanding protects them from experiencing the feeling. Until they actually experience it full measure, it commands a kind of magic, magnified by years of building defensive barriers, so that it appears out of all proportion to what it is. Because such a distortion affects how one functions in the world, it is essential to learn to see the feeling for what it is, recognize that it comes from misprogrammed distortion, and struggle to keep this in mind so one does not give in to the feeling or "act it off" distortedly in everyday life.

Mindy, in her mid-twenties, was well aware of her inadequate feelings in relation to her mother. The mother was beautiful, and the father would always point that out to Mindy: "Isn't your mother beautiful? She was the prettiest gal at school, and she doesn't look a day older." In reality, Mindy's mother felt very insecure herself, and she was jealous of her daughter. (Mindy and her father were very close, as long as Mindy maintained a kind of "buddy" relationship with him, for example, by enjoying spectator sports together.) The mother would dress Mindy in tomboy clothes. She had scoffed when Mindy wanted to get a bra because all her friends had one. However, Mindy's mother was very loving and supportive of Mindy in other ways. Significantly, people didn't get angry in that house. Anger meant "non-love."

As Mindy grew up, she could see the rivalry between her mother and herself and accepted her mother's superiority. To Mindy's mind (and from her conditioning), her mother *was* more beautiful, and Mindy was even proud of everybody's response to her mother. Besides, her mother loved her. Yet by the time she was twenty-three, Mindy's life style had settled into a vicious pattern. Although she held down a good job responsibly, she was sleeping with almost every man she met, and she had had four abortions. In our groups, she was able to talk about the fact that she loved her mother but felt her mother had done her harm with her jealous feelings. Mindy guessed she was angry about that. We started her on a simple anger exercise, and the feeling mounted. Suddenly she jumped out of her chair screaming, "I love her! I hate her! I love her! I hate her!" over and over. Her alternate rage and pain were intense for a couple of minutes, then she collapsed in tears from the sheer relief of having let out such bottled-up feelings. Afterwards, she told me: "You know, I knew I had those contradictory feelings about my mother, but I never really understood them—or believed them—until that moment."

One of the greatest values of our groups is that we provide a safe place to show feelings, however distorted. It is a place to let out years of pent-up emotion which could not be released in the world. A great deal of the pressure escapes forever when someone first penetrates into a deep feeling. But then he must practice. Through group exercises and their attendant insights, the feeling becomes easier and easier to reach, and its magic fades away. We learned this fact first through the "I'm angry" exercises, but it is also true of other basic feelings.

Despite the safety of group, few people can learn right away to trust the atmosphere enough to drop defenses and go right through to the depths of anger (or any feeling). It takes struggle and several attempts. If someone is having trouble, the group helps in a number of ways. They may shout encouragement, goad with insults, suggest specific actions on how to change a stance or gesture. The main feeling the group will not allow is "helplessness." They know that everyone is capable of expressing assertive depths of anger. Anything short of struggling toward that goal is considered a "cop-out" and invokes impatience or anger from others. But if a group member tries hard, yet misses, he will be let down gently. Many people cut themselves off in the midst of an exercise because they feel they are taking too much time. This could be an escape route from the feeling, but it often is a genuine worry, and the person needs reassurance. He needs to hear: "There is plenty of time. If you can't get to it this time, then maybe next time." In such ways, the group has the ability to both encourage and reject. Both actions have value, depending upon the person and the situation.

There are several variations on the basic anger exercise. The words "I hate" often raise particularly forceful fear and rage. I have seen patients able to get angry freely, but when they connect to "I hate," they tremble all over in terror and guilt. They are close to a feeling about some significant loved person. Sometimes getting them to jump up and down, Rumpelstiltskin-fashion, while yelling "I hate" helps them get through the fear to a confident assertion of anger.

Eye contact is almost always important in anger exercises (except on the mat). It means the person is taking full responsibility for his feeling. This is especially significant with anger because our society so often teaches us that anger is a forbidden feeling; one dare not show it if one wants to remain socially acceptable. In our groups, through eye contact, the person does dare to show anger. He is taking full responsibility for it by focusing on specific human beings rather than protecting himself in a kind of isolated rage. Sometimes even more specific eye-to-eye assertion is valuable: "I hate *you*, Charlie. I'm angry at *you*, Jean." With each assertion to individuals, a chance is taken. They could be hurt by his attack. There could be angry retaliation. There could even be humiliating laughter. But the person learns that no assertion of his anger is as powerful as what his childhood programming taught him to fear. His anger causes neither the annihilation of the person he is focusing upon, nor the destruction of himself. Anger is not magic; it is a feeling.

Throwing an actual tantrum on the floor often helps people connect to angry feelings. The person starts out lying on his back on a mat, with group members crouching around him. This is a very vulnerable position; one feels helpless and frightened like a baby (it's hard to defend oneself while flat on one's back). The tantrum may start with the words "I'm angry," but the important part of the exercise is to get the body moving naturally into the signals of a tantrum. The object is basically to go out of control, like a raging infant. By rolling the head from side to side and becoming slightly dizzy, adult controls begin to go. The person also moves his arms and legs rhythmically, hitting his fists on two pillows at his sides, flexing his knees in a suggestion of bicycle-pumping. When the feeling begins to connect, this bodily rhythm becomes spontaneous. It moves faster and faster, but more loosely, too, and the words of anger change to screams. As the feeling takes over, the group member may roll around the floor, writhe and gasp and pound his fists. (Other group members take care to see that he does not hurt himself.)

Once the anger is spent, usually there will be pain, a soft, whimpering, vulnerable pain. Then more anger may shoot out of this pain. Then more pain. Finally, a quiet peace and loving need as the person looks around at the tender, concerned faces surrounding him.

The release of anger through a tantrum often brings deep sensual and sexual feelings. I have seen women who have never had orgasms go through this exercise, and as their whole body loosens up, their pelvis becomes unlocked in a way they had never known before. They are delighted with this new freedom. They will wriggle happily on the floor as they take account of their new feelings. No one is offended by this reaction; it is a vital, joyful thing to watch. The tantrum exercise can be tremendously freeing, especially for Acceptor types who have trouble with anger and with asserting themselves as well-defined, adult identities.

# Pain Exercises

All our psychological defenses are designed to avoid emotional pain one way or another. Depending upon the particular hurts of our early years, each of us developed specific defenses to protect us from having to experience such pain again. Whenever a situation suggests the danger of pain such as we subconsciously remember from the circumstances of childhood, our defenses come into action. But we are adults now, not helpless children. We are realistically able to fend for ourselves much better. Still, the defenses of childhood remain, walling us off from the chance for emotional health. An addict will shoot dope rather than feel how lonely he is, or how inadequate he felt in the face of his father's emotional rejection. A phobic neurotic will stay out of elevators, which terrify him, rather than chance feeling the pain he experienced when he was locked in a closet or in his parent's emotional control as a little boy. A grown man will stoically avoid shedding tears rather than show his pain, because he was taught that men do not cry. Whatever the programming, we prevent ourselves from exposing our deep pain. It feels too vulnerable; the price would be too great, it seems.

Yet pain is a common human experience which can be understood and shared by other people. We can receive valuable support from them by showing honest pain. To stuff pain away only makes it grow to unbearable proportions, forcing us to cut ourselves off from meaningful emotional contact with others. It must be released; otherwise we suffocate from it, or wither away emotionally, or waste a lifetime in frantic psychological ploys to avoid feeling pain.

The words, "I hurt," said louder and louder can help people release pain. The person may sit in his chair and tell each group member, "I hurt," looking directly in their eyes in order to be as vulnerable as possible. As he goes around the room, he gradually opens up. The tears flow as the words gain force. When the pain really comes, he may double over, clutching his stomach and sobbing or covering his face with his hands. But it is important to share the feeling, and group members will gently pull him back upright in his chair so his legs are stretched out, his chest and belly exposed, his head thrown back, eyes closed tight. In this position—usually grasping someone's hand on either side— most people's sobs turn into screams of pain, wordless howls that pierce the air again and again. Some people writhe about, turn their heads and bodies away as they attempt to escape the feeling. Others feel that they will faint. A prickly blackness rushes behind their eyes. They feel as if they were receding into a long, lonely tunnel.

It is very difficult for most people to open their eyes at the end of this feeling. They are sure that no one will be there, or that they will see nothing but hostile, disapproving looks or expressions of uninterest from the rest of the group. But when they finally look around, they see open love on some faces, tears on many, embarrassment or fear on a few. It is important for the person to focus on other people at this point—he must bring himself back into the room, in effect, and realize that his feeling of pain is acceptable. He has not disappeared. And neither have the other human beings in the room.

Lying on the floor also helps the patient to get to pain. Again, the vulnerable position makes him feel as helpless as an infant. If he can take the chance of relaxing and allowing that vulnerable sensation to take over his body, he often will connect up to the words "I hurt" and be able to release the feeling in tears and screams.

In either position, the feelings sometimes become angry: "I hur-r-rt," a clenched-jaw wail which bespeaks the unfairness of what has happened to the individual. Sometimes the anger disconnects him from the pain. Then he must try to feel the pain again. But if it is an open, vulnerable anger, the signals are not protective. They are, instead, a reaction to all he has suffered, and an assertion of how it was not fair. Other group members are quick to tune in on the signals and help him stay with the deepest feelings.

Pain often comes up in exercises of other feelings, such as the anger tantrum. The fact is, people frequently feel pain when they let out any deeply buried feeling. The release makes them realize how much they have gone through to protect their feelings from exposure. It is as though one's whole life passes in review when the catharsis of an important feeling happens, and the person sees clearly all at once how emotionally deprived much of his life has been. It is an excruciating insight, one with which everyone in group can empathize. Many people weep openly when they see someone at this point of self-awareness. Some people reach for others, hold their hands, cry on their shoulders. Other group members cry in lonely isolation (as they have their whole lives), afraid to reach out or to be touched.

When I speak of "unfairness" in someone's life and the pain it causes, I am not trying to make a scapegoat out of mommy or daddy or whoever caused pain in a patient's life. Pain is inevitable in life. No doubt we can all cite some kinds of painful experiences—such as the early childhood loss of a parent, or the tyranny of a drunken father, or being born into poverty—as being more unfair to one person than to others. What we are tackling in our groups is *how one deals* with pain, *not how unfortunate* one is.

A primary goal of our process is to lead people to see that they can do nothing about their past except rid themselves of it. Then they will be free to live the future as they choose. But to gain this freedom, one must feel in a full sense one's entitlement as a human being to all his feelings. To that end, the misprogrammings and unfairnesses of childhood must be faced and felt, so they can be removed from power. Our exercises attempt to tap fully such historic feelings so that their magic is taken away and healthy feelings can take their place. Only then can a person be master of himself, rather than slave to childhood experiences. Only then can he be open enough to let in others' feelings and to establish healthy, adult relationships which are meaningful and fruitful to his growth and happiness.

# Love Exercises

Accepting love maturely is probably the hardest feeling of all for anyone in our culture to manage. Surprisingly, the difficulty

is not to give love, but to *let love in.* It is as though the thing we
most need—to be loved—is the thing we most defend against.
Because love is so important, I suspect, it feels to us subconsciously that we would be too vulnerable if we were to admit
openly our need for love. The hurt would be too great if that
need were rejected. And if love were let in, the subconscious
reasoning goes, to have it taken away again would be too painful. The need is too big, the danger too great, the price too costly.

In order to let love in, we must feel that we are entitled to be
loved for ourselves, not for our performance, appearance, or
relationship to others. We must feel strong enough to trust that
others will not hurt us or take advantage of us if we accept their
love. We must feel strong enough to sustain ourselves healthily if
that trust is betrayed. We must feel confident enough to reach
out to others, consistently risking rejection and hurt.

Feeling "lovable" is what we all were denied in some way or
other in childhood. Feeling "lovable" is a kind of self-esteem
that says I have value for myself and can give pleasure to others.
It is something all of us can gain through learning how to be
open emotionally, while we see both ourselves and others realistically. Feeling "lovable" allows us to experience the vibrant,
joyful excitement of being alive.

Most people today have a great deal of trouble asking vulnerably for love. People will demand love with angry, threatening
signals; use "blackmail" tears to force love out of the other
person; pretend they do not need love; perform "good deeds" to
ensure the other person's love. In fact, many people will do
anything but openly admit the need for love. "I need love" is an
important confession for everyone to make. It must be made
openly—linked up to a vulnerability to pain and tears, and
accompanied by the emotional and attitudinal sense of entitlement which is expressed physically through eye contact with
other people.

One often-used exercise in my New Identity groups involves
someone who simply stands up, looks another group member
directly in the eyes, and asks: "Am I lovable?" Or the
request might come in the form of the statement, "I *need* love."

Many resist this exercise as a sign of weakness. The need for
love is a personal "secret" many people have hidden since

infancy. Actually, showing the need is the reverse of weakness; it is an especially important exercise for Rejectors. When the need for love is revealed honestly, a defensive gate opens. The person shows the most painful secret of all—that he needs the concern, understanding, acceptance, and *love* of other people. Without exposure of that need, it is impossible to sustain honest, trusting, relationships with peers. As human beings, we all need such bondedness.

People must learn to ask for love. If the request is not expressed vulnerably, others find it hard to respond. They sense a cocked fist or manipulation behind the statement of need. A difficult responsibility for each group member is to refuse to give love if he does not feel like giving it to the person who asks. But when the person asking for love is truly open, showing his human needs, people jump up instinctively, feel love for him, and openly give him love. They hug him, hold him, stroke his hair as he shows the painful feeling. At last he can be as vulnerable as the hurt, lonely child he was. He can cry openly in someone's arms, give in completely to his need while supported by the loving response of others in the group.

Embracing to show love and support originated spontaneously in my groups. Many people shied away from such embraces. They certainly disturbed *me* to begin with; the open expression of loving feelings was absolutely at odds with my training, as well as my sense of personal emotional security. The fear of touch is great in our society, yet when you see people embrace in groups you see so clearly how such contact is part of our nature. It is a basic need, one we see acted out naturally in simians, and one which civilization has denied us more and more. The child needs to be held and cuddled. So does the adult.

Many people fear sexuality in such embraces. True, people sometimes have sexual reactions. But they know they do not have to act on them. Usually the experience is really one of sensuality— the emotional-tactile pleasure of bodies in contact with each other—rather than the anticipation of sexual relations and all the overtones that we have learned in our society. This is an important distinction for everyone to make in his group education, for embracing others openly is a beautiful experience.

# Pleasure

When people overcome the fear of embracing and can take in and give love freely, their joy is intoxicating. It sets other people to hugging spontaneously, sharing the pleasure of feeling alive, lovable, loving. This kind of group experience happens at the height of marathons, when most people are especially vulnerable because they have shared other people's feelings and have worked through their own feelings which stood in the way of letting in love. The bond between people is immense at these times. Love fills the room in a way few of us have ever experienced it before. People giggle, smile, laugh out loud, jump up and down with joyful whoops. They hop about from one person to another. Several hug at once. They stand in arm-locked circles and weave from side to side, eyes closed serenely, heads touching, contented humming coming forth in communal cadences drawn deep from within and matching instinctively with others' sounds.

We first experienced such group love only in marathons. Now these communal feelings arise sometimes even in short group sessions. Our exercises more and more cut right through to the heart of human feelings, so that all can share them easily and naturally.

Most of our exercises, when worked through to the end, bring a feeling of pleasure. The person feels the pleasure of being himself, in touch with his real feelings, able to face and deal with his misprogrammed feelings. He feels the ability to have much more choice in his life. He feels the pleasure of being bonded with other human beings. This is his new identity, the goal of our group process. Although such pleasure may be reached at first only after going through painful, fearful exercises, we strive to reinforce the good feelings so that the individual learns to reach them without having to struggle through bad feelings first. Such reinforcement comes from taking in the group's love. It also comes from an open assertion, repeated again and again, of "I am me." As that realization connects, the person really comes alive—open, vibrant, strong, joyous. Often the historic deprivation of this sense of himself will bring up pain as he feels his new identity. But the pleasurable feeling of self soon takes charge again.

Most of the exercises described above developed through trial and error as our group process progressed. A few entail techniques we borrowed from other group disciplines which are going on throughout the country. Several of our exercises came about through the imagination and sensitive insight of the peer catalysts who have helped run my groups. Group members themselves have also made important contributions.

Recently, we have tried some totally nonverbal groups, mostly for experienced group members. We start with someone making the sound of what he feels. Through signals and touch, other group members become involved. This generates many intense feelings. Not to be allowed to use words is very threatening in our culture. This threat can lead people deep into feelings which they would have avoided expressing if they had had words to defend themselves from the feelings. The nonverbal groups have been a means to crack through to a number of people who had otherwise avoided showing their feelings.

We have also made some fascinating discoveries in these groups. Running one's fingers lightly over someone's lips, for example, has brought out spontaneous reactions which clearly relate to preverbal experiences. One man I remember, an alcoholic, began to purse his lips in distaste and to gag as though someone were forcing something into his mouth. Then he began to cry uncontrollably. I later learned that he had been force-fed as a child—a fact he did not remember until that nonverbal group.

On another occasion a lovely girl in her twenties, who had been in and out of hospitals six times, diagnosed as schizophrenic, started to cry deeply for the first time in her adult life in one of our nonverbal groups. When I walked over to her silently with open arms to embrace her, she turned away from me in absolute panic. I was able to hold her anyway, and she finally relaxed. She told me afterward that she was convinced that I was going over to her to commit her to the hospital. She had never been allowed to show her feelings in her well-educated, highly verbal family, and the experience of releasing those feelings in our group felt to her as though she must be insane. After that breakthrough, she made tremendous progress in our groups.

I know that such experiences are a prelude to other discoveries. Our exercises and techniques are constantly being refined and new ones tried. We recognize that the process must remain a growing, viable dynamic. The basic tenets of the New Identity Groups are well established. But our exercises and techniques will always be changing to some extent, just as the nature of human interaction is constantly shifting and opening up to spontaneous, new experiences.

# CHAPTER 15 | *From Now On*

GROUP THERAPY has become a widely-accepted activity today. The Manhattan Board of Mental Health in early 1970 estimated that more than five thousand experiential groups were being conducted in Manhattan alone. And while nobody seems to know the exact number, several authorities have estimated that over six million Americans are participating in encounter groups.

The literature on group therapy has increased enormously, from professional texts to journalistic treatments like Jane Howard's *Please Touch*. Indeed, encounter groups have become part of our pop culture. A shirt commercial on television takes place in an encounter group. And a popular movie, more or less featuring group therapy, has been acted in and written by a couple who participated in group sessions at the Casriel Institute.

There is no question about the importance of group activity in the United States. Massive individual anxiety and alienation exist in our country, and drive more and more Americans to search for more than a high income and a flashy automobile. They are seeking an improved quality to their lives; a sense of community with others; careers that provide a genuine fulfillment; and more intensive and meaningful emotional contact with mates, parents, children, and other significant persons. The group experience is positioned close to the center of most of these desires.

Today, the group experience is available in places like Esalen; in communes; in weekend retreats; in a few school systems; in the offices of psychiatrists and psychologists; in body-movement classrooms; in encounter or sensitivity-training sessions; and in specialized groups for homosexuals, addicts, married couples, clergymen, and many others. For the most part, public school systems do not offer groups. Nor to my knowledge, do the Y.M.C.A., the P.A.L., the Boy Scouts and Girl Scouts, trade unions, veterans' organizations, the Kiwanis, Lions, Rotarians, and so forth.

I believe the involvement in groups will increase from the current estimated 3 percent of our population to 10, 15, or even 20 percent. The need for psychological help in our character-disordered society is too pervasive for high-cost individual psychotherapy to be able to do the job. Group therapy is the most effective treatment method available. Its rate of expansion depends upon many factors, and I foresee a number of problems.

For one thing, there is the question of publicity. Groups have already received a great deal of attention in books, magazines, newspapers, movies, and on television. Favorable publicity will accelerate the expansion of groups; unfavorable publicity will slow it down. My fear is that ineptly-administered, nontherapeutic groups will make better copy for journalists than professionally-administered group systems. Of the many encounter groups estimated to be operating in Manhattan, many are badly run, and some are actually harmful. The problem is, the publicity focused on a harmful group could give a bad name to the entire group-therapy process.

For that matter, it is easy for someone who is not familiar with groups to distort what he sees even in a responsible practice. In my groups, for example, there are daily encounters which any tabloid reporter could destructively describe. He could use patients' angry, fearful, or pained screams and sobs to paint a damaging word picture of what goes on. Any group system is vulnerable to such misinterpretation, particularly because writers who take on such a project may be unable to see the emotional communication which is taking place. They may choose to be aware only of the verbal content or only of the physical activity—screaming, fist-pounding, frequent embracing, and so forth. Such reporting could be sorely misleading. Imagine the field day a feature writer could have with screams such as, "Fuck you, Mother;" "Shove your approval up your ass;" or, "Me first!" Yet such screams *do* provide valuable techniques for reprogramming distorted and maladaptive feelings and attitudes.

Further publicity about groups is inevitable as more and more people become involved. It is important that the techniques of group therapy be reported fairly, as startling as some of these techniques may seem to many of our culture today. I do not mean, however, that all groups should be accepted without question. There are many harmful systems in operation, and I feel all groups should be able to submit to close, responsible scrutiny.

Especially when encounter techniques are being employed, scrutiny is important. The lives of some unsuspecting group members might—literally—be at stake. It is my belief that the vast majority of people have more than enough ego strength to withstand the verbal assaults of encounter groups. But a few individuals do not, and the process may do them psychic damage. In some extreme cases, suicide or homicide attempts are possible. Before a newcomer is permitted to enter a group, someone who is trained to know what to look for should interview him. People with possible suicidal or homicidal tendencies should be identified. Then the judgment about whether or not such a personality is to be exposed to encounter therapy should be made by a fully qualified professional.

This leads to a second important issue about the expansion of groups—the licensing of therapists. Today, in most states, *anyone* can set himself up as a group leader and start conducting "groups" for emotionally discomforted people. (In New York State a nonprofessional who runs groups without supervision cannot legally use the word "therapy" to describe what goes on.)

Such a situation breeds opportunities for nonprofessionals to establish a group following—and a lucrative group practice. Although I believe that many people experienced in a group process such as mine are capable of running groups responsibly—more so than *some* emotionally-closed professionals—I believe every group system should have an affiliation with a psychologist or a psychiatrist. This is important for the screening of new members, so that psychotics and other severely disordered people are not allowed in the groups. It is also important to keep a professional check on the progress of group members. Furthermore, I believe that nonprofessional group leaders should be trained within the practice of a professional. And there should be some form of licensing to ensure the knowledge and skill of the group leader.

Many groups today are responsibly run. But others are not. As group activity grows, so will the number of destructive group methods, nontherapeutic group leaders, charlatans, profiteers, and emotionally distorted people who try to work out their own problems by setting up faultily-run groups. In New York, you need a license to be a barber, but you do not need a license to run groups that tamper with people's emotions, bodies, and psyches. The ramifications of such a situation wherever it may be can cause consternation to anyone seriously considering getting involved in group.

Clearly, the lack of licensing requirements will permit more groups to exist. A continuation of the existing situation will surely generate problems that will diminish public confidence in group therapy. No one can predict all the forms group therapy will take. It is safe to say that methods will vary and that the techniques of some groups will advocate unlawful or antisocial actions. Public nudism, for example, is against the law in most places in the United States. So are the use of certain drugs, the act of assassination, stealing from giant corporations, and so on But already "groups" that call for such actions are coming into existence.

The problems inherent in expanding group therapy are part and parcel of the difficulties of improving human relations in our society. Group therapy is no cure-all. At its best, it is an organized and disciplined way in which people can share each others' feelings in an honest and safe atmosphere, develop a better understanding of their own emotions and attitudes, and improve their ability to relate to others. By establishing meaningful communication among individuals, groups can also establish bonded friendships. In my judgment, the other benefits which group therapy can bring depend upon the way the meetings are run, and who runs them.

Truly effective groups can bring about significant behavioral and personality changes when participants are motivated to become healthier emotionally. But emotionality by itself is not enough. In-the-world changes of a positive nature are not an automatic result of intense emotionality. Effecting such changes demands sustained effort, insight, and purposefulness.

Group therapy entails many questions, many complexities. How is a "group" different from a social gathering, for instance? Is "encountering" an essential part of the process? What if you are considering forming a group with a few close friends? Isn't it wise to include at least one or two outsiders? How do you prevent the candor of angry encounters from breaking up long-time friendships? What qualifications should you seek in a group? How do you go about finding a group that can help *you?* How do you locate one in your area? How do you avoid a group which might be dangerous?

The word "group" can encompass an amazing variety of human get-togethers. When four people hold hands in a room and discuss their feelings, are they involved in a therapeutic experience? What credentials should a group therapist have? Must there always be a professionally trained group leader? What sorts of rules or discipline are required, if any, to make the gathering a "group?" Can't anger be destructive, even dangerous? What about gossip? Is it inevitable? The number of questions generated is enormous.

I'll start with gossip first, since it is a consideration that one must face before making a decision to enter a group system.

By its nature, group therapy involves dynamic, unguarded interactions. A personal fact divulged in a group is not the same thing as an intimate fact revealed privately to a psychologist or psychiatrist. In a group, a lot of people will know. Even if the "ground rules" require secrecy about the confidences of other group members, people are all too human about telling *other people's* secrets. How can you stop it, even with the best controls? A group member confidentially tells his wife, she inadvertently "leaks" the fact to her closest friend three months later, and the secret is out.

I do not know the answer to this problem. Generally, in my judgment, too many people are involved to permit secrets to be kept. Even if a group decided to keep in confidence all information divulged, anyone would be naive to expect everything to remain secret. In small towns, in particular, where standards of morality are considerably more rigid than in large cities, I believe that gossip flowing out of a group could be a serious problem. In my groups (which are run in the largest and most cosmopolitan city in the United States), I purposely set up no rules about confidences. But I can truthfully say that, with the thousands of patients I have treated and the tens of thousands of group-patient hours I have observed, I do not personally know of any truly damaging situation resulting from the divulgence of facts revealed in group. By this, I mean a job lost, a marriage broken, a deep friendship permanently severed.

I know of instances in which gossip was feared. Finding himself in a group with a female copywriter who worked for the same large advertising agency for which he worked, a homosexual named Sidney immediately transferred to a different group. Then, he began telephoning the woman (whom I will call Connie), asking her not to tell anyone at work about his symptom. The woman replied that she would not tell; and she did not. But, from her viewpoint, the request was ridiculous: "Sidney's very swishy," she later told the group. "Everyone at the agency considers him a queer. The only weird thing is, *he* doesn't know it."

Sidney continued to hound Connie about gossip, until she came into his new group to encounter him about his phone calls. The encounter proved painful to Sidney. The group, en masse, told him he talked and walked, even cried and shouted, like a homosexual. Out of this painful confrontation, Sidney developed new maturity that ultimately was to become the starting point in changing his life.

In another instance, a husband heard about his wife's infidelity through group gossip. Fortunately, he and his wife were in my process (in different groups); and the infidelity had happened several years before. By entering the same group and working through the problem together, the couple became closer. He recognized that her infidelity had grown out of his criticism and rejection of her. She began to understand that her household sloppiness and free-spending had provided a legitimate basis for his criticism.

My group system currently contains over 500 patients. Thousands have participated in it over the past few years. Among present and past patients are doctors, dentists, lawyers, corporate vice presidents, communications executives, personalities from the entertainment world. In one sense, it is surprising that gossip does not run rampant.

There are several reasons why it does not. First, most patients share an understanding that the group system is designed to help people reprogram maladaptive feelings and attitudes. Vindictive or idle gossip simply does not fit into such reprogramming, and people are likely to be challenged for irresponsible chatter. Second, the basic platform of trust which is indigenous to the dynamic for the most part transcends the problem of irresponsible exposure. People who come to know and trust each other in groups do not want to damage each other. And, third, members use only their first names, not their full names. This provides surprising security. One nationally-known man completed a marathon without being identified.

We *do* ask group members, however, to talk about their out-of-group activities with other group members. This is not a policing action intended to discover whether people have been behaving themselves. As I have noted before, I accept socializing among adult group members. When they are adults, we try to treat them like adults. If a couple meets out of group and has sexual intercourse, for example, that is their business. What we are interested in is the emotions such a relationship generates, not the actual actions. Behavior concerns us if it is irresponsible. When that is so, the truth about the behavior comes out and can be dealt with. As for the person who is just "tattling" or gossiping about other group members, he will be confronted immediately by the group: "What's in it for you?" "Why don't you deal with your own problems?" And so forth. Responsible group members and leaders will make sure these questions arise.

But there's no foolproof way in group therapy to bypass

gossip. If you feel you cannot risk it, opt for individual therapy, or hand-select a group to which you wish to relate.

After the question of gossip, the next query is: How do you go about locating a group which will help you? (The reciprocal question, of course, is: How do you avoid *harmful* groups?)

The question is easier to ask than to answer—especially so because of my conviction that groups which focus on feelings are more effective than groups that go in for extensive verbalizing.

One starting point is to contact the American Psychiatric Association or the American Psychological Association, requesting the names of qualified professionals who run psychotherapy groups in your area. A better approach is to ask a psychologically-oriented professional whose judgment you respect—your family doctor, perhaps, or a minister, marriage counselor, school administrator, or social worker—to help you locate a responsible group.

It may be difficult to find groups which focus on expressing repressed emotions. An all-too-real problem is that, without additional training, many of today's psychologists and psychiatrists would be terrible at leading such groups. The U.S. educational system has long tended to produce emotionally turned-off people. Higher education often conditions emotionality out of its graduates. Medicine is as much a turn-off process as law. Psychology, by and large, is not as bad; but it is bad enough. Psychiatrists and psychologists have discipline and knowledge, but they are also most likely to approach groups through intellectualized perceptions about *others*. In my groups, nobody is permitted to remain an observer for long. A professional who tries to do so will come under severe attack—provided there is enough time (as there is in a marathon) for him to reveal how barren of emotionality his sit-on-the-fence perceptions can be.

Let's face it: Relatively few professionals are capable of running emotionally charged encounter groups without special training in the process that is involved. To run my groups, a leader must be able to participate actively as an emotionally open person. Otherwise, group members won't trust him. Unfortunately, professional training sets up structures which avoid emotional openness.

In most psychiatric disciplines, professionals are selected for training primarily on the basis of their intellectual capacity. Perception about others and sensitivity to others matter. And, in the last stage of training, so does a professional's insight into his own distortions. But emotionality is never really a criterion. A psychologist or psychiatrist may have accurate and useful perception about the feelings and attitudes of others, but lack the ability to express his own emotions full measure. Despite intelligence, knowledge, perception, and sensitivity, a professional may remain extremely closed emotionally.

In my process, the criteria for selecting a group leader are almost reversed. Emotional openness is an absolute must. How can a person who is closed instruct others about how to be emotionally open? The ability to empathize with the feelings of others is essential, of course, since the process is built on it. And accurate perception (even though a few areas of distortion may exist) is crucially important. However, intellectual capacity is not a prime consideration. The group process is, after all, a person-to-person dynamic relying heavily on emotional communication, not upon understanding based on theory and a knowledge of case histories. (This is not to suggest that my group leaders are low in intelligence. The contrary is true. All have high IQ's.) The point is that, with proper supervision, an emotionally open and perceptive person does not need to be given years of specialized training in order to become an effective group leader. His lifetime training as a human being has prepared him for the role. This is fortunate, I believe, because if we are to meet the expansion in group-therapy treatment which I anticipate, we must involve nonprofessionals as group leaders. The numbers of persons involved will be too massive for professionals to fill the need and there will be no alternative to having nonprofessionals lead groups.

Knowing the risks, I nevertheless cautiously advocate the use of nonprofessional group leaders as assistants. If a group leader has a need to control other people, problems will rapidly arise. I try to avoid this problem through our check-and-balance system of having patients switch periodically from one group to another. I also sit in regularly on groups with my group leaders. And, of course, I receive written reports from group leaders on the progress of each patient.

The biggest danger of using group leaders who have not had extensive, formal training in psychiatry is this: They may become extremely skilled at dealing with people's emotions, opening group members up to their deep feelings, yet they may be unable to deal effectively with the next stages of therapy. It is one thing to help people open up their repressed feelings. It is quite another to be able to reinforce new, healthy feelings and deal therapeutically with distorted feelings.

Most important for lasting change, a group leader must be able to help the person sift through and deal with the hundreds of attitudes which must be identified and changed to ensure true growth toward health. To learn these more subtle and complicated aspects of psychotherapy, a group leader needs extensive training in psychology. That's why I believe groups should only be run under the over-all direction of a psychiatrist or psychologist, experienced with groups, who has trained the leaders and who takes responsibility for the treatment that goes on.

With the expansion of groups, I expect that many people will consider starting their own groups together—several married couples, for instance, or friends at work. There are many important questions to consider:

1. *Should a psychologist or psychiatrist be asked to "sit in"?* By all means, I think this would be a good idea—although I would reiterate my warning that such professionals can be extremely controlling, nonemotional, and inhibiting. The chief advantage is that a psychologist or psychiatrist can talk to everybody *before* groups begin and "screen out" those who are best advised not to participate.

2. *If the participants cannot get a psychiatrist or psychologist involved, how about a minister, priest, or rabbi, a social worker, or some other "people person"?* The same basic problems exist as for a psychiatrist. "People persons" tend to talk too much, and to rely on perception instead of their emotions. Nevertheless, if you can include one professional "people person" in your group, I advise doing so.

3. *What about the dangers of anger?* Anger is an extremely difficult feeling for new group members to handle. Many people have built up a giant load of what we psychiatrists call "historic

anger." Usually distorted, this kind of anger is—in terms of the individual it is focused on—invariably excessive. When someone who cannot accept anger enters a group with defenses that stir group anger, the individual may be in for a very painful experience.

It takes training to know how to accept anger. When a person has been misprogrammed about receiving anger, he is in trouble in groups. Group anger can be damaging to an individual on the receiving end. A "group dump" can cause someone to want to snub everybody in the group, leave town, or even commit suicide. At the very least, it can be an excruciatingly humiliating and hurtful experience.

I try to combat these dangers in four ways. First, I interview people before they enter groups. (This would seem an obvious prerequisite for any therapy, but a surprising number of groups do not have a diagnostic interview. Certainly anyone interested in participating in a group should look for a group system which requires such a preliminary meeting.) In this diagnostic interview, I determine that the individual is not schizophrenic. I evaluate him in terms of the series of criteria important in my process. I am especially alert to self-destructive tendencies, and all group leaders who deal with the person are advised of any such problems, in advance. If I personally do not hold the diagnostic interview, then a staff psychiatrist or psychologist, or occasionally a staff member among my group leaders, will prepare a case history. The patient will then automatically be placed in my group for his first group experience. This gives me the opportunity to do my own diagnostic evaluation of him within the process. (I will already have read the case history background.)

Second, I emphasize to my group leaders the dangers of anger. Though the use of angry confrontation can be effective for many people, I recognize that my leaders and I are human and can err. We all must be aware that everyone is capable of dredging up historical anger, which sometimes will be brought to bear under the guise of therapeutic confrontation with some hapless group member. When several others join in, each mixing his historic anger with the outrage of the moment, the target of the "group dump" can be in for a rough time. I try to put a stop to such excessive and inappropriate confrontations.

Third, the nature of my groups tends to minimize the dangers of anger. Our recognition of love as a therapeutic tool offers a kind of support which group members can count on. The sharing of experiences, the feeling that others have been in the same spot, also gives strength to group members. And, most important of all, the way we challenge people to change and grow stems from a profound faith that each person *can* change, that he is a valuable, vital human being full of potential and respected for his desire and ability to struggle with his problems. It is difficult for someone to recognize this faith in his potential when he is defending against a particular confrontation. But the assumption has been there throughout his group experience. He has seen it with others, felt it for others, and it is rare that its implications for his own life have not filtered in to some degree.

Fourth, I try to put newcomers into groups which I personally lead. When I cannot do this, I see that they are assigned to at least two or three groups with different group leaders. If at least two group leaders can discuss a newcomer, there is a safeguard against distortions. Also, the patient has an opportunity to evaluate his feelings and attitudes in different groups. (I tell the patient that if one group leader calls him a horse's ass, ask the leader why he has said it—or leave the group. But if three group leaders call him a horse's ass, he should either change or buy a saddle.)

4. *Are there physical dangers in group?* This suggests another reason why I believe a professionally-trained person—preferably an M.D.—should be in charge of any group-therapy system. Certain group exercises can be physically exerting. Human bodies are affected by violent emotions. I am concerned about people with specific physical infirmities, such as a damaged heart or emphysema. Such physical infirmities should not be toyed with. I make a point of eliciting a medical history when I interview new group members, and I share my decision about the risks with the group leaders so that we may take all necessary precautions.

I began to observe an interesting fact about the body's stresses and strains as we encouraged more intense expressions of feelings. There are myriads of ways people use their bodies to cut off or control feelings—holding their breath, tightening muscles, constricting their throats, and so forth. One of the signals we have learned to trust, for instance, is this: we know someone is getting very deeply into a feeling when he begins to cough or gag as he shouts "I'm angry," or whatever. When that happens, the group encourages him to "push through" that control. If he makes the extra effort, he will get through to the deeper, truer feeling, and his whole body will loosen up so there is no strain at all. Many people in psychology, such as Wilhelm Reich and Alexander Lowen, have noted such physical controls, of course; I do not purport to have discovered them. But I can corroborate that when the human being is truly open emotionally, his body is not his enemy. His feelings and his body express themselves in concert. That is a lovely state of humanness to behold. It also is an observation which lessens my worries about physical dangers related to group therapy.

5. *How do you avoid letting potentially dangerous people into group?* Again, it is crucial that someone with professional perception see a person before he enters a group. My fear is that psychotics will get into groups (though I have admitted a few for experimental purposes). I think anyone running groups should share this fear and take all precautions to avoid the problem. Needless to say, a group containing three or four psychotics could be an extremely destructive social instrument, especially if one of the psychotics were the group leader. (Remember the group started and led by a borderline schizophrenic? He merely ran ads in a local newspaper, and dozens of people asked to join— knowing nothing at all about the leaders!) Provided a leader has a sufficiently powerful personality, and provided a path of action is made sufficiently enticing, people can be found who will join even a criminally destructive group. A frightening example is seen in the girls who followed Charles Manson into multiple murder. If groups continue to multiply rapidly in the next few years, "crime groups" will be a social problem generating extensive newspaper headlines.

6. *What about group touching and embracing? Can't this get "out of hand"? Can't it promote promiscuity?* Emotionally, human beings need to touch each other. Yet it is not accidental that our culture has tended to repress our desires to touch. Especially

when men and women (and boys and girls) are involved, touching is extremely delicate. The demonstration of love is a wondrous, beautiful, yet subtle thing. When a man and woman embrace, it can readily result in sexual excitement—for one or both of them. Sensuality can become sexual sensation; then, unless there are restraints, the path might lead to subsequent coitus.

Recognizing the common-sense reality of this situation, I still feel the overriding factor we must countenance is the human need to touch. I advocate *more touching in groups.* Admittedly, it creates the need for restraints. We observe the social rules regarding sex. We rule against sexual mouth-to-mouth kissing, or other modes of touching which are erotic or which might offend anyone who is not socially in tune with the times. When group members are teen-agers, some limitations on in-group and out-of-group embracing seem wise. And there are adults whose symptoms involve sexual actions which are offensive to most group members. For instance, there are women accustomed to being seductive with their friends' husbands, fathers who enjoy being seductive with their daughters' girl friends, and so on. Despite such possibilities, I believe that the need to touch and embrace should be encouraged. It is a natural human activity too long restricted and distorted in our culture.

As a matter of fact, encouraging people to embrace and touch out of genuine concern and empathy is not just a freeing, fulfilling therapeutic activity. Often it opens new avenues for solving specific sexual abberations. A homosexual, for example, will often break into deep, painful sobs when a male group member embraces him with love and concern as a human being. A male homosexual's need to "act out" with others of the same sex frequently connects specifically to not having had direct, honest expression of love from his father when he was a child. Taking in the love and concern of a male group member through an embrace often begins to free the homosexual from the "magic" he has attributed to relationships with men.

7. *Can "group" become a way of life? Doesn't it tend to make participants dependent on it?* If someone is not committed to getting well, he will stay sick. This is true of any kind of therapy;

my groups are by no means exempt from that problem. We find, however, that the combination of support and challenge in our groups tends to keep people moving forward toward better emotional health. No one will be allowed to stay in groups for months, without effective behavioral changes. If someone is clearly dedicated to avoiding change, we sometimes challenge him to leave groups. His time with us is doing neither him nor the other group members any good. Groups are not conversational get-togethers, mutual contract sessions, or any other social ritual or routine. Groups which are therapeutic demand honesty and emotionality. They are a special exercise, a demanding discipline, designed to stretch your emotional muscles and to help you develop new insight.

The idea cannot be stated too often: *Group is not a cure-all.* It offers no magic formula for emotional health. It requires the utmost involvement and dedication on the part of the individual if he is to gain anything from group. He must stay in the struggle, and if group itself becomes too comfortable, he is not struggling in the outside world. Group is, very simply, an educational tool which can lead people to realize the greatest *potential* to live responsible, adult, rewarding lives. But group cannot solve the problems of in-the-world living. Life is a struggle, and any therapy that provides escape from that struggle is not truly therapeutic. Our group system can only bring people, well-equipped, to the threshhold of life. Thereafter they are in the struggle. But—unlike the retreat from real struggle which each person's symptoms and emotional withdrawal or distortions allowed—this struggle as an adult promises great rewards.

8. *What about the possibility of cultism?* "Cultism" is a danger of any group-oriented approach to living. Many individuals are at an adolescent or childish stage of personality integration. If they are emotional children, they want to have their cake and eat it, too. If emotional adolescents, they want to have their cake without paying the price. In either case, they want to blame or rebel against Daddy, Mommy, and the authorities. This creates programmed, ready-made followers for leaders who are proficient at manipulation.

Treatment is for the good of the patient; cultism and brainwashing are for the good of the leader. Groups should be looked at in the light of such questions as these: Do the patients get well and leave the group with the group's blessing? Or is there an atmosphere of betrayal? Is a guilty feeling fostered if a person says he is finished? Does the group leader pull professional rank and say, "You're too sick and helpless to make it without me?"

I do not mean to imply that social evils do not exist that will lead people to band together in "causes." There are many social wrongs to correct, and youthful groups can be expected to focus their energies in trying to correct them. Such activity can be very constructive. However, in a cult, the members may lose contact with the realities. They can disregard the laws, institutions, ideas, and people which curtail their activities. Ignoring consequences, they can ride roughshod over others in order to pursue objectives they believe desirable. Too often, the results are disastrous—not only for some of the institutions and people they encounter, but chiefly for members of the cult.

Reality-testing is healthy. It is desirable to know what the law says, how others feel about a subject, what the consequences of one's actions are likely to be. By insulating groups of people from the mainstream of thought and feeling in a culture, cultism accomplishes exactly the reverse. It isolates its members, reduces the possibilities open to them, and causes them to misgauge the results of their individual and collective conduct.

Cultism can lead to violence and revolution, conditions that many thoughtful Americans think are inevitable in the United States. I am hopeful that violence and revolution can be prevented. But how? It seems absolutely clear to me that one place to start would be in improving one-to-one human relationships. After all, society is made of human beings. And any society creates the nature of its human beings to an immeasurable, but unmistakable, degree. Freud's Victorian world produced many neurotics. Our world has produced millions upon millions of emotionally disturbed people, the vast majority of them character-disordered personalities retreating ever further into emotional isolation and unproductive, frequently destructive, lives.

Psychiatry as it evolved from Freud can no longer cope with the problems of emotional health as they exist today. Disciplined, responsible group therapy is the only way I see that can possibly begin to deal with the emotional problems which are corroding our world. The most brilliant of plans to handle the major social problem—our cities, the blacks, student unrest, rising divorce rates, generation gaps, war, job depersonalization, conspicuous consumption, ethnic prejudice, crime—must fail if our society continues to produce emotionally isolated human beings. Quite simply, comprehensive solutions to particular social problems cannot be made to work permanently if we do not first deal with the problems of individual human interaction and identity.

*We must find ways to make people human again.* Groups can provide the way to bring about re-humanization in our society. I would like to see assumptions and techniques such as ours woven into the fabric of American life. We must hasten to train as many qualified people as possible, so that others, and still others, in geometric progression, can benefit from the process and spread it further.

I believe that a group-therapy practice should be set up so that people have access to all modalities of treatment. There can be regular groups for most people. Intensive groups for the initial involvement with the process and for the training of group leaders. A day-night center such as the one recently established at the Casriel Institute, so that someone having trouble functioning with his work life can become part of a structured program during the day, and someone having problems with his social life can have a place to go during the evening. There should be a therapeutic community such as AREBA, where someone can be involved with a twenty-four-hour-a-day program. And the leader of the practice should have access to all medical facilities—from laboratories and hospitals to the thoughts and experience of his colleagues.

Furthermore, psychiatric schooling needs to be revamped. Today, a psychiatrist must be enough of a generalist to grasp at least the rudiments of a number of disciplines—medicine, ethnology, semantics, primatology, sociology, psychology, pharmacology. He should be a doctor of psychiatry, not merely a doctor of medicine. We cannot blame the people practicing psychiatry today for their failures. They have done the best they can, based on their training. Nor can we blame patients who fail to respond to certain modes of therapy. It is time, instead, to change the psychotherapeutic process itself. Better processes are available. We now have the knowledge and experience to develop these processes. It is time we created schooled professionals to do the day-to-day work.

Although I have relied upon paraprofessionals to a great degree, I see that paraprofessionals by themselves are not the answer. We need more trained professionals—trained to the new techniques rather than stifled by the old—to set up group-therapy systems. These professionals should be like superintendents of school systems. Professional training demands too many years to limit practitioners to the number of patients they are able to treat on a face-to-face basis.

One truth about group therapy is that it *works*. In its *initial* stages, it is astonishingly simple, dramatic, and therapeutic. The beginning stages do not require a well-trained professional, any more than the distribution of penicillin (in most cases) requires an M.D. However, the final stages of psychotherapy require the skills and understanding of someone trained in what I call attitudes" (which, in toto, are really the analytic process). In its final stages, the technique of effective psychotherapy also demands considerable life experience, most particularly of a successful character. How can a professional whose career has been spent in a university, hospital, and cloistered private office truly understand the problems a highly-responsible executive faces in a competitive business? How can a psychologist without children appreciate the problems of raising kids in our complex, multifaceted culture? It behooves psychiatrists and psychologists to leave their closeted world and find out what is truly going on in the society they live in.

Two doctors whom I know have broadened their approaches to their fields. One, a general practiner in Flint, Michigan, spent a year in my groups developing an understanding of the group process so that he could apply it in his practice. A second, a psychiatrist from Paris, is now in my groups to learn about the process. He had become so discouraged about the effectiveness of classical approaches to psychotherapy that he gave up his profession for a year. These men are doing the same thing *I* began to do in 1963, when I first visited Synanon. The Frenchman will soon be taking the method to Paris, and will start a group system on the continent.

I would like to see children learn how to be emotionally honest in classrooms run by teachers trained in sensitivity and group methods. I would like to see preadolescents meeting in special groups—not because groups are a fad or promise them a way of denying their parents and avoiding responsible adulthood, but because groups can teach young people how to expand as human beings. The group process can help young people learn who they are, sense their own potential, share their feelings with others, and become bonded for a while to other young persons who also dare to expose their true feelings.

I would like to see such institutions as the YMCA, the YWCA, the Boy Scouts, the Girl Scouts, and welfare departments set up programs run by people trained to lead therapeutic groups and supervised by professionals who have also had special training in group methods. I would like to see the facilities for group meetings used widely by businesses, counseling services, social clubs, and other kinds of organizations.

I am pleased by the thought that business may find humanization a profitable activity. Executives interacting in an emotionally open atmosphere are significantly more productive in a very measurable sense. I envision such corporate benefits as increased efficiency, a reduction in wasted effort, improved morale, less job turnover, a better understanding of company problems and objectives, and more time for each individual employee to be creative.

Most of all, I would like to see the principles of humanization take root within the family, so that a child is given his natural right to feel lovable and will feel entitled to express his emotions honestly without the threat of punishment. I would like to see the nature of emotions, and the limitations of attitudes, better understood by those who assume the responsibility of being parents.

In the largest sense, I would like to see two new "Rs" added to the traditional three. These two "Rs" are "Relationship" and "Responsibility." The first subject would focus on how to understand, communicate with, and get along with other human beings. The second would teach the discipline of how to be responsible—not only to other people and institutions, but also *to oneself.*

These are the subjects all of us practice throughout our adult lives, regardless of our profession or socioeconomic position. When we set bad examples for our children, we transmit emotional ill health to the next generation. "Responsibility" and "Relationship" are essentials for human interaction. We invest major time acquiring and sharpening less important skills, whereas these foundation skills are ignored by formal educators and misconditioned by parents.

It is a fact that human beings need emotional contact with others. We need to relate to the vulnerable feelings of others, not to the prideful facade or distorted conduct that is too often presented to us. Genuinely satisfying emotional contact requires that each individual not only feel and show honest emotions, but also be sensitive to the emotions of other people. Meaningful emotional contact is based on responsible concern for oneself *and* for others, concern that is based on knowing one's own investment in a situation.

A pivotal reason for the expansion of encounter and sensitivity groups is that they provide the milieu for direct, honest interaction among people. Regretfully, it is an interaction which most facets of our culture do not permit.

In my practice, I consistently hear sophisticated and intelligent people—successful businessmen, college students with promising futures, middle-class housewives, professionals of high standing in their fields—tell me that the group process gives them something that is lacking in the rest of their lives. A lawyer told me that he knew and understood many fellow group members better than he did lifelong friends and professional associates. A chief executive officer of a substantial corporation returns to group for a few sessions each year to "take in some love" and "get away from the ivory tower." (Those in his groups do not know who he is.) A couple (whom I would characterize as extremely healthy emotionally) comes into groups two or three times a year—whenever they "feel the need for a breath of fresh air."

The words describing what emotionally-oriented groups can give vary from individual to individual. But they come down to one common denominator: emotional contact.

It is emotional contact that is the antidote to alienation and loneliness. It involves the ability to trust, the capability of dropping one's defenses against "nonpeople." And it is based on a hominid past that verges on being two million years old.

# Bibliography

Alexander, Franz, M.D., and Ross, Helen, *Dynamic Psychiatry*, Chicago: University of Chicago Press, 1952.

Arthur, Ransom J., *An Introduction to Social Psychiatry*, Middlesex, England: Penguin Books, 1971.

Bach, George Robert, *Intensive Group Psychotherapy*, New York: Ronald Press, 1954.

Berne, Eric, *Principles of Group Treatment*, New York: Grove Press, 1969.

——, *Transactional Analysis in Psychotherapy*, New York: Grove Press, 1961.

Bieber, Irving, et al., Eds., *Homosexuality: A Psychoanalytic Study*, New York: Basic Books, 1962.

Boyers, Robert, and Orrill, Robert, Eds., *R.D. Laing & Anti-Psychiatry*, New York: Perennial Library, Harper & Row, 1971.

Braceland, Francis J., M.D., and Stock, Michael, O.P., *Modern Psychiatry, A Handbook for Believers*, New York: Doubleday, 1963.

Breuer, Joseph, M.D., and Freud, Sigmund, M.D., *Studies in Hysteria*, New York: Nervous and Mental Disease Monographs, 1950.

Brill, A. A., M.D., *Basic Principles of Psychoanalysis*, New York: Doubleday, 1949.

Byrd, Oliver E., Ed., *Medical Readings on Drug Abuse*, Reading, Mass.: Addison-Wesley, 1970.

Casriel, Daniel, M.D., *So Fair A House: The Story of Synanon*, New York: Prentice-Hall, 1966.

———, and Amen, Grover, *Daytop: Three Addicts and Their Cure*, New York: Hill & Wang, 1971.

Chance, Michael R., and Jolley, Clifford, *Social Groups of Monkeys, Apes, and Men*, New York: Dutton, 1971.

Clark, W. E. Le Gros, *The Fossil Evidence for Human Evolution*, Second Edition, Chicago: University of Chicago Press, 1964.

Coles, Robert, M.D.; Brennen, Joseph H., M.D.; and Meagher, Dermot, *Drugs and Youth: Medical, Psychiatric and Legal Facts*, New York: Liveright, 1970.

Coon, Carleton S., *The Hunting Peoples*, Boston: Little, Brown & Co., 1971.

———, *The Living Races of Man*, New York: Alfred A. Knopf, 1965.

———, *Origin of the Races*, New York: Alfred A. Knopf, 1962.

Deutsch, Helene, *Neuroses and Character Types*, New York: International Universities Press, 1965.

Eisenberg, J. F. and Dillon, Wilton S., Eds., *Man and Beast: Comparative Social Behavior*, Smithsonian Annual III, Washington: Smithsonian Institute Press, 1971.

Evans, Richard I., *Dialogue with Erik Ericson*, New York: Dutton, 1969.

Farber, Seymour M., Mustacchi, Piero, and Wilson, Rodger H. L., Eds., *Man and Civilization: The Family's Search for Survival*, New York: McGraw-Hill, 1965.

Fast, Julius, *Body Language*, New York: M. Evans and Co., 1970.

Flescher, Joachim, M.D., *Dual Therapy Triadic Principle of Genetic Psychoanalysis*, New York: D.T.R.B. Editions, 1966.

Freud, Sigmund, *The Basic Writings of Sigmund Freud*, New York: Random House, 1938.

———, *The Problem of Anxiety*, New York: Norton, 1936.

Fromm, Erich, *The Art of Loving*, New York: Harper & Row, 1956.

Greenson, Ralph R., *Technique and Practice of Psychoanalysis*, Volume 1, New York: International Universities Press, 1967.

Hahn, Emily, *On the Side of the Apes*, New York: Thomas Y. Crowell, 1971.

Hall, Edward T., *The Silent Language*, New York: Doubleday, 1959.

Hanna, Thomas, *Bodies in Revolt*, New York: Holt, Rinehart & Winston, 1970.

Howard, Jane, *Please Touch: A Guided Tour of the Human Potential Movement*, New York: McGraw-Hill, 1970.

Janov, Arthur, *The Anatomy of Mental Illness,* New York: Putnam, 1972.

——, *The Primal Scream: A Revolutionary Cure for Neurosis,* New York: Putnam, 1970.

Jones, Ernest, M.D., *The Life and Work of Sigmund Freud,* Volume 1, New York: Basic Books, 1954.

——, *What is Psychoanalysis?,* New York: International Universities Press, 1948.

Kardiner, Abram, M.D., *The Individual And His Society,* New York: Columbia University Press, 1949.

——, *Sex and Morality,* London: Routledge & Regan Paul, Ltd., 1955.

——, et al., *Psychological Frontiers of Society 1945-1963,* New York: Columbia University Press, 1950.

——, and Spiegel, Herbert, M.D., *War Stress and Neurotic Illness,* New York: Paul B. Hoeber, Second Ed., 1947.

Laing, R. D., *The Divided Self,* New York: Pantheon, 1969.

Levitas, G. B., Ed., *The World of Psychology,* Volumes I and II, New York: George Braziller, 1963.

Lorenz, Konrad, *On Aggression,* New York: Harcourt Brace & World, 1966.

Louria, Donald B., M.D., *The Drug Scene,* New York: McGraw-Hill, 1968.

Lowen, Alexander, M.D., *The Betrayal of the Body,* New York: Macmillan, 1967.

May, Phillip R. A., M.D., *Treatment of Schizophrenia: A Comparative Study of Five Treatment Methods,* New York: Science House, 1968.

May, Rollo, *Love and Will,* New York: Norton, 1969.

Mead, Margaret, *Culture and Commitment: A Study of the Generation Gap,* New York: Natural History Press, 1970.

——, *Male and Female: A Study of the Sexes in the Changing World,* New York: William Morrow, 1949.

Menninger, Karl, M.D., *Theory of Psychoanalytic Technique,* New York: Basic Books, 1958.

Moltz, Howard, Ed., *The Ontogeny of Vertebrate Behavior,* London: Academic Press, 1971.

Moore, Ruth, *Man, Time and Fossils,* New York: Alfred A. Knopf, 1965.

Morris, Desmond, *The Human Zoo,* New York: McGraw-Hill, 1969.

——, *Intimate Behavior,* New York: Random House, 1971.

——, *The Naked Ape: a Zoologist's Study of the Human Animal,* New York: McGraw-Hill, 1967.

Perls, Frederick S. *Gestalt Therapy Verbatim,* New York: Bantam Books, 1971.

Reich, Charles A., *The Greening of America,* New York: Random House, 1970.

Reisman, David, Glazer, Nathan, and Denney, Reuel, *The Lonely Crowd: A Study of the Changing American Character,* New York: Doubleday Anchor Books, 1953.

Rado, Sandor, *Adaptational Psychodynamics,* Jameson, Jean, Klein, Henriette, Eds., New York: Science, 1969.

————, *Psychoanalysis of Behavior,* New York: Grune and Stratton, 1956.

————, and Daniels, George E., M.D., *Changing Concepts of Psychoanalytic Medicine,* New York: Grune and Stratton, 1956.

Reik, Theodor, *Masochism in Modern Man,* New York: Farrar, Strauss, 1941.

Rinkel, Max, M.D., *Biological Treatment of Mental Illness,* New York: L. C. Page and Co., 1966.

————, and Denber, Herman C. B., *Chemical Concepts of Psychosis,* New York: McDowell, Obolensky, 1958.

Rogers, Carl R., *Carl Rogers on Encounter Groups,* New York: Harper & Row, 1970.

Rosenberg, Bernard; Gerver, Israel; and Howton, William F., Eds., *Mass Society in Crisis: Social Problems and Social Pathology,* New York: Macmillan, 1964.

Ruitenbeek, Hendrik M., *The New York Group Therapies,* Avon Books, New York: 1970.

Salter, Andrew, *Conditioned Reflex Therapy: The Direct Approach to the Reconstruction of Personality,* New York: Capricorn Books, Second Ed., 1961.

Schutz, William, *Joy: Expanding Human Awareness,* New York: Grove Press, 1967.

Slavson, S. R., Ed., *The Fields of Group Therapy,* New York: Schocken Books, 1971.

Tiger, Lionel, *Men in Groups,* New York: Random House, 1969.

————, and Fox, Robin, *The Imperial Animal,* New York: Holt, Rinehart, and Winston, 1971.

Toffler, Alvin, *Future Shock,* New York: Random House, 1970.

Van Lawick-Goodall, Jane, *In The Shadow of Man,* Boston: Houghton Mifflin, 1971.

Vernon, Raymond, *Metropolis, 1985, An Interpretation of the Findings of the New York Metropolis Region Study,* Cambridge, Mass.: Harvard University Press, 1960.

Washburn, Sherwood L. and Jay, Phyllis C., *Perspectives on Human Evolution,* New York: Holt, Rinehart & Winston, 1968.

# Index

Abreaction, 61

Accelerated Re-education of the Emotions, Behavior, and Attitudes. *See* AREBA

Acceptor, 73, 74, 76, 201, 209, 210, 212-16, 263, 268

"Acting-out," 158, 175, 183, 184, 187, 191, 193, 217, 289

Adaptational Psychodynamics, 152, 153-54, 181, 182, 203

Adler, Alfred, 163

Affect, 9, 116, 120

Aggression, 109-10, 112

Alcoholism, 86, 92, 148

Alienation, 95, 114, 115, 129

American Academy of Psychoanalysis, 168

American Medical Association, 86

American Psychiatric Association, 283

American Psychoanalytic Association, 168, 169

American Psychological Association, 168, 283

American Society of Psychoanalytic Physicians, 166

Anesthesized feelings, 58, 63, 73, 95, 128-29, 130

Anger, 53, 54, 55, 57, 60-61, 63, 69, 73, 75, 76, 80, 84, 91, 93-94, 109-10, 112, 142, 144, 153, 187, 188, 190, 237, 285-87

Anger exercises, 91, 190, 219, 261-68

Anxiety, 137-38, 157, 202

AREBA, 7, 12, 16, 62-63, 65, 134, 151, 200, 292

"As if" behavior, 9, 93, 149, 189, 197, 258

Association for Humanistic Psychology, 54

Attitudes, 62, 68, 189-92

*See also* Maladaptive attitudes

Bach, George A., 58

Bassin, Alex, 47, 51

Behavior
"as if," 9, 93, 149, 189, 197, 258
character-disordered personality, 67-68, 92, 148-49
group therapy, 50-51
out-of-control, 256
out-of-group, 282, 288-89
primate, 104-6, 111, 113, 114
sexual, 102-3, 113
Triangular Man, 182-86

"Belly emotions," 95, 157, 250, 263, 264
Berne, Eric, 70 n
Birdwhistle, Dr. Ray, 243
Body language, 100, 242, 243, 288
*Body Language,* 100
Bonding
  emotional peers, 5, 6
  group therapy, 8, 25, 113, 115, 116-19, 172
  love and, 110, 113, 234, 273
  in marathons, 234, 238, 239, 273
  in marriage, 122, 124
  need for, 10, 44
  sexuality and, 110
  survival-value, 112
  trust and, 113
Brancato, Ron, 7

Casriel, Daniel H., 2, 4, 45-66, 93, 120, 121, 128, 166, 169, 174, 179, 181, 205, 210, 231
Casriel Institute, 2, 7, 11, 12, 29, 62, 63, 65, 69, 152, 196, 246, 251, 272, 276, 281, 284, 286, 287, 292-96
Catalysts, 53, 55, 56, 57, 59, 230, 231, 274
  *See also* Group leaders
Chance, Michael, 111
Character, 147-48
Character-disordered personality
  anesthesized emotions, 58, 63,128-29
  definition, 2-3, 73
  detachment, 153, 154, 157, 159
  encapsulation of emotions, 3, 4, 63, 159, 160-61, 202
  examples, 146-52
  freeze, 64, 73, 153, 154, 158-61, 203
  and neurotic personality, 132-61
  symptoms, 3, 58, 66-67, 73, 76, 120-21, 146-52, 158-61, 183-86
  tension, 159-60
  types, 146-52, 216-18
  therapy, 2-4, 58, 63, 121, 128, 171-72, 173, 174
  withdrawal, 159
  *See also* Alcoholism, Drug Addiction, Homosexuality
Children, 129-30, 203-10, 233, 247-48, 294
Civilization, effect on man, 115, 116, 117, 243

Closed individual, 70, 81
Communication, 99-101, 116, 124
Concept House, 57
Confrontation, 50-51, 52, 53, 55, 61-62, 95, 174-75, 187-88, 227, 261-62, 286, 287
Contracts, 227-28, 229, 237, 239, 290
Control, 159
Conversion reaction, 144-45
Coon, Carleton, 103
Counter-signals, 248-49, 250
Crying, 17, 20, 24-25, 26, 30, 34, 36, 37, 55, 58, 76, 84, 139-40, 188-89, 269
Cultism, 290-91
Culture, 82, 84-85, 98-99, 101-3, 107-8, 109, 111, 113, 152

Danger, 207, 208, 214, 258
Daytop Lodge, 4, 7, 47, 51-52, 134
Daytop Village, 57, 58, 62, 151-52, 172
Dederich, Chuck, 48, 52
Deitch, Dave, 56, 57, 58
Depression, 76, 77, 139-40, 216
Detachment, 153, 154, 157, 159
Diagnostic interview, 69-76, 286
Dissociative reaction, 145-46
*Divided Self, The,* 137
Dominant behavior, 104, 105, 111, 112
Dropouts, 87, 90, 115
Drug addiction, 2-3, 7, 46-51, 57, 58, 62-63, 72, 85, 134, 148, 151-52
Drugs, 87-88
Dynamic level of person, 202-3, 219

Ego-alien symptoms, 3, 137
Ego-syntonic symptoms, 3
Emotional health, 66-67, 68, 69, 71, 77-81, 113, 135, 209
Emotional "high," 4, 234, 239
Emotional honesty, 249-50
Emotionality, 1, 2, 4, 6, 175-76, 179, 196, 223
Emotions
  anesthesized, 58, 63, 73, 95, 128-29, 130
  "belly feelings," 95, 157, 250, 263, 264
  civilization and, 94-95
  encapsulation, 3, 4, 63, 64, 120-21, 159, 160-61

full measure expression, 2, 24, 43, 62, 80, 188, 222, 264
"gut-level," 95, 116, 254
historic, 61, 138, 246, 254, 285-86
repression, 157, 158-59, 164-65, 175
responsibility for, 240-41
signals, 245-46, 247, 252, 254, 288
Triangular Man, 187-89
"turn-off," 64
universality of, 4-5
*See also* Character-disordered personality, Neurotic personality, New Identity Group Process, *specific emotions*
Encapsulation, 3, 4, 63, 64, 120, 159, 160-61, 202
Encounter groups, 4, 8, 43, 49, 223-24, 226
*See also* Confrontation, Daytop Lodge, Synanon
Enculturation, 101-2, 107, 113
Esalen, 7, 54, 244, 277
Ethnology, 97, 99, 103, 107-8
Exercises
anger, 261-68
eye contact, 257, 259
fear, 256-61
function of, 253-56
"image-problem," 260-61
love, 270-72
on mats, 20, 22, 61, 261
pain, 268-70
Eye contact, 18, 33, 257, 259, 266-67, 268, 271
Eysenck, Dr. H. J., 178

Fast, Julius, 100, 243
Fear, 77, 83, 84, 94, 95, 117, 137, 138-39, 143-44, 153
Fear exercises, 256-61
"Feedback," 259, 260
Feelings. *See* Emotions
Ferenczi, Sandor, 163
"Fight" or "flight" reaction, 73, 79, 153, 154, 202
Forming a group, 278-79, 285-91
Fox, Robin, 111
Framingham Study, 86
"Freeze," 64, 73, 153, 154, 158-61, 203
Freud, Sigmund, 74, 97, 98-99, 102, 103, 112, 115, 121, 125, 131, 152, 153, 162-63, 167, 172, 215, 291
Fromm, Eric, 130

Full-measure expression of emotions, 2, 24, 43, 62, 80, 188, 222, 264
*Future Shock,* 124

Gardenzia Houses, 57
Gateway, 57
Gestalt therapy, 54, 182
"Getting off" the feeling, 261, 264
"Go-around," 246, 256
Gossip, 280-83
Greenson, Ralph R., 166-67, 170
"Group dump," 198, 250, 251-52, 286
Group leaders, 6, 9, 12, 27, 56, 58, 59, 61, 186, 198, 222, 229, 230-32, 234, 246, 256, 279, 283-86, 288
*See also* Catalysts
Group-survival patterns, 106-7, 108-9
Group therapy. *See* New Identity Group Process
Guilt feelings, 127-73
"Gut-level" feelings, 95, 116, 254

"High," 4, 234, 239
Historical emotions, 61, 138, 246, 254, 285-86
Homosexuality, 82, 86, 92-93, 94, 148, 151, 196-98, 289
Horney, Karen, 152
Howard, Jane, 276
Hugging, 18, 24, 25, 26, 28, 30, 34, 35, 37, 55, 56, 58, 106, 234, 272-73, 288-89
Human Potential Movement, 54, 114, 118

Identity anger, 263-64
Identity development, 203-10
Identity level of person, 203, 219
Identity pain, 61
"Image problem," 260-61
*In the Shadow of Man,* 114
Individual therapy, 2, 7, 9, 53, 92, 115, 133, 164-76, 177-79, 229, 283
*See also* Psychoanalysis
Interaction, 95, 97, 113, 226, 235, 262
Interview, 69-76, 286
Isolation, 159, 270

Janov, Arthur, 164, 226
Joint Commission on the Mental Health of Children, 129

Jung, Carl Gustav, 163

Kardiner, Abram, 45, 152, 153, 166, 203
Kinesics, 243

Laing, R. D., 137
Laughter, 94, 118
Lawick-Goodall, Jane Van, 114
Lay therapists, 174
Leakey, L. S. B., 103-4
Leakey, Mary, 103-4
Licensing of therapists, 278-79
Love
    character-disordered personality and, 121
    emotional health and, 80, 96, 110
    identity level and, 74-77
    pleasure-pain constellation, 207-8, 209
Love exercises, 270-72
Lowen, Alexander, 164, 288

Maladaptive attitudes, 69, 121, 137, 180, 182, 192, 193, 194, 196, 201, 209, 219, 278
Manhattan Board of Mental Health, 276
Manson, Charles, 288
Marathon Houses, 57
Marathons, 27, 57-59, 144, 145, 188, 223, 234-40, 273, 283
Marriage, 88-89, 122-23, 124, 131
Maslow, A. H., 54
Mendel, Werner, 178
Morris, Desmond, 110, 113
Multiple groups, 229-30
Murphy, Michael, 54

*Naked Ape, The*, 110
National Institute of Mental Health, 47, 51
National Training Laboratories, 7, 54
Neubauer, Peter, 129-30
Neurotic personality
    anxiety, 137-39, 157, 202
    attitudes, 68-69
    and character-disordered personality, 132-61

    classification, 70-72, 73, 137-46, 216-18
    conversion reaction, 144-45
    defense mechanism, 73, 79
    depression, 76, 77, 139-40
    dissociative reaction, 145-46
    evaluation interview, 69-76
    obsessive-compulsive, 140-43
    pain, 137, 138, 139-40, 150-51, 153, 157
    phobic reactions, 143-44
    relationships with peers, 72
    symptoms, 3, 7, 64, 66-67, 69, 73, 120, 121, 137, 150-51, 202
    therapy, 133
    *See also* Individual therapy, Psychoanalysis
New Identity Group Process
    affect, 9, 116
    basic rules, 210-22
    bonding, 8, 25, 113, 115, 116-19, 172
    contracts, 227-28, 229, 237, 239
    cultism, 290-91
    dangers of, 277, 278, 279, 280, 283, 285-91
    development of, 8, 46, 54-55, 56-57, 64, 115, 165-66, 276-77
    drug addicts, 134, 151
    duration of, 289-90
    dynamic level, 219
    emotional contact, 116-17, 170
    emotional "high," 4, 234, 239
    emotional honesty, 249-50, 259-60
    emotionality, 1, 2, 4, 6, 175-76, 179, 196, 223
    encounter technique, 223-24, 226
    exercises, 222-23, 253-75
    "feedback," 259, 260, 261
    first session, 11-12
    forming of, 278-79, 285-91, 293
    future of, 276-96
    "getting off" the feeling, 261, 264
    "go-around," 246, 256
    gossip about, 280-83
    "group dump," 198, 250, 251-52, 286
    guilt feelings, 172
    historical emotion, 61, 138, 246, 254
    homosexuals, 148, 151, 152
    identity levels, 203, 209, 219
    identity pain, 61
    "image problem," 260-61
    individual therapy, 9, 53, 54, 179, 180

interaction, 95, 97, 113, 226, 235, 262
licensing of therapists, 278-79
marathons, 27, 57-59, 144, 145, 234-40, 273
members, 9, 12, 53-54, 282
multiple groups, 229-30
nonverbal groups, 274-75
"out-of-control" behavior, 256
out-of-group activities, 282, 288-89
paraprofessionals, 293
personality levels, 219
pleasure, 273-74
post-group stage, 180
post-marathon groups, 239
projection, 226-29
promiscuity, 282, 288-89
psychotics, 135, 136, 137
publicity, 277-78
"push through," 259, 288
responsibility, 240-41
as a "safe place," 256, 265, 266, 279
"secret sin" revelation, 260-61
self-image, 259-60
signals, 116, 117
size, 222, 223, 238
special groups, 232-34, 294
structure and dynamic, 93-94, 222-26, 240-41, 246-47, 249, 259, 260, 275, 282
subgrouping, 26-28
supervision, 7-8, 55, 56
symbols, 241
symptomatic level, 219
tantrum, 23, 24, 144, 267-68, 270
teenagers, 232-33, 294
touching, 106, 114, 117, 288-89
transference, 228-29
Triangular Man, 64-65, 69, 182-201
typical session, 12-28, 30-42
value, 276-77, 279-80
verbal repetition, 255
verbalization, 1-2, 13-14, 27, 43, 59-60, 118, 143, 181, 226, 246, 255, 257
videotaping, 233-34
*See also* Anger, Catalysts, Character-disordered personality, Confrontation, Crying, Emotions, Fear, Group leaders, Hugging, Neurotic personality, Pain, Pleasure, Screaming, Symptoms, Trust
"Nonpeople," 113, 116, 296

Nonverbal groups, 274-75

Object pleasure, 212
Obsessive-compulsive neurosis, 140-43, 148
Oedipal theory, 98-99, 112, 172
One-to-one therapy. *See* Individual therapy, Psychoanalysis
"Open" individual, 69-70, 81
"Out-of-control" behavior, 256
Out-of-group activities, 282, 288-89
Overweight, 86-87

Pain, 76-77, 80, 88, 90, 94, 95, 110, 137, 138, 139-40, 146, 150-51, 153, 157, 160, 171, 201, 203-4, 207, 209, 267
Pain exercises, 268-70
Paraprofessionals, 293
Passivity, 87
Peer process, 5-6, 7, 27
Perls, Frederick S., 54, 182, 244
Personality, 147, 202-3, 210-13
Phobic reaction, 143-44
Phoenix House, 57
*Please Touch,* 276
Pleasure, 77, 80, 90, 110, 142, 153, 201, 203-4, 207, 209, 212, 273-74
Post-group stage, 180
Post-marathon groups, 239
Preverbal signals, 245
Price, Richard, 54
Primitive behavior, 104-6, 111, 113, 114
Programming, 203, 204, 209, 253, 267, 268
Projection, 226-29
Psychiatry, 77, 97, 98, 279, 283-84, 285, 292-93
Psychoanalysis, 92, 133, 165, 166-76, 177-79, 181-82, 229
Psychodynamics, 152-54, 181, 203
Psychosis, 133, 135, 136-37, 167, 279, 288
"Push through," 259, 288

Rado, Sandor, 74, 141, 152, 153, 203, 215
Rank, Otto, 163
Reich, Wilhelm, 163, 288

Rejector, 73, 74-76, 201, 209, 210-16, 258, 272
Relationship, 2-3, 295
Repression of emotions, 157, 158-59, 160-61, 164-65, 175
Residual attitudes, 68-69
Responsibility, 2, 6, 240-41, 295
Rogers, Carl, 54, 182

Sadism, 74
"Safe place," 72, 256, 265, 266, 279
Schizophrenia, 72, 121, 135, 136, 145, 167, 286, 288
Screaming, 1, 2, 4, 11, 16-17, 18, 20, 23, 24, 26, 27, 33-34, 42, 43, 49, 55, 59-62, 94, 116, 135, 138, 141, 144, 151-52, 156, 164, 185, 186, 223, 238, 254, 261, 262, 278
Secondary encapsulation, 158-61, 202
"Secret sin" revelation, 260-61
Self-image, 259-60
Sensitivity groups, 4, 54
Sexual behavior, 102-3, 113
Sick society, 82, 85-94, 114-15, 120-31, 291-92
Signals, 67, 68, 100, 116-17, 242-50, 252, 254, 260, 288
Significant person, 204, 206, 208, 209, 228
Signs, 100
Simmel, Georg, 125-26
Skinner, B. F., 177
Slavson, S. R., 46, 166
Smith, Robertson, 98
*So Fair a House,* 51
Special groups, 232-34, 294
Stoller, Frederick, 58
Subgrouping, 26-28
Sullivan-White school of psycho-dynamics, 152
Survival-based feelings, 94-96, 107, 109-10, 115, 138, 153-54, 156-57, 158-61, 208, 211
Survival patterns, 104-7, 148
Survival-value bonding, 112
Symboling, 100-1, 107, 243
Symptomatic level of person, 202, 219
Symptoms
  "acting-out," 158, 175, 183, 184, 187, 191, 193, 217, 289

  character-disordered personality, 3, 58, 66-67, 73, 76, 120-21, 146-52, 158-61, 183-86
  classical treatment, 92-93
  conversion reaction, 144-45
  culture and, 82, 84-85
  definition, 82-83
  diagnosis, 133-35, 137
  dissociative reaction, 145-46
  ego-alien, 3, 137
  ego-syntonic, 3
  neurotic personality, 3, 7, 64, 66-67, 69, 73, 120, 121, 137, 150-51, 202
  New Identity Group Process approach, 65, 93-94, 219
  obsessive-compulsive, 140-43, 148
  phobic reaction, 143-44
  and residual attitudes, 68-69
  of sick society, 82, 85-92, 114-15, 120-31, 291-92
  survival-based feelings, 94-96, 115-16
  *See also* Anger, Depression, Fear, Pain, Pleasure
Synanon, 4, 7, 47-50, 51, 52, 53, 57

Tantrum, 23, 24, 144, 154, 155, 267-68, 270
*Technique and Practice of Psycho-analysis, The,* 166
Teenagers, 232-33, 294
Tension, 159-60, 214
"T-groups," 54
*Three Faces of Eve, The,* 145
Toffler, Alvin, 124
*Totem and Taboo,* 98, 112
Touching, 106, 114, 117, 288-89
Transactional analysis, 70n
Transference, 3, 93, 163, 164, 171, 174, 182, 220, 228-29, 233
Triangular Man
  attitudes, 189-92
  behavior, 182-86
  definition of, 9, 64, 67, 181
  dynamic of, 192-201
  feelings, 187-89
  therapy, 65, 69
Trust, 113, 114, 115, 116, 121, 221, 260, 266
"Turned-off" emotions, 116

Unconscious, 43, 112, 121, 144, 164-65, 210, 243
Underachievers, 90, 148

Verbalization, 1-2, 13-14, 27, 43, 59-60, 118, 143, 181, 226, 246, 255, 257

Videotaping groups, 233-34
Vocal expression, 245, 253, 255
  *See also* Anger, Crying, Screaming

Washburn, Sherwood, 111, 112
Withdrawal, 159
Wolf, Alexander, 46